IMAGES
of America

Galveston's Historic Downtown and Strand District

On the Cover: This photograph was taken from Twenty-second and Strand Streets, looking east before the 1900 Storm. The Mensing Building is on the left, with its shaded second story, which is followed by the Mallory Building. The First National Bank Building is to the right, showing the Oppermann, Brown, and Clara Lang Buildings with their intact upper floors. (Courtesy of the Galveston Historical Foundation.)

IMAGES
of America

GALVESTON'S HISTORIC DOWNTOWN AND STRAND DISTRICT

Denise Alexander

ARCADIA
PUBLISHING

ISBN 978-0-7385-6685-6

Published by Arcadia Publishing
Charleston, South Carolina

Printed in the United States of America

Library of Congress Control Number: 2010925044

For all general information, please contact Arcadia Publishing:
Telephone 843-853-2070
Fax 843-853-0044
E-mail sales@arcadiapublishing.com
For customer service and orders:
Toll-Free 1-888-313-2665

Visit us on the Internet at www.arcadiapublishing.com

To Daniel Carey, Vince Michael, and Anne Sullivan for teaching historic preservation in a humorous and thoughtful way

Contents

ACKNOWLEDGMENTS

A very special thank-you goes to the kind, patient, and resourceful staff of the Briscoe Center for American History at the University of Texas Austin, especially Aryn Glazier in Photograph Reproduction. The Mary Moody Northen Endowment and Larry Wygant also played an integral part by donating city directories to Galveston Historical Foundation and by loaning *Picturesque Galveston*. Also, thank you to the Galveston County Historical Museum, Rosenberg Library, the Paul Verkin family, and Fred Huddleston; Margaret and V. J. Tramonte for allowing us to use their copy of *Art Work of Galveston*; Ellen Beasley and Stephen Fox for their copious research in the *Galveston Architectural Guidebook*; and Peter Brink and others who took photographs and documented buildings and contributed these resources to the Galveston Historical Foundation. Without a Hurricane Ike Relief Grant, received from Humanities Texas, the Galveston Historical Foundation would not have been able to purchase and rebuild our Galveston and Texas section of the Preservation Resource Center. Unless otherwise indicated, images in this volume appear courtesy of the Galveston Historical Foundation's Preservation Resource Center.

Special acknowledgments go to the following: Matthew Farragher for his scanner, Lisa Lowry for keeping me sane and merry, my mom for not asking too many questions but always being there, Dwayne Jones for his trust, Lauren and Kevin Scott for their love of Galveston, Laurie and Tom Hesser (and the girls, too) for loaning me their beach house, and Peter Ketter.

This book could not have been written without the architectural history memory bank of my good friend Brian M. Davis. He answered hundreds of questions for me and was a good influence on me finishing this book. Unless otherwise indicated, all images appear courtesy of the Galveston Historical Foundation.

INTRODUCTION

Galveston has many names: "Treasure Island," "Queen City on the Gulf," "Playground of the Southwest," "The Ellis Island of the West," and the Strand was once noted as the "Wall Street of the Southwest." Galveston, due to its natural deepwater port, provided this small barrier island with an economy in the late 1800s that was unmatched in the Southwest. Because of new businesses forming at lightening pace on the Strand and then Ships Mechanic Row, Market Street, Postoffice Street, and the cross streets, Galveston's architectural identity was born. Lucky for those that visit and live here, most of it is still standing. All activities in Galveston radiated from the Strand. Churches lined Church Street, the medical center was a few short blocks away, and civic buildings including the U.S. Custom House, post office, courthouse, and city hall were all within the block area of Twentieth to Twenty-fifth Streets. Galveston has a wealth of historic commercial buildings that is evident in a walk around Galveston's streets.

Immigration played a major role in the city's history, with over 200,000 immigrants entering the United States through Galveston. Although many of these immigrants did not settle in Galveston permanently, these diverse people brought with them their culture and influenced everything from architecture to cuisine. Many of the influential leaders of Galveston, like Henry Rosenberg, immigrated to Galveston and made a fortune in business and then made early philanthropic gifts to the city.

Galveston's rich history has been influenced not only by the businesses that grew here and the people, but also by fire and hurricanes. The buildings on the Strand have withstood major hurricanes in 1900, 1915, 1943, 1961, 1983, 2005, and now 2008; three great fires; the Civil War Battle of Galveston; the Great Depression; and urbanization of the 1950s and 1960s. Most notably, the fire of 1885 burned 42 city blocks that included both residential and commercial buildings, and the 1900 Storm killed between 8,000 and 12,000 Galveston residents and a good portion of housing stock while flooding the entire Island. Commercial architecture in Galveston has withstood most of these ebbs and flows, with a few exceptions, and when given a chance, new uses were found for buildings, and they remained a part of Galveston. It is fascinating to watch as our buildings change uses; one year it is a grocer, the next a cotton warehouse, and so on. Local historic preservation laws have not only kept the Strand Mechanic National Historic Landmark District cohesive, but also adaptable like the old days, since multiple uses for these buildings will inevitably come in the future.

Attempting to find little known or unpublished photographs and drawings of commercial downtown buildings proved to be a difficult task. Galveston's earliest building stock—the Hendley, Berlocher, Davie, and Pix Buildings—were not photographed with the zeal of the Ball, Hutchings, and Sealy Buildings or the first Galveston Cotton Exchange. Only rare images exist, because when photography was all the rage, these "old" buildings were reaching 40 or more years of age and were not as appealing to photograph as the new designs of Nicholas Clayton or Alfred Mueller. The photographs that remain of these buildings have been widely published, and now it is apparent why.

Architecture in Galveston is highly influenced by Victorian styles, but there is still evidence of the Greek Revival, art deco, and Second Empire styles across the downtown streets. Cast iron was a major building element; cast-iron storefronts were in vogue in the 1860s, 1870s, and 1880s all across America. Galveston, eager to show its financial success, employed these designs on buildings throughout the downtown. There are 36 buildings in downtown with cast-iron elements. Some buildings used it on the interiors, which was when cast iron was used as structural supports. Galveston had a wealth of wooden buildings, but again, like many cities in America, frequent fires plagued Galveston, and new building codes made way for stronger and sturdier brick structures. There are still several of the old wooden buildings left; take a close look at the Central Hotel on Market Street and a few of the buildings on Postoffice Street. There are still remnants of the old, old Galveston.

By including *Galveston City Directory* advertisements, my attempt is to show how business and commerce was the focus of Galveston's downtown and the breadth of the goods for purchase and trade. In 2010, as a consumer, we can go to any number of locations within miles of home to get even the most obscure items. While writing, I had to constantly remind myself that Galveston was the center for retail for men and women within 100 miles of the island.

This book is not intended to be an architectural guidebook to downtown Galveston, since that book has already been published, and nothing can compare to the work of Ellen Beasley and Stephen Fox in their book *Galveston Architectural Guidebook*. This book is meant to give visitors and lovers of Galveston a quick glimpse of Galveston through a multifaceted lens of architecture, history, culture, and even some fun facts thrown in. Most of the buildings in the book are extant, but in my attempt to give an indication of Galveston in its heyday, I have included some of Galveston's most notable architectural masterpieces that are no longer standing—Old City Hall and the Masonic Temple, for example. This book does focus on what can be seen today, while giving the backstory of the architects, owners, and cultural influences that surround the built environment.

Galveston has heart, and one of the reasons might be its vulnerability. Vulnerability has not made Galveston weak, but stronger. Anyone thinking about making a home or starting a business here is well aware of the stormy and fiery history. To take that chance, a person has to recognize that heart and be willing to possibly leave a little bit of yourself here. The people that built this island and those that have continued to respect and love it, your work and dedication does not go unnoticed. It is seen in each rehabilitated house, the brick streets, and the waterfront, as well as every shutter slat and open door along the Strand, and the cast-iron columns; your love for the city surrounds people. There is no other way to describe that, but to call it heart. Thank you.

One

DOWNTOWN GALVESTON

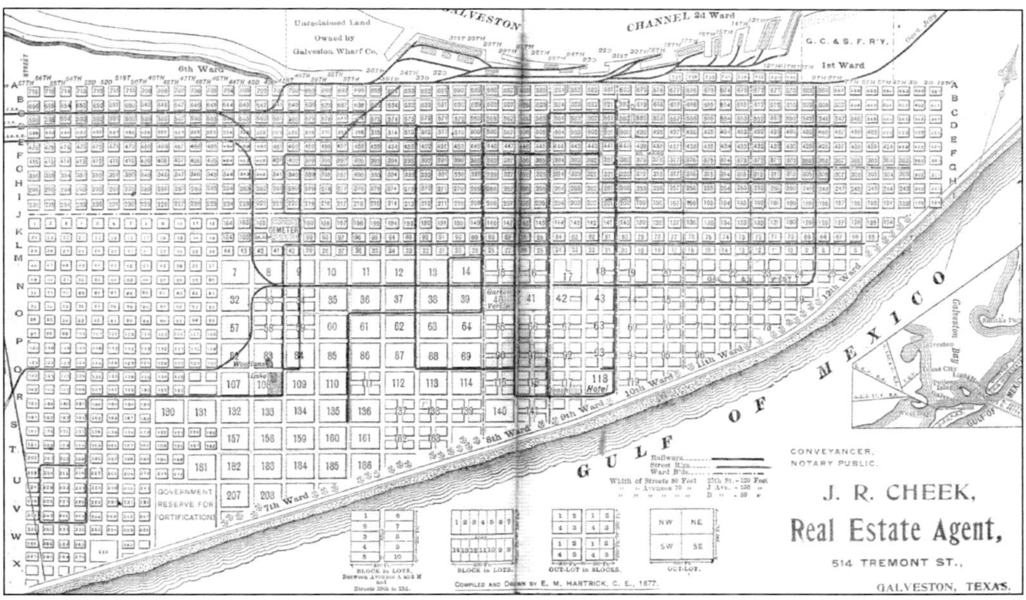

The time between 1870 and 1900 was an important period of growth for Galveston. With 37,000 residents by 1900, Galveston was expanding at a rapid pace. It was a busy port with immigrants arriving daily. Downtown Galveston was the center of all activity, and banks, merchants, public buildings, and churches radiated from the Strand area. This map from the 1897 *Galveston City Directory* shows the complex trolley lines that connected the residential areas to downtown.

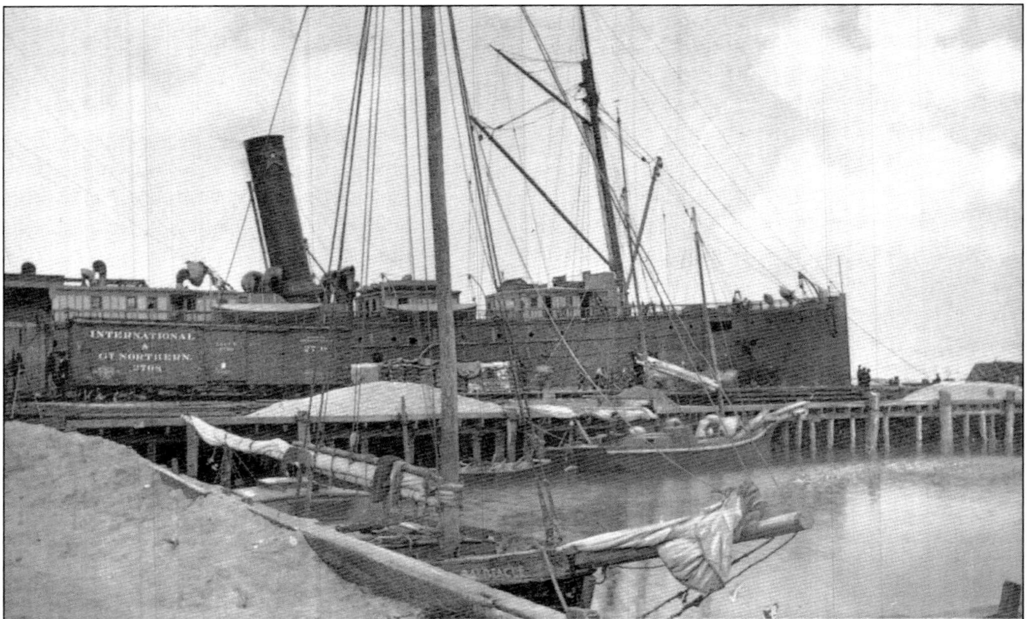

MALLORY LINE STEAMER "NUCCES."

By 1825, the Port of Galveston was a small trading post. The city was established by an act of the Mexican Congress in 1825, when the land was still part of Mexico. The site of the future Port of Galveston was long reported as the best natural harbor in the Texas Colony, and it is the oldest port in the Gulf of Mexico, west of New Orleans.

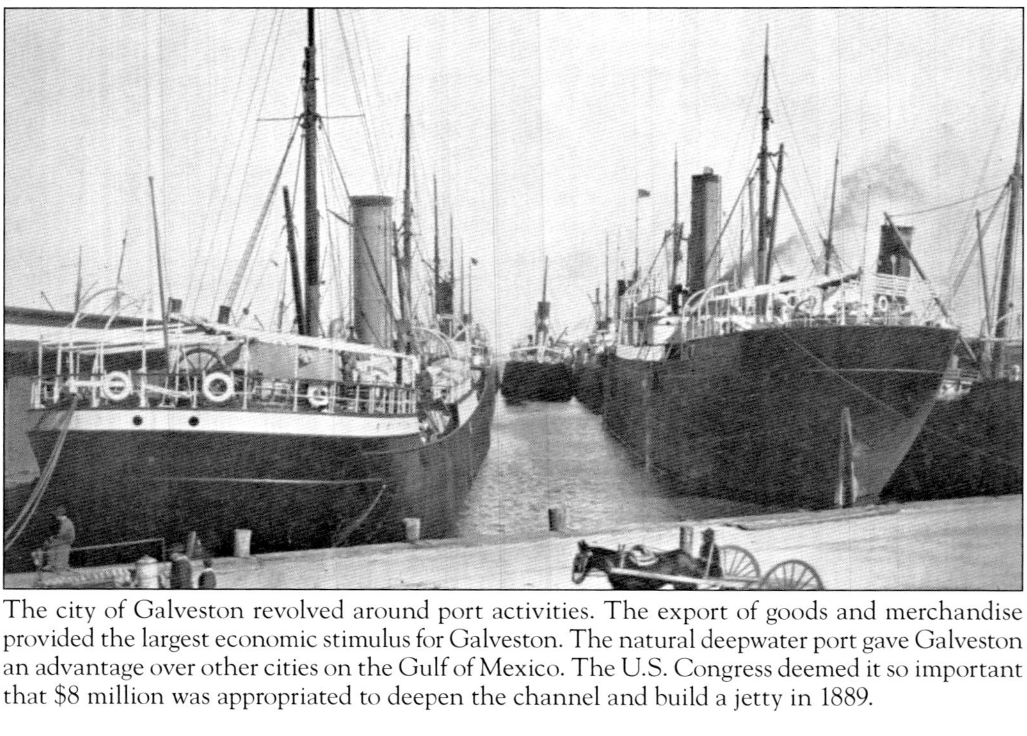

The city of Galveston revolved around port activities. The export of goods and merchandise provided the largest economic stimulus for Galveston. The natural deepwater port gave Galveston an advantage over other cities on the Gulf of Mexico. The U.S. Congress deemed it so important that $8 million was appropriated to deepen the channel and build a jetty in 1889.

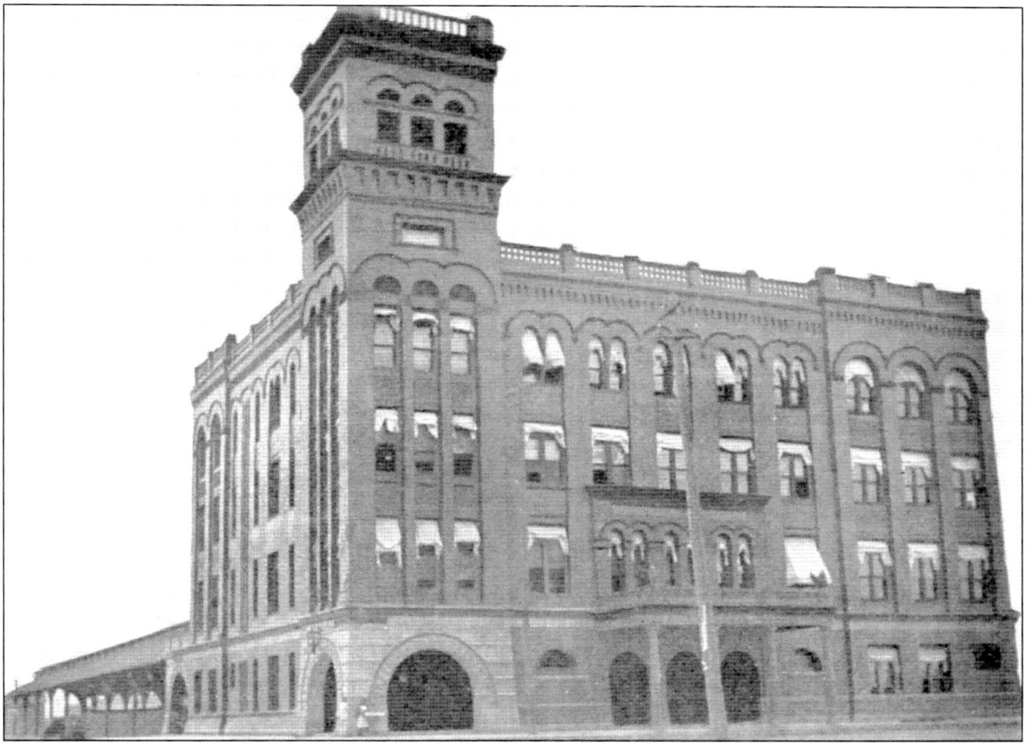

This photograph is of the original Union Depot, built in 1897. The purpose of this building was to separate passenger traffic from the freight traffic of the port. As the demand for railroad transit increased, the Union Depot was soon too small and was demolished in the 1930s. The railroad remained as a way to reach Galveston and a way for thousands of immigrants to move into Central Texas and cities beyond.

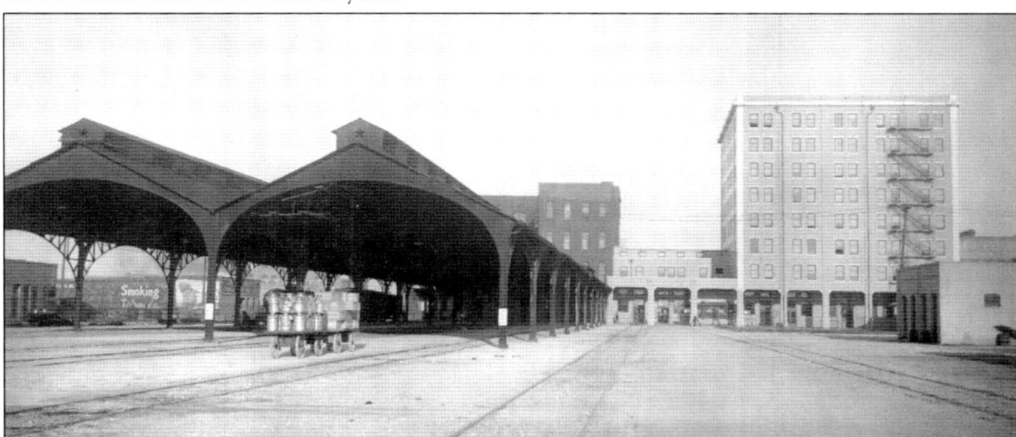

The first railroad to reach Galveston was the Galveston, Houston, and Henderson Railroad in 1860. Competition for extending lines beyond Texas in order to get the valuable exports elsewhere was somewhat out of Galveston's hands, but it was not without trying. Henry Rosenberg founded the Gulf, Colorado, and Santa Fe Railroad in 1873 and remained competitive by investing in connecting lines to the West. (Courtesy of the Galveston County Historical Museum, Galveston, Texas.)

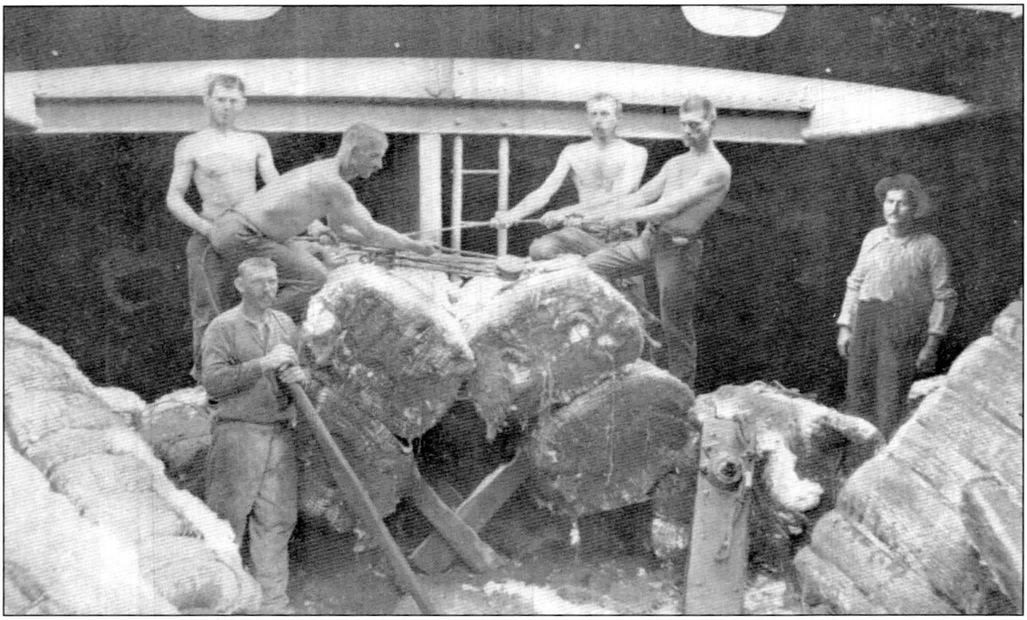

Cotton was king in Texas, and thus in Galveston. By 1900, the Port of Galveston had cotton receipts totaling 2,278,000 bales. In 1878, Galveston was third in the country in cotton exporting and fifth in 1882. The port exported 10 to 11 times greater value of goods and merchandise than it imported in the mid-1870s.

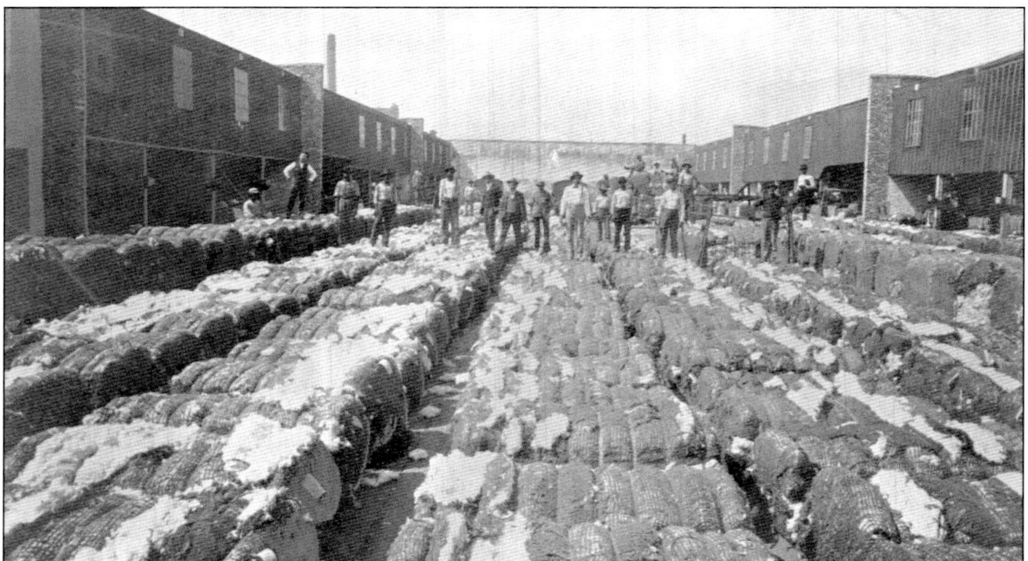

Galveston had a large cotton compress industry. For cotton to be easily transported overseas and into the interior of the United States, it had to be compacted. Huge machines reduced 500-pound bales to about half their ginned, or flat bale, size for convenience in shipping. The cotton industry grew up along the area west of downtown with many local industrialists, including W. L. Moody, leading the way. Cotton mills, cotton shipping, and brokerages were the basis of many businesses in downtown.

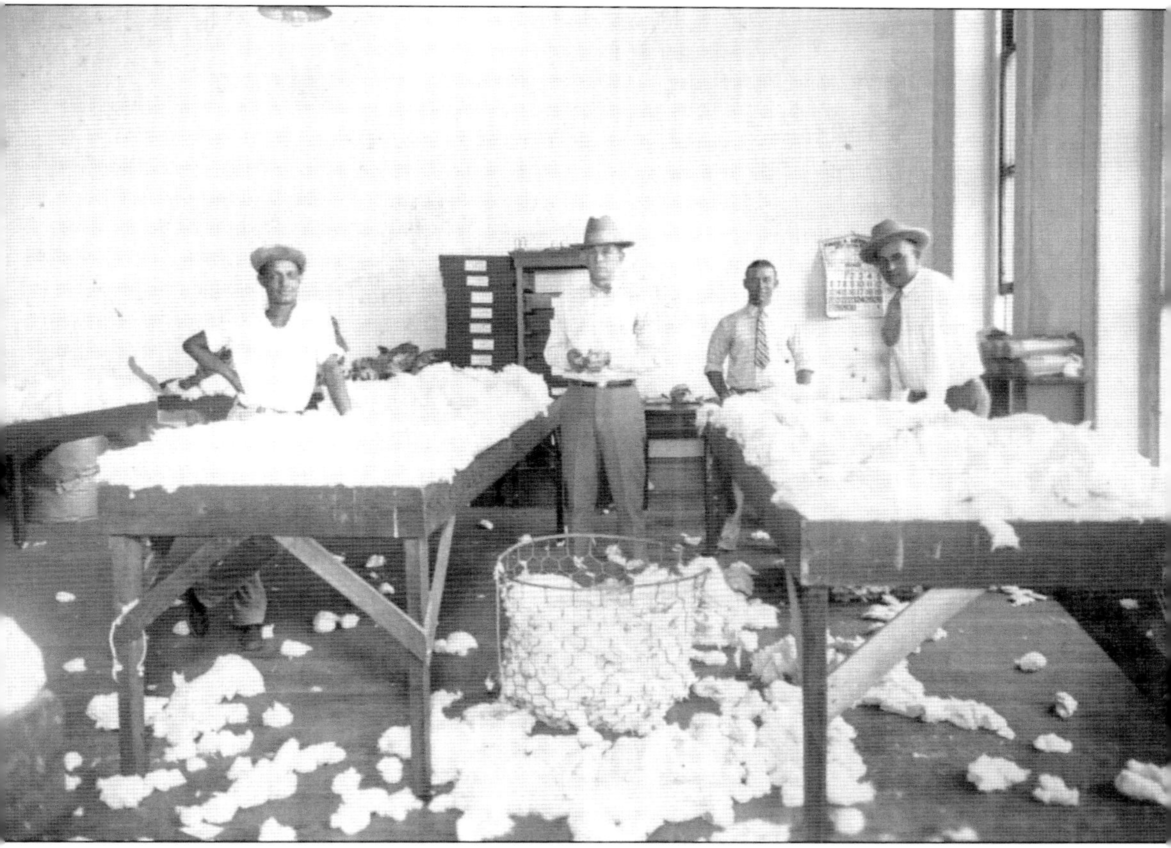

In this photograph, taken inside the Mensing Building on Twenty-second and Strand Streets, unknown workers of the Estene Brothers Cotton Company are classing cotton to be sold. Cotton buyers cut samples from bales and classed the cotton according to grade, staple length, color, and character (smoothness and cleanliness). Classing determined the quality, and thus the value, of cotton. Galveston remained a leader in cotton exporting well into the 1920s and still has a small cotton industry in 2010. In 1900, Galveston's largest employers and manufacturers dealt with cotton. Some of these employers were Galveston City Cotton Mill, Galveston Bagging and Cordage Company, Clark and Courts, and Galveston Rope and Twine Company. In particular, the Galveston City Cotton Mill was the largest in the state of Texas in 1900 and employed over 500 people. (Courtesy of the Galveston County Historical Museum, Galveston, Texas.)

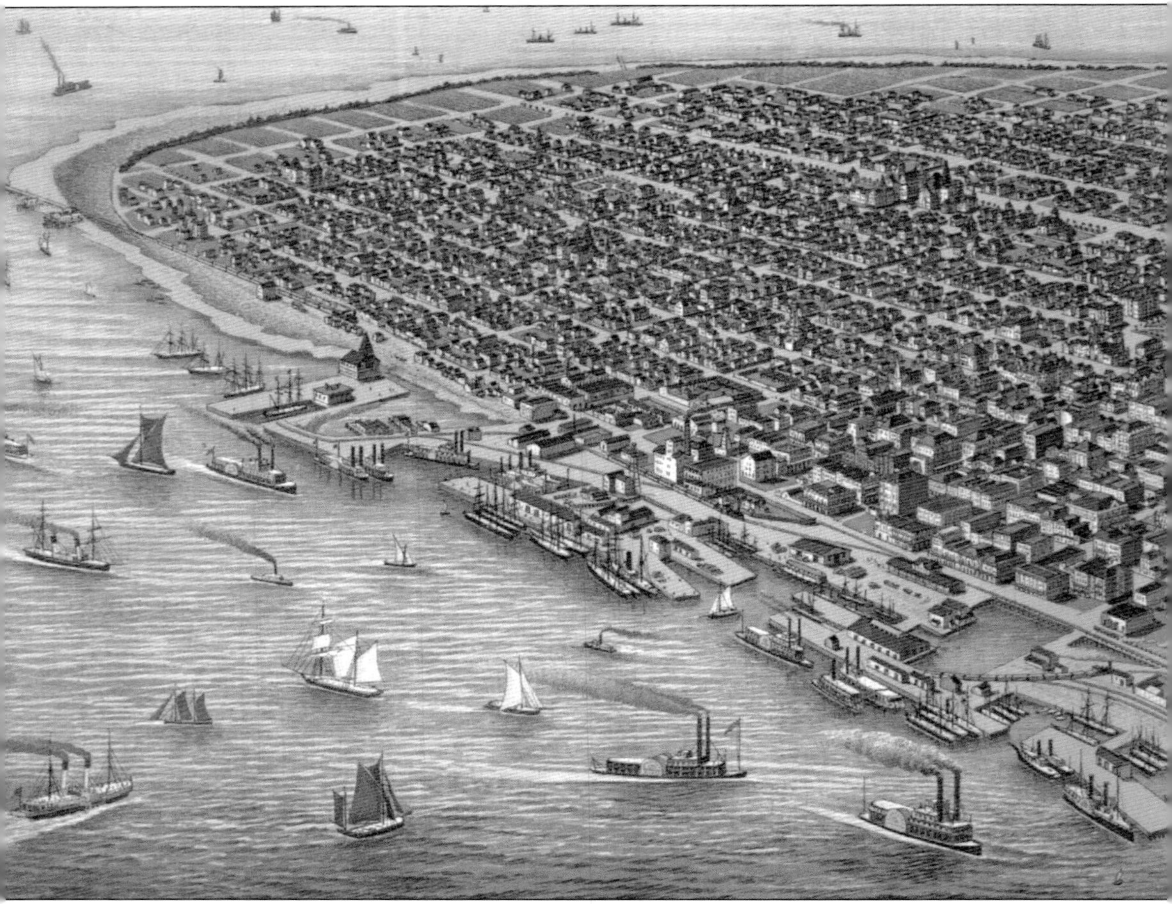

This bird's-eye-view drawing from 1880 shows the density of Galveston. Galveston grew by being a city of many firsts in the state of Texas. These firsts include the following: first post office (1836), first naval base (1836), first bakery (1838), first chapter of the Masonic Order (1840), first military company (1841), first cotton compress (1842), first law firm west of the Mississippi River (1846), first Catholic convent (1847) and first cathedral (1847), first grocery store (1851), first railroad locomotive (1852), first insurance company (1854), first use of telegraph (1854), first

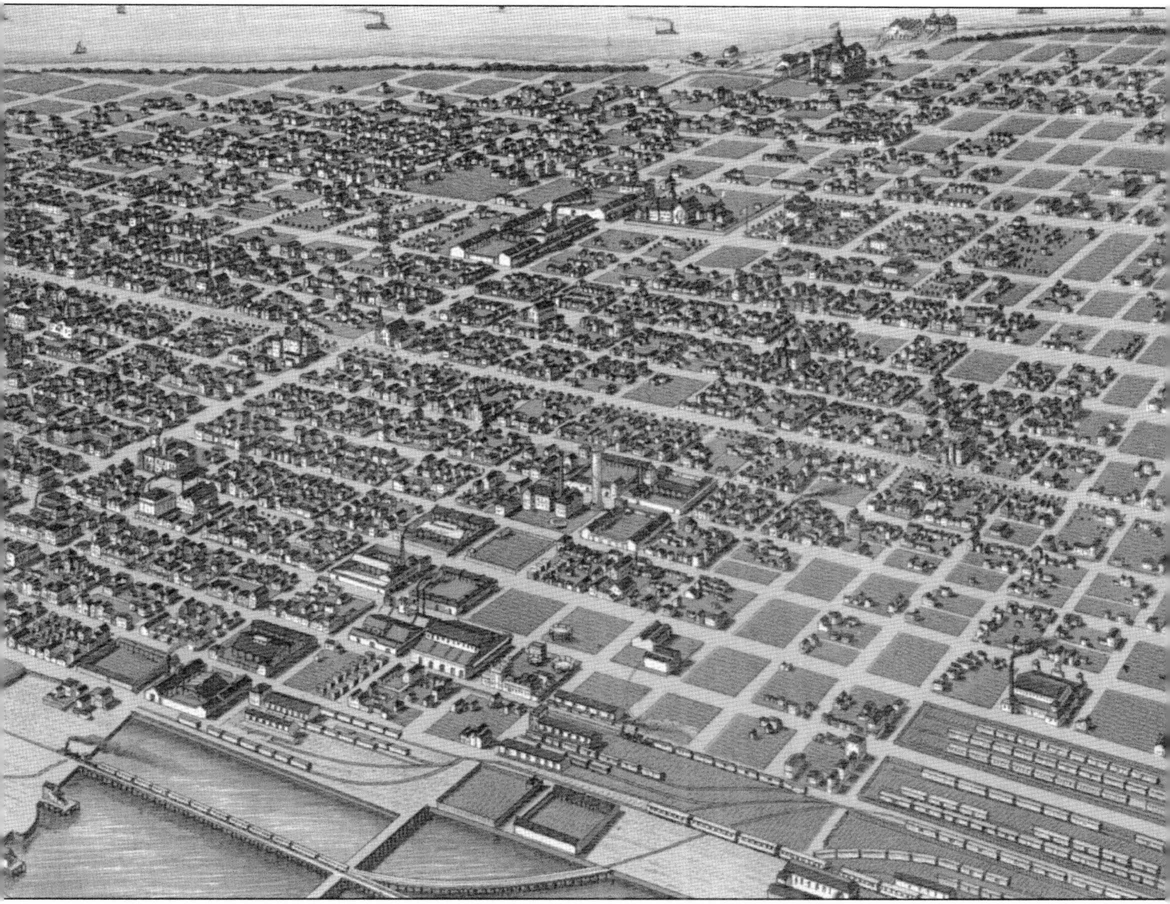

private bank (1854), first jewelry store (1856), first gaslights (1856), first real estate firm (1857), first hospital and trade union (1866), first drugstore (Star Drug Store 1867 and still standing), first opera house (1870), first cotton exchange (1872), first orphanage (1876), first telephone (1878), first electric lights (1883), first medical college (1886 and still standing), first electric streetcars (1893), first school for nurses (1894), first golf course (1898), and first country club (1898).

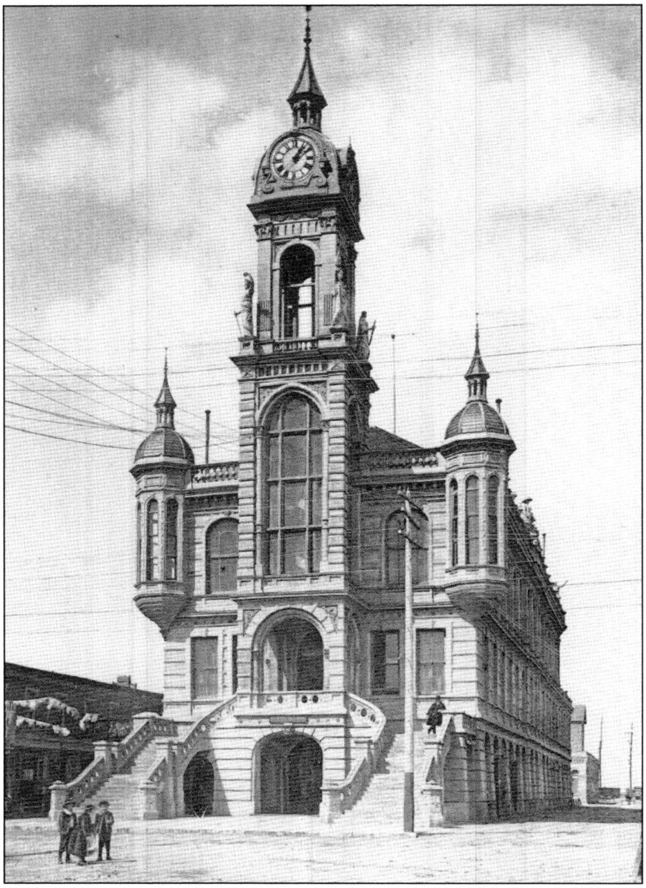

This amazing building, designed by Alfred Mueller, was a showcase for city government in Galveston. Located on 2002 Market, this building was constructed in the French Renaissance Revival style. Damaged heavily in the 1900 Storm, the tower and the third floor were removed. In 1966, this dramatically altered building was demolished.

As this aerial view shows, Galveston was a very dense and populous city in the late 1800s. The population grew from around 5,000 in the 1850s to 22,000 in the 1880s, which ranked Galveston number one in the State of Texas. By 1890, Dallas, San Antonio, and Houston's populations passed Galveston. The 1900 Storm saw Galveston with a loss of population, while other cities in the state soared.

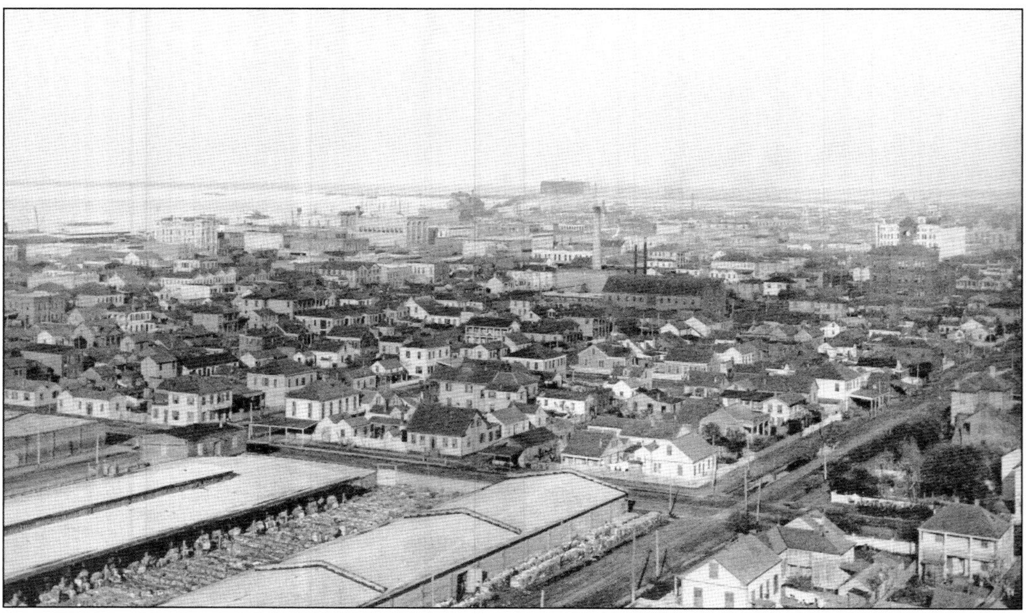

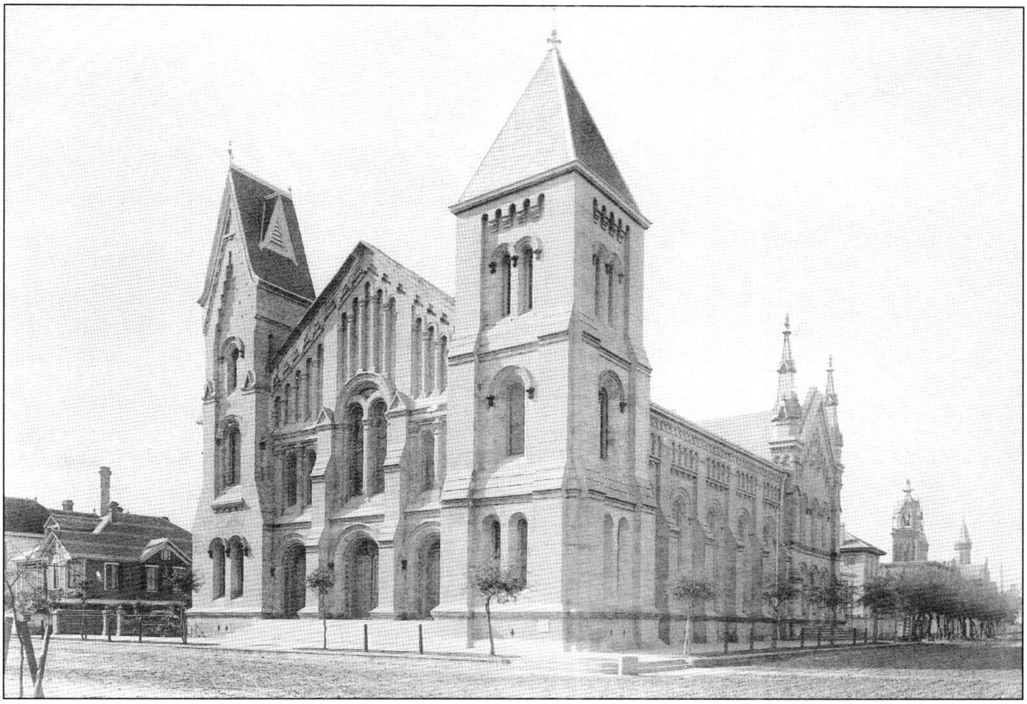

In addition to commercial activities, downtown Galveston was also the center of religious activities in the late 1800s. The First Presbyterian Church, located at 1903 Church Street, began construction in 1876 and finished in 1889. Architect Nicholas Clayton came to Galveston to oversee construction. Jones and Baldwin of Memphis, Tennessee, were the architects.

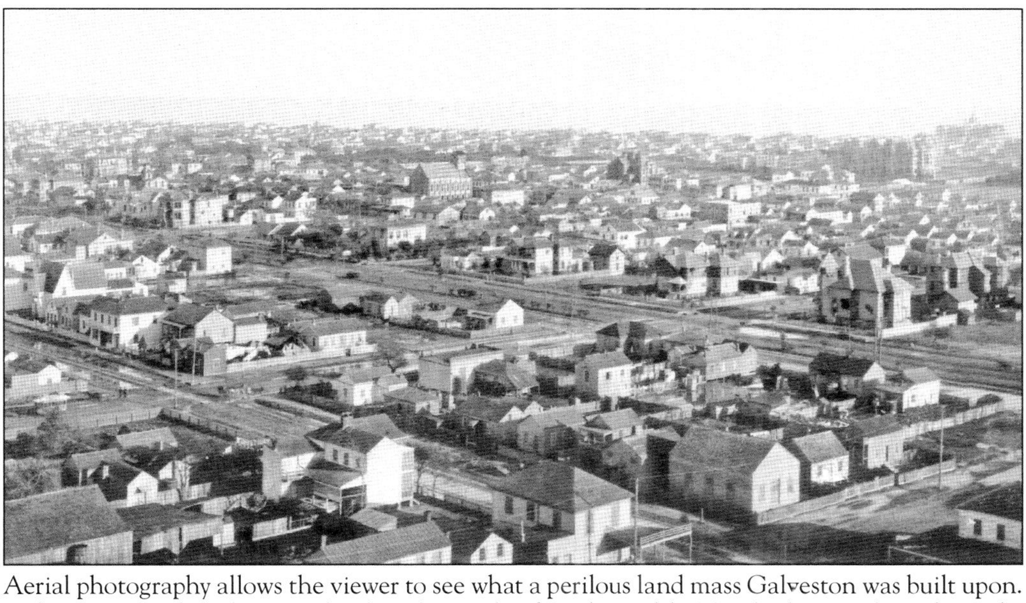

Aerial photography allows the viewer to see what a perilous land mass Galveston was built upon. Galveston Island is a barrier island made mostly of sand, roughly 35 miles long and 3 miles wide. With very little natural vegetation and no natural dunes, Galveston, prior to construction of the Seawall, had very little to stop the water surges that hurricane season often brought.

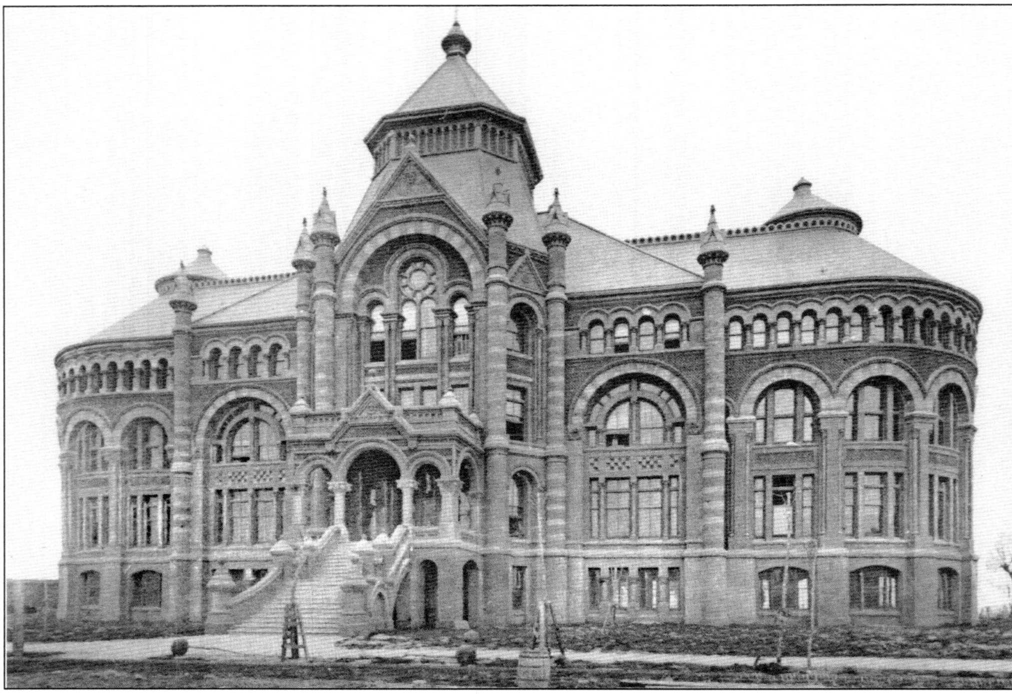

Galveston had a city hospital in 1845, but it was not until 1881, when a statewide vote was cast to locate the University of Texas Medical School on Galveston Island. Galveston enjoyed top-notch medical care, and in 1891, Nicholas Clayton designed the University of Texas Medical Department Building, now known affectionately as "Old Red." The center tower was lost during the 1900 Storm, and Clayton oversaw its repairs in 1901.

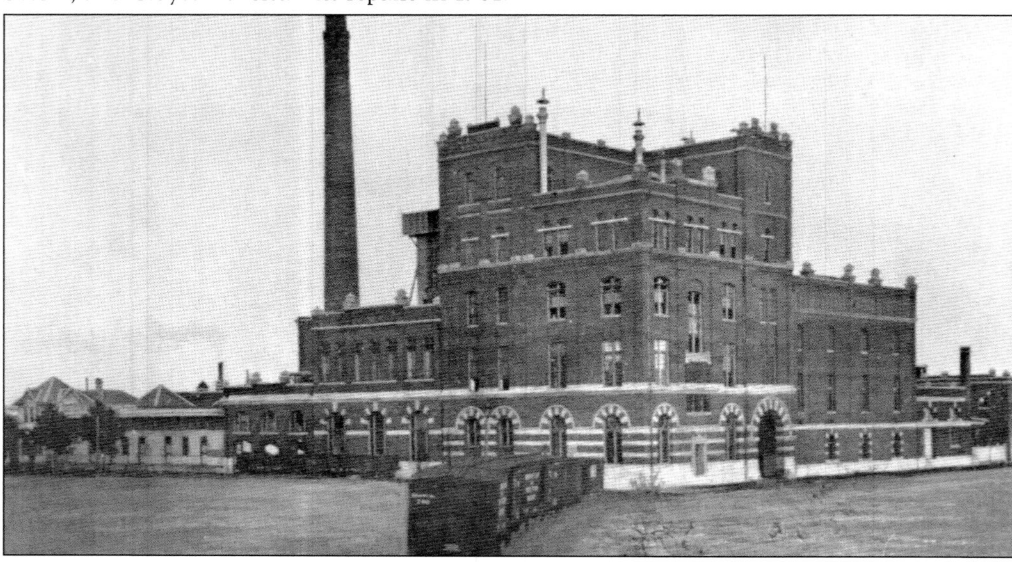

The Galveston Brewing Company was located at Thirty-third and Postoffice, built in 1895. This photograph shows the brewery in 1900. The brewery produced beer for almost 80 years, most notably as the Falstaff Brewery. The original brewery was a project of Adolphus Busch. The building is still standing today and is one of the last factory buildings in Galveston.

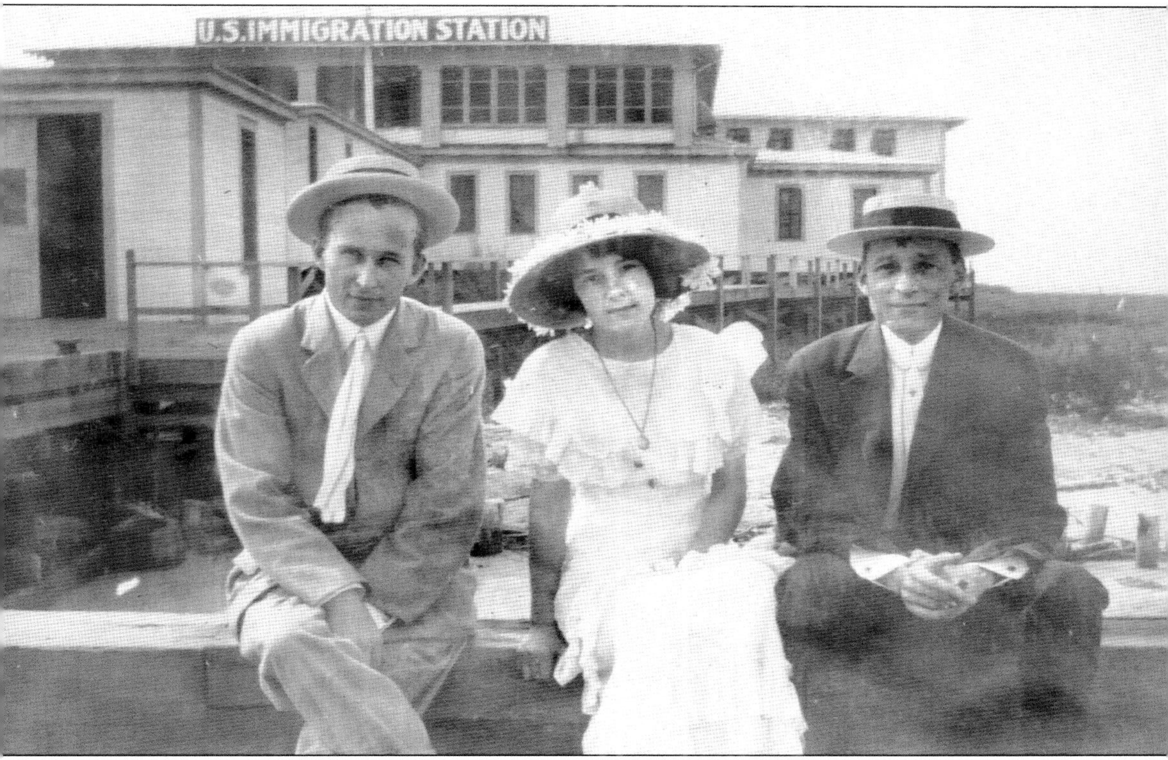

It was not until the early 1830s that Europeans started immigrating to Texas. Traveling to Texas, the different ethnic groups took divergent routes. The Germans and the Czechs exited Europe through the Northern German Lloyd Line ports, either in Bremen or Hamburg. The Swedes departed from a Swedish town called Goteborg, while the Norwegians immigrated from either Stavanger or Christiansand. The Irish departed from the west coast of England and then transferred to ships sailing to America. The Belgians, Dutch, and some French immigrated from L'Havre, France, and the Italians left from Naples. Once the immigrants arrived in Galveston, they were faced with drought, hurricanes, disease, loneliness, the lack of basic necessities, and homesickness. Galveston was a port of entry for hundreds of thousands of immigrants. While the New York counterpart made it a natural port for Europeans, Galveston attracted a diverse group of people from Europe, Mexico, South and Central America, and even Asia. (Courtesy of the Galveston County Historical Museum, Galveston, Texas.)

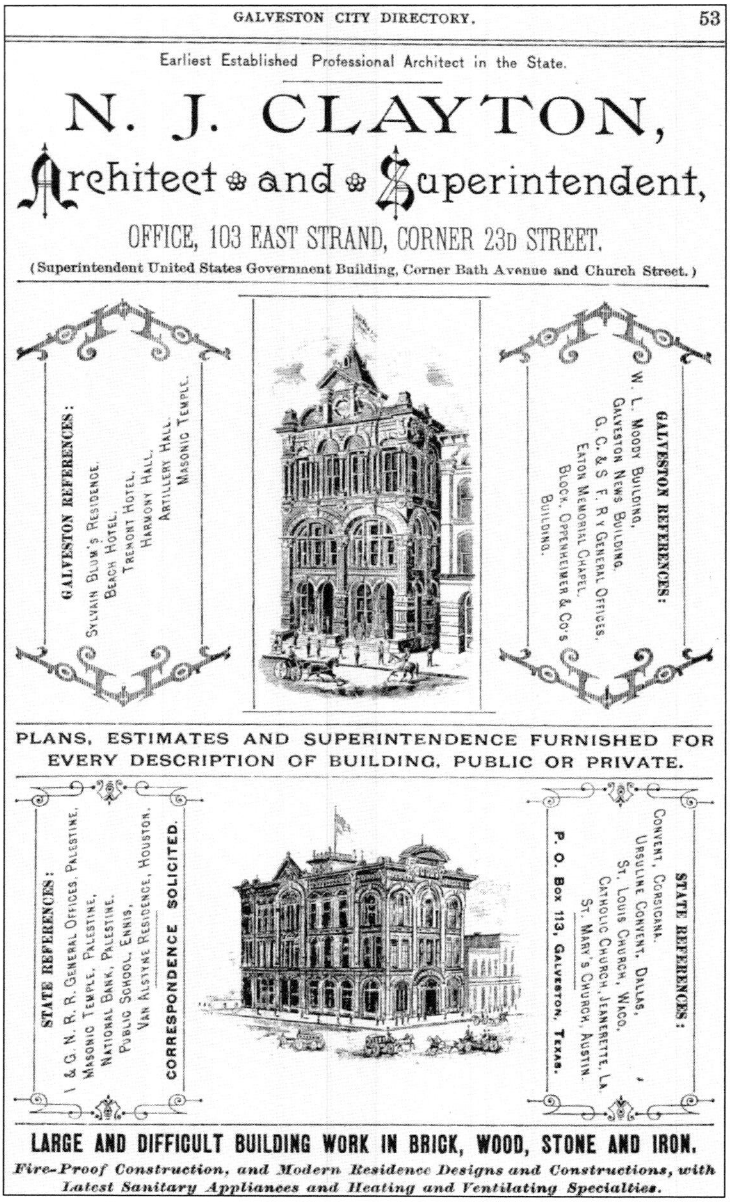

Nicholas Clayton was born in 1840 in Ireland and immigrated to Boston with his mother, Margaret, in 1848. From Boston, they moved to Cincinnati, which was where Clayton graduated from high school. Clayton fought for the Union in the Civil War and lived in Memphis, St. Louis, and Louisville. He married Mary Lorena Ducie in 1892, and the couple had five children: two daughters, who never married, and three sons. Clayton had interests in structural improvements, often using the newest technology at the time of construction. He also was keen on interiors and used new devices such as folding windows and doors, which can both be found in the Gresham House. Clayton worked in the Victorian and Gothic styles. His work has been called "alluring" and "sparkling," and he has a noted feel for proportion. He used layers and multiple building materials (brick, tile, glass, cast iron) to add subtle detail to his designs.

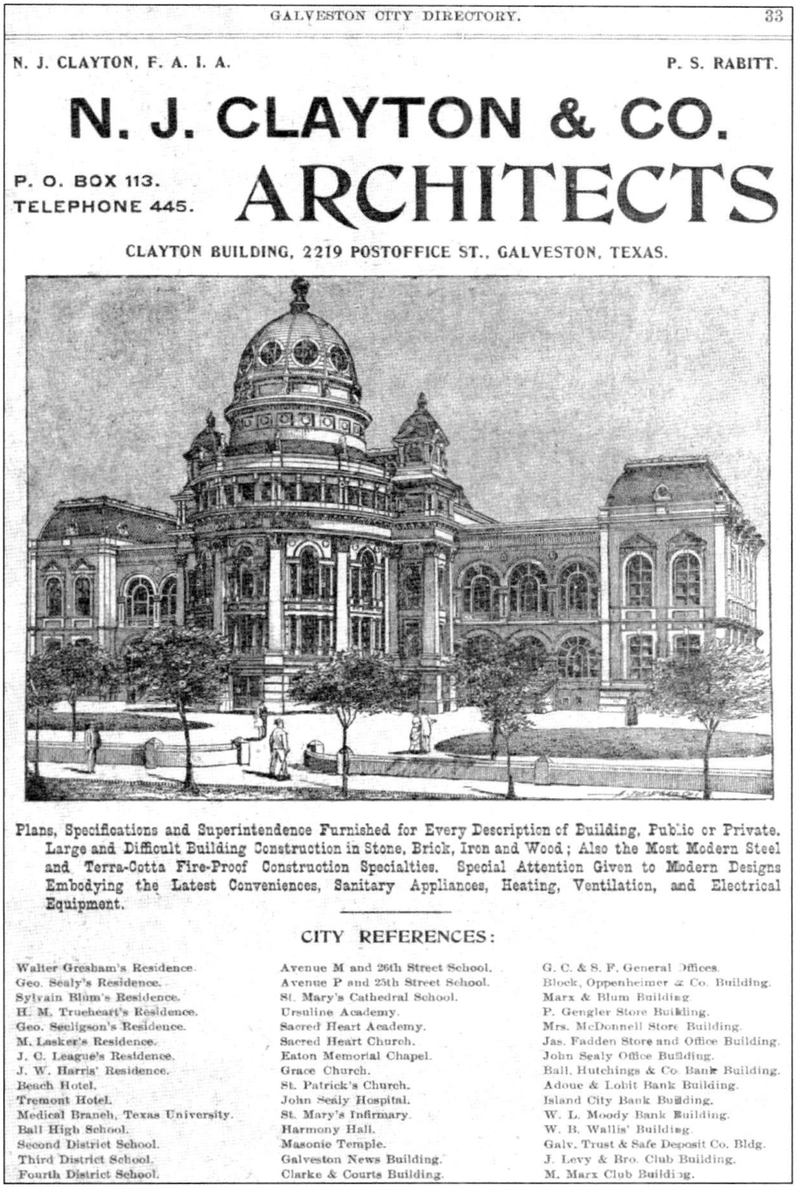
GALVESTON CITY DIRECTORY. 33

N. J. CLAYTON, F. A. I. A. P. S. RABITT.

N. J. CLAYTON & CO.

P. O. BOX 113.
TELEPHONE 445.

ARCHITECTS

CLAYTON BUILDING, 2219 POSTOFFICE ST., GALVESTON, TEXAS.

Plans, Specifications and Superintendence Furnished for Every Description of Building, Public or Private. Large and Difficult Building Construction in Stone, Brick, Iron and Wood; Also the Most Modern Steel and Terra-Cotta Fire-Proof Construction Specialties. Special Attention Given to Modern Designs Embodying the Latest Conveniences, Sanitary Appliances, Heating, Ventilation, and Electrical Equipment.

CITY REFERENCES:

Walter Gresham's Residence.
Geo. Sealy's Residence.
Sylvain Blum's Residence.
H. M. Trueheart's Residence.
Geo. Seeligson's Residence.
M. Lasker's Residence.
J. C. League's Residence.
J. W. Harris' Residence.
Beach Hotel.
Tremont Hotel.
Medical Branch, Texas University.
Ball High School.
Second District School.
Third District School.
Fourth District School.

Avenue M and 26th Street School.
Avenue P and 25th Street School.
St. Mary's Cathedral School.
Ursuline Academy.
Sacred Heart Academy.
Sacred Heart Church.
Eaton Memorial Chapel.
Grace Church.
St. Patrick's Church.
John Sealy Hospital.
St. Mary's Infirmary.
Harmony Hall.
Masonic Temple.
Galveston News Building.
Clarke & Courts Building.

G. C. & S. F. General Offices.
Block, Oppenheimer & Co. Building.
Marx & Blum Building.
P. Gengler Store Building.
Mrs. McDonnell Store Building.
Jas. Fadden Store and Office Building.
John Sealy Office Building.
Ball, Hutchings & Co. Bank Building.
Adoue & Lobit Bank Building.
Island City Bank Building.
W. L. Moody Bank Building.
W. B. Wallis' Building.
Galv. Trust & Safe Deposit Co. Bldg.
J. Levy & Bro. Club Building.
M. Marx Club Building.

Clayton was the first person to practice architecture as a profession in Galveston. He came to Galveston in April 1872, with little professional training. It is not known exactly how Clayton became trained in architecture. Clayton designed more than 150 buildings, and 50 additions are attributed to him. Known as "Galveston's Architect," he designed buildings for Galveston's elite between 1875 and 1902. More than any other architect, Clayton shaped Galveston's architectural identity. Commercial commissions included Adoue and Lobit; W. L. Moody; Ball, Hutchings, and Sealy; and McFadden Buildings (all on the Strand). His best-known residential design is the Walter Gresham House at 1402 Broadway. He also designed most of the public schools and medical buildings in Galveston in the late 1800s. Clayton's adeptness is most noted in his design of churches. As a devout Catholic, he was often the choice for many commissions from dioceses around Texas.

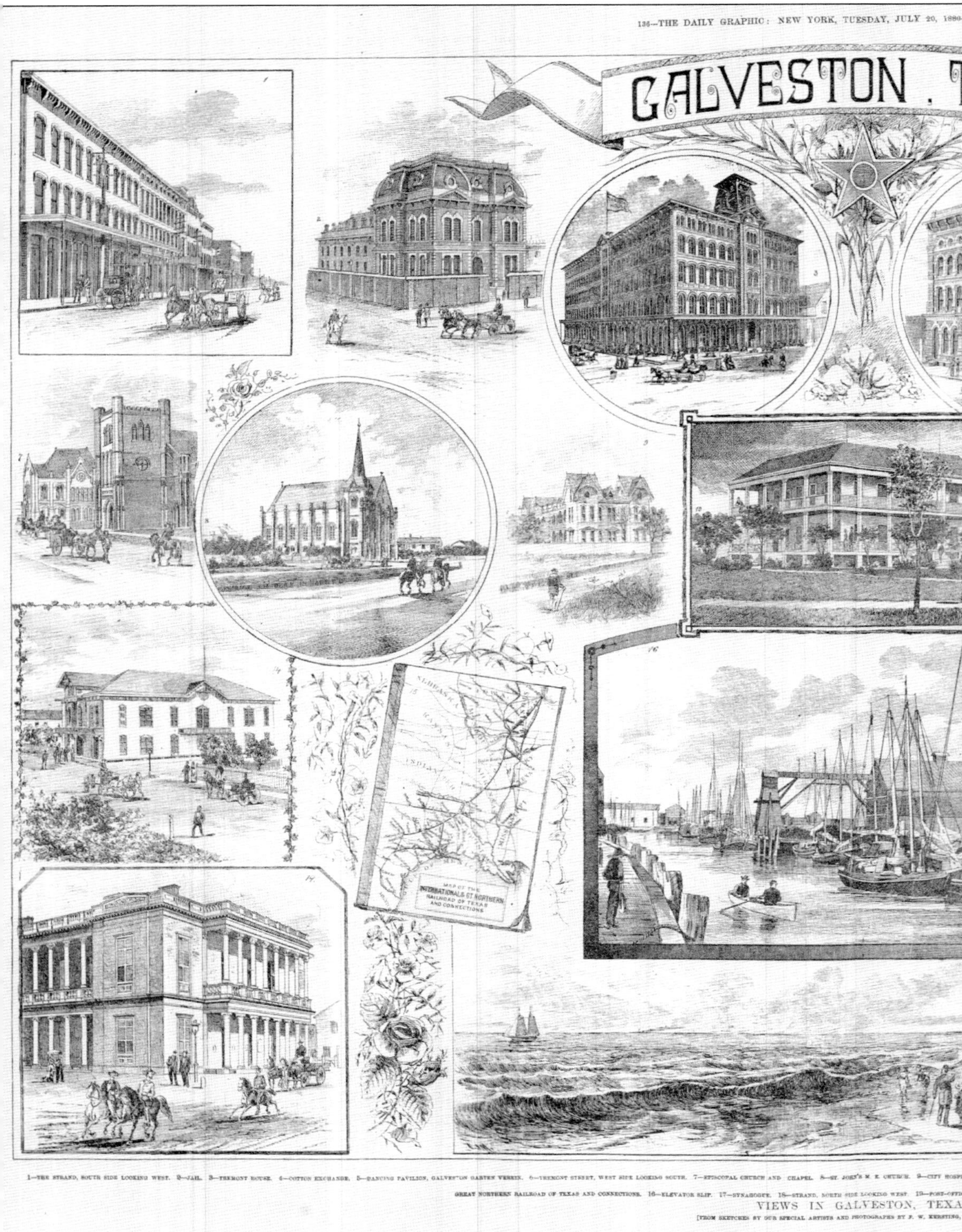
136—THE DAILY GRAPHIC: NEW YORK, TUESDAY, JULY 20, 1880—

GALVESTON, T

1—THE STRAND, SOUTH SIDE LOOKING WEST. 2—JAIL. 3—TREMONT HOUSE. 4—COTTON EXCHANGE. 5—DANCING PAVILION, GALVESTON GARTEN VEREIN. 6—TREMONT STREET, WEST SIDE LOOKING SOUTH. 7—EPISCOPAL CHURCH AND CHAPEL. 8—ST. JOHN'S M. E. CHURCH. 9—CITY HOSPI

GREAT NORTHERN RAILROAD OF TEXAS AND CONNECTIONS. 16—ELEVATOR SLIP. 17—SYNAGOGUE. 18—STRAND, NORTH SIDE LOOKING WEST. 19—POST-OFFIC

VIEWS IN GALVESTON, TEXA

[FROM SKETCHES BY OUR SPECIAL ARTISTS AND PHOTOGRAPHS BY F. W. KERSTING,

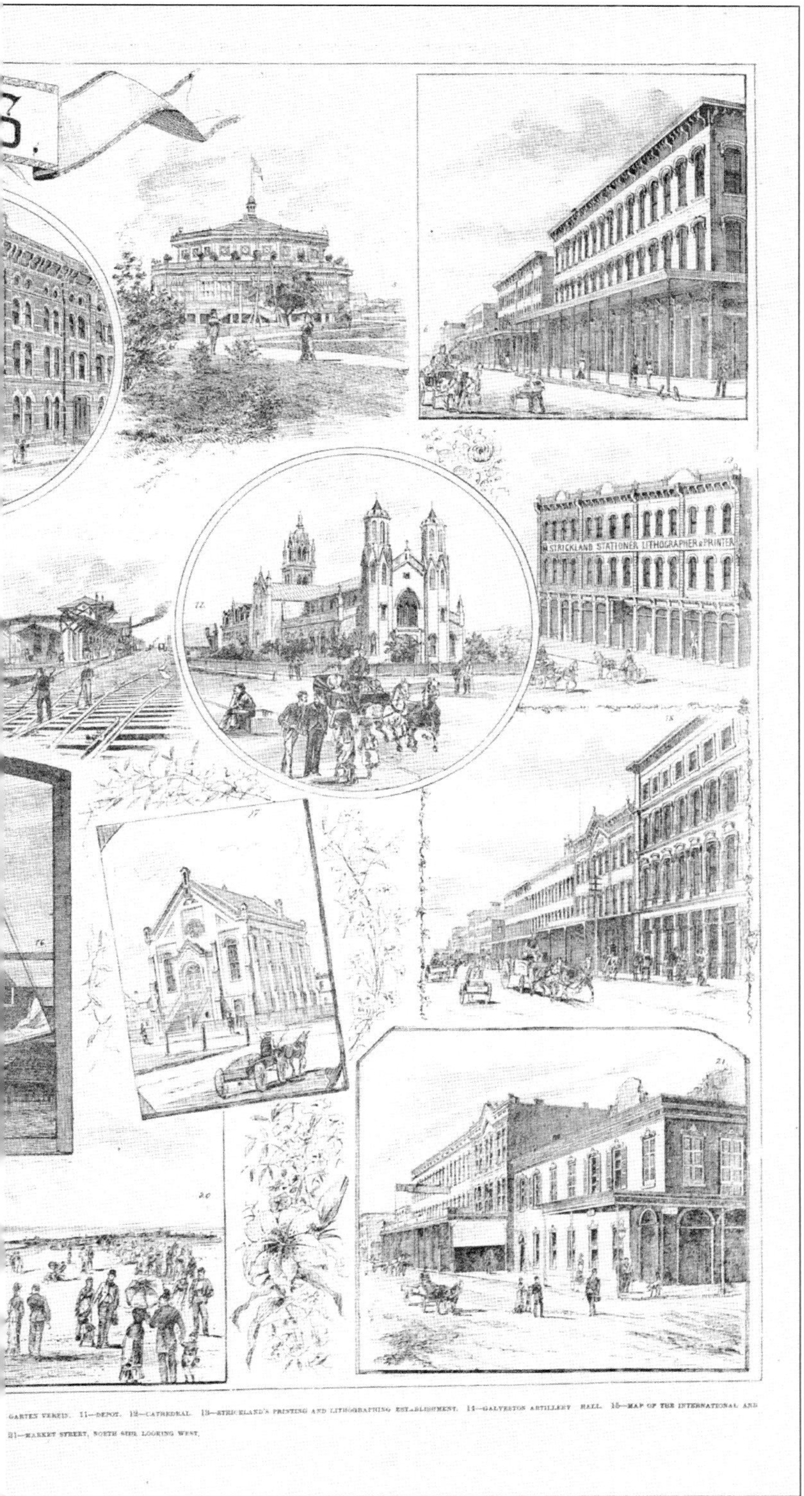

The New York Daily Graphic published these Galveston scenes in on July 20, 1880. Showing a variety of scenes from entertainment, civic, industrial, and residential, these detailed etchings interpret Galveston as a cosmopolitan city. Galveston in 1880 was a thriving port city, full of sophistication and architectural beauty. Many of the buildings still stand today; the Custom House, Garten Verein, The Lasker House, Trinity Episcopal Church, St. Mary's Cathedral, and many of the buildings in the Strand, Tremont and Market scenes. *The Daily Graphic: An Illustrated Evening Newspaper* was founded in New York in March 1873. The Daily Graphic published daily illustrations of news around the country. *The Daily Graphic* ceased publication on September 23, 1889. (Courtesy The Dolph Briscoe Center for American History, The University of Texas at Austin.)

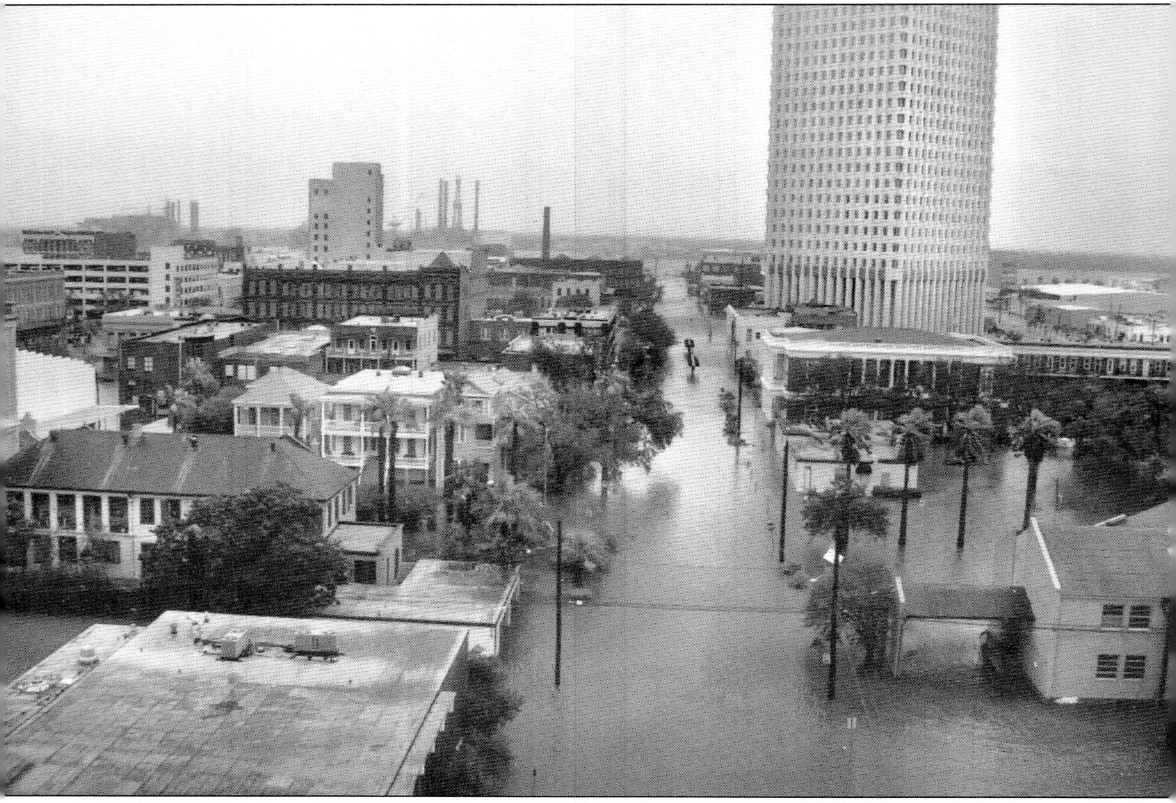

Galveston is no stranger to disaster. In September 2008, Hurricane Ike hit Galveston. Even though Galveston has a seawall to protect the beachside of the island, the bayside has no such barrier. The flooding in Galveston occurred from the bay, inundating downtown with up to 13 feet of water on the Strand to 3 feet on Broadway. Hurricane Ike was the third costliest hurricane to ever make landfall in the United States. As a Category 2 hurricane, with winds of 110 miles per hour, Ike made U.S. landfall at Galveston, Texas, on September 13, 2008, at 2:10 a.m. (Central Daylight Time). The storm surge was projected at Category 4 height. The National Hurricane Center advisory cited tropical storm and hurricane force winds extending 275 miles and 120 miles respectively, from the center. A 10- to 14-foot storm surge washed over Galveston Island. The water was 15–20 feet above sea level along Galveston Bay. (Ron Shelby.)

Two

Avenue B, Strand

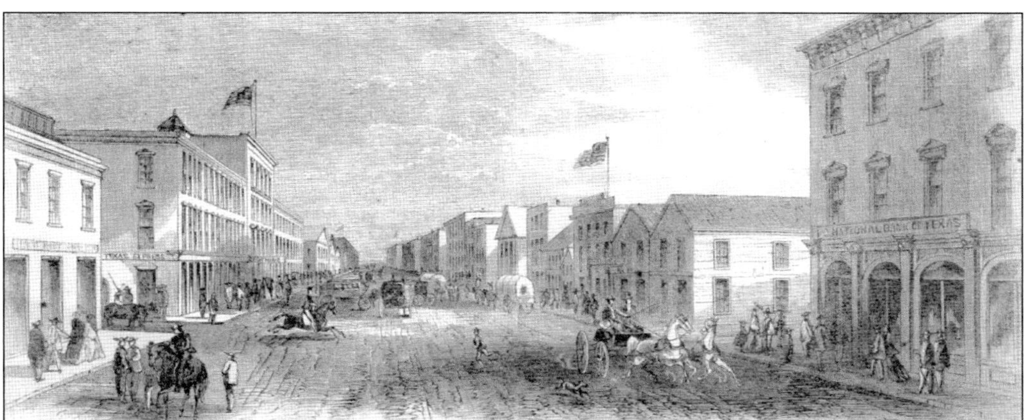

This engraving illustrates the Strand in 1866. The engraving, sketched by Theodore R. Davis, was published in *Harpers Weekly* on October 27, 1866. Looking from approximately Twenty-second Street, this view, shows how early Galveston had an abundance of wood-framed buildings and depicts the time before architectural styles became more refined with the help of architects and trained craftsmen. Most of this area was destroyed by fire in 1869.

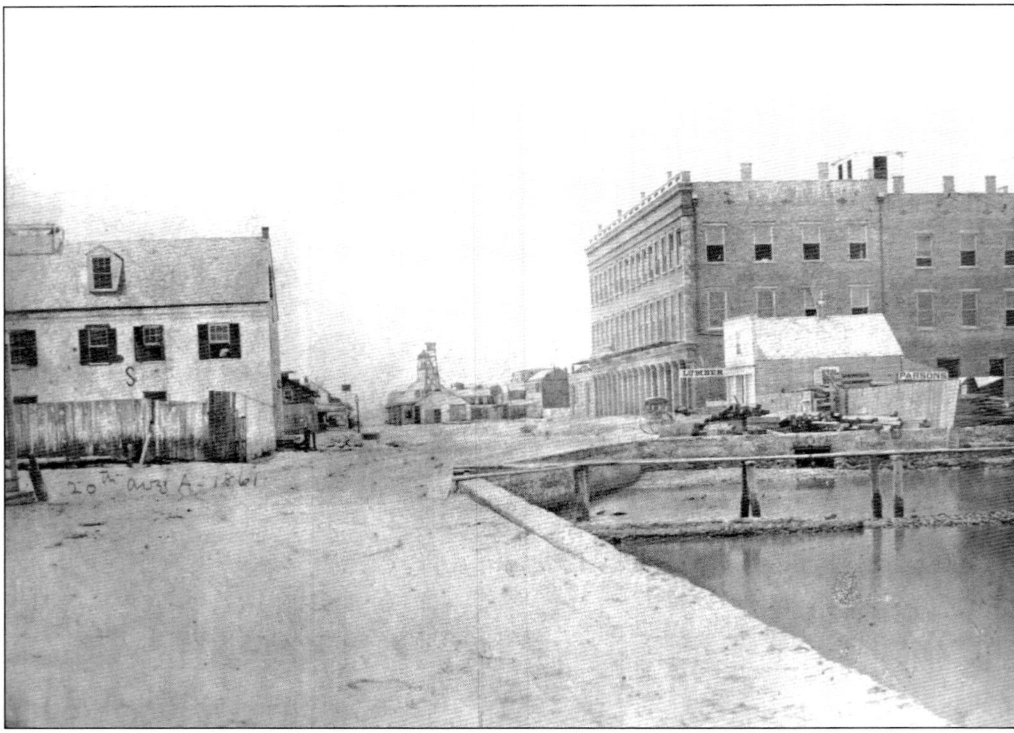

Looking south to the old city Market, this photograph shows the Hendley Building (1859) and the Market House. Taken around 1861, this image depicts Galveston during a period of growth, which took place before the Battles of Galveston during the Civil War. The photograph also shows how far Kuhn's Wharf came into the city. (Courtesy of the Rosenberg Library, Galveston, Texas.)

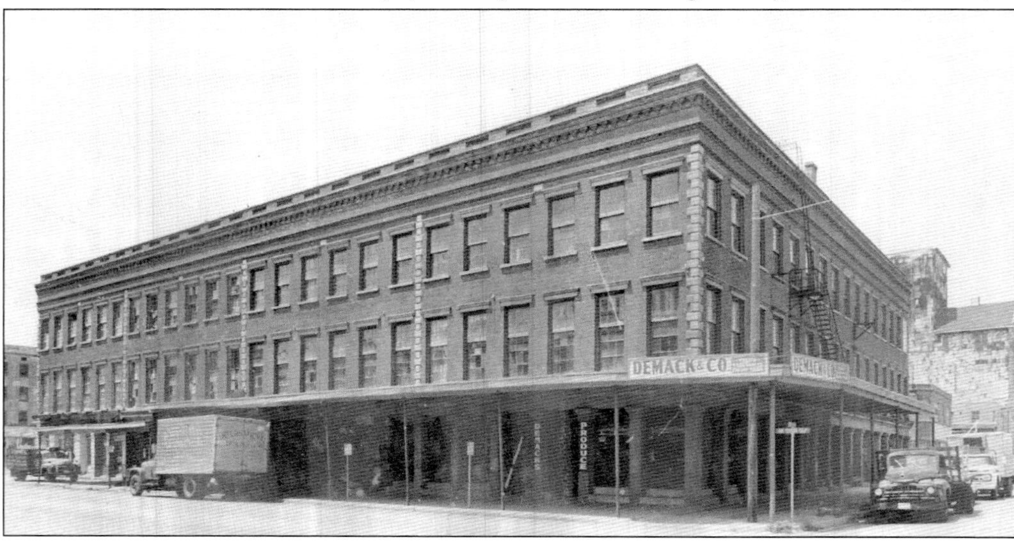

This mid-1970s photograph shows how the Hendley Buildings continued to be used, retaining their character, even when the Strand was experiencing a decline in business and traffic. Even at over 100 years old, the Hendley Buildings still retained much of their character and charm. Though this building might look like one single unit, it is actually four separate buildings.

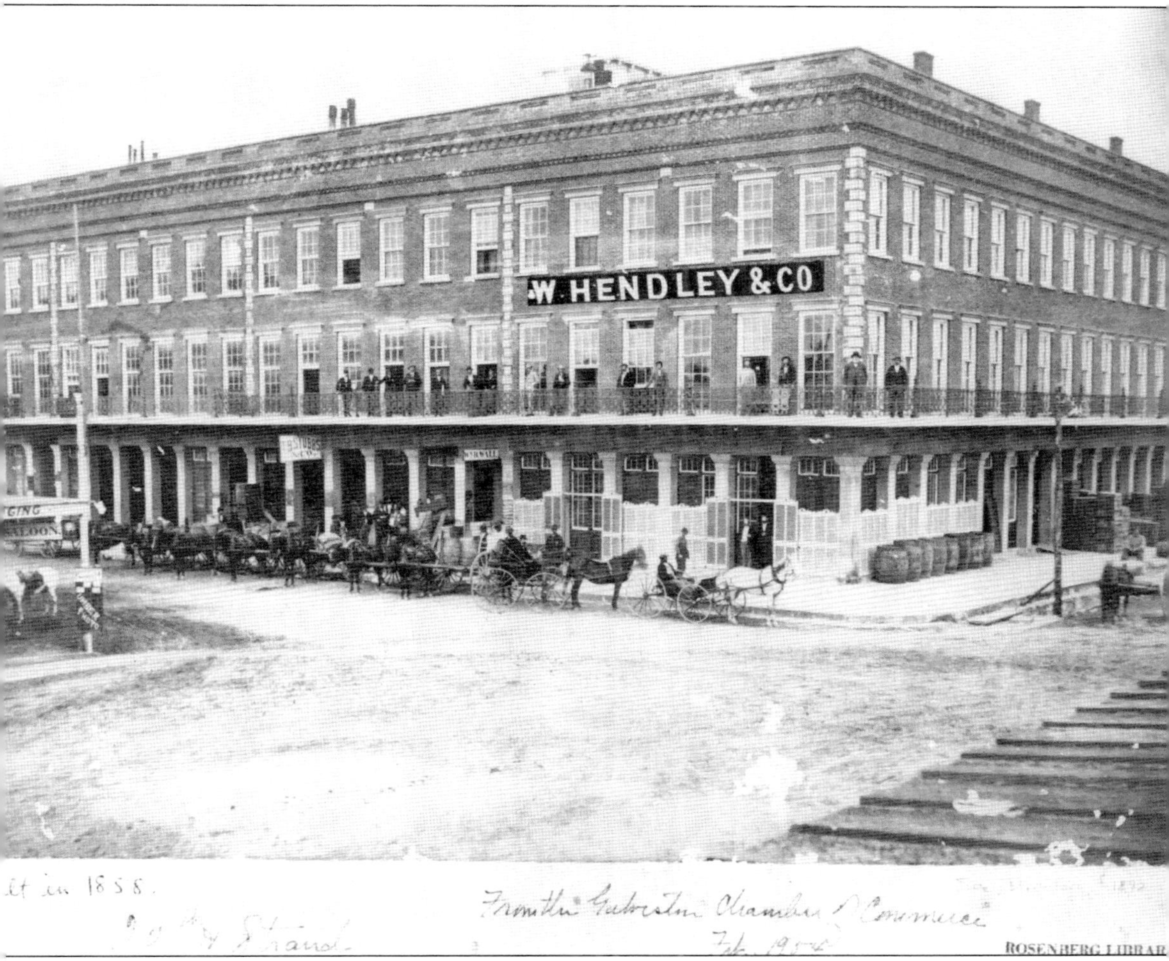

Hendley Row at 2000–2016 Strand was built from brick and cast with iron interior supports. This block is one of the earliest surviving commercial blocks in downtown Galveston. During the Civil War, a wooden cupola served as a lookout for the Confederates to spy on what the Federals were doing in Galveston Harbor. The Federal blockade of Galveston began on July 2, 1861, with the arrival of USS *South Carolina*. The Federal move on the island was delayed, but when it finally came in October 1862, Comdr. Jonathan M. Wainwright, commanding the Navy gunboat *Harriet Lane*, took possession of the city and raised the U.S. flag over the U.S. Custom House. In the early hours of New Year's Day 1863, however, Confederate forces, commanded by John Bankhead Magruder, launched a bold attack to recapture the city. The attack ended with an almost complete Confederate victory. *Harriet Lane* and three Union transports were captured, and Wainwright was killed. The Federals never tried to retake Galveston but reinforced the blockade around the Island. (Courtesy of the Rosenberg Library Galveston, Texas.)

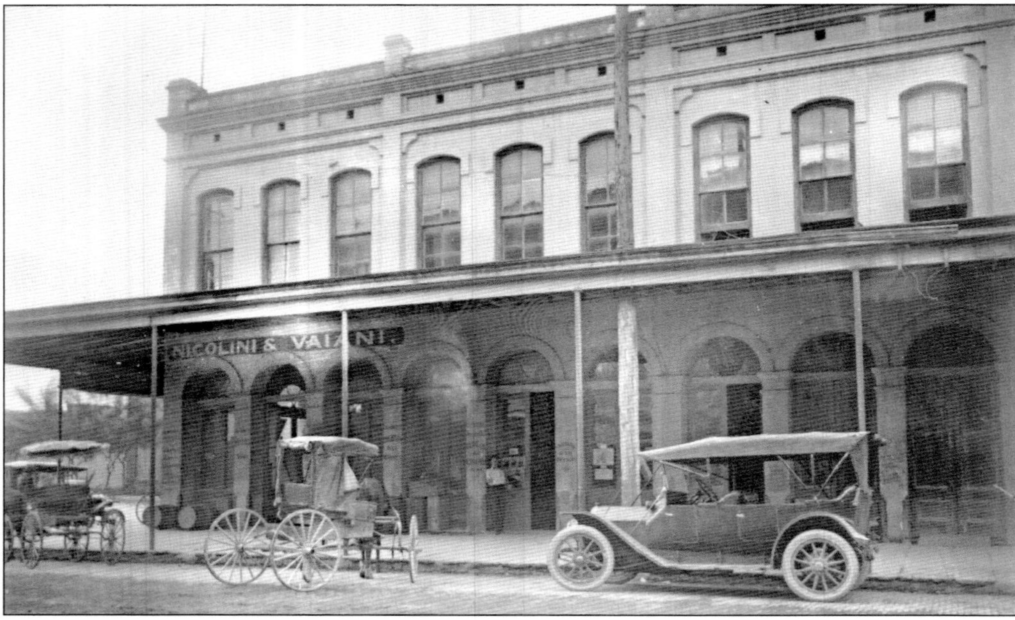

Nathaniel Tobey Jr. designed the Rosenberg Building in 1876 as an investment for Swiss-born banker, Henry Rosenberg. Henry Rosenberg built several investment properties in downtown Galveston. The brick building cost Rosenberg $20,000 to build. Rosenberg was one of Galveston's first philanthropists. He built water fountains, the library, local schools, and church buildings. (Courtesy of the Dolph Briscoe Center for American History, The University of Texas at Austin.)

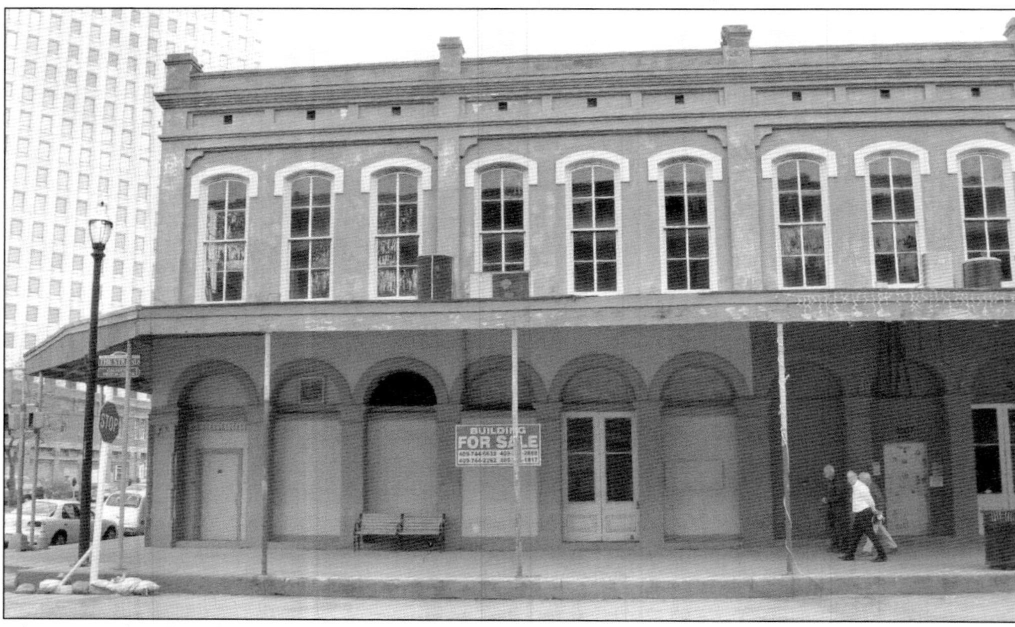

The Strand suffered a steep decline after the Great Depression, and many buildings along the Strand were turned into warehouses. The Rosenberg Building is no exception, and this present-day photograph shows it has yet to reach its potential. As an anchor for the easternmost section of the commercial district, at Twentieth and Strand, reinvestment is needed.

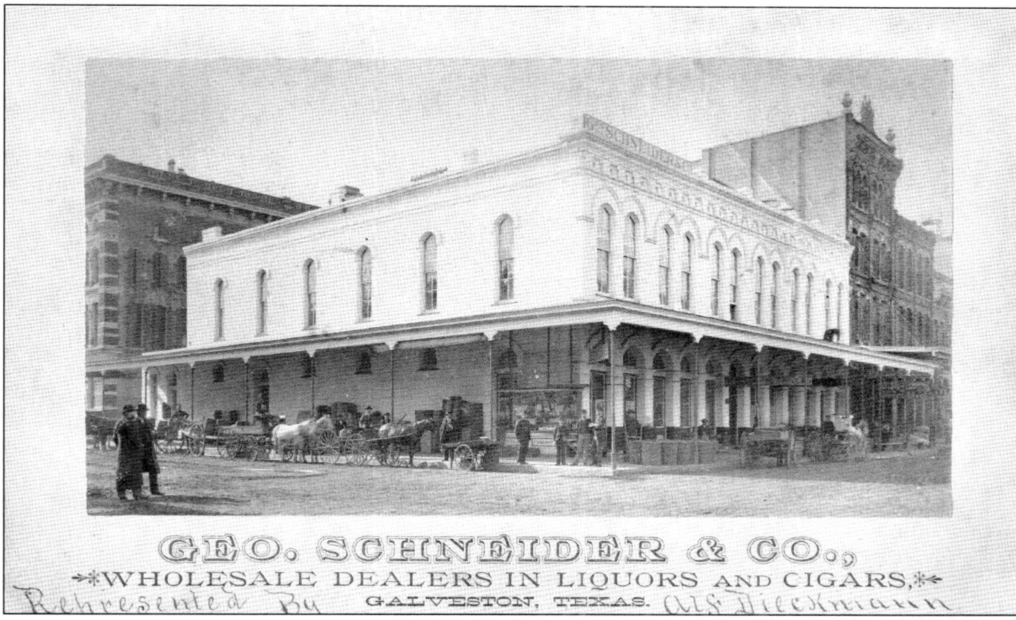

The Schneider Building was constructed in 1878. The building was an investment property for Ball, Hutchings, and Company. Nicholas Clayton and his partner of the time, Michael Lynch, designed this building with four grouped ground-floor doors and pairs of matching windows. This photograph, taken prior to the 1900 Storm, also shows the Clara Lang Building to the right with all four floors intact. (Courtesy of the Rosenberg Library, Galveston, Texas.)

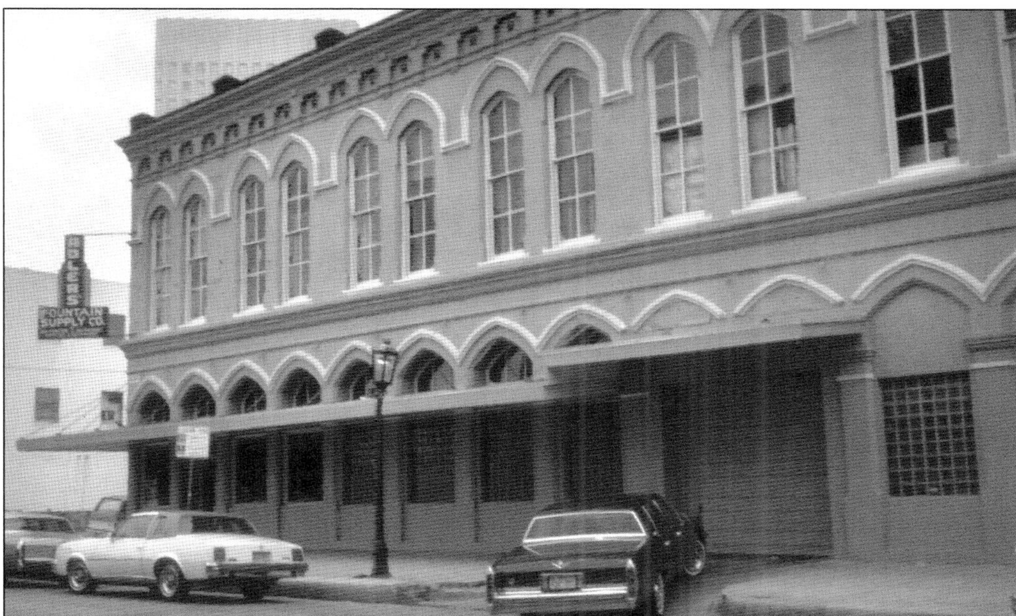

The George Schneider and Company were local agents for Schlitz bottled beer, and they handled many varieties of bourbons, wines, and brandies. George Schneider's three sons, Louis, William, and Fred, continued to run his business after his death.

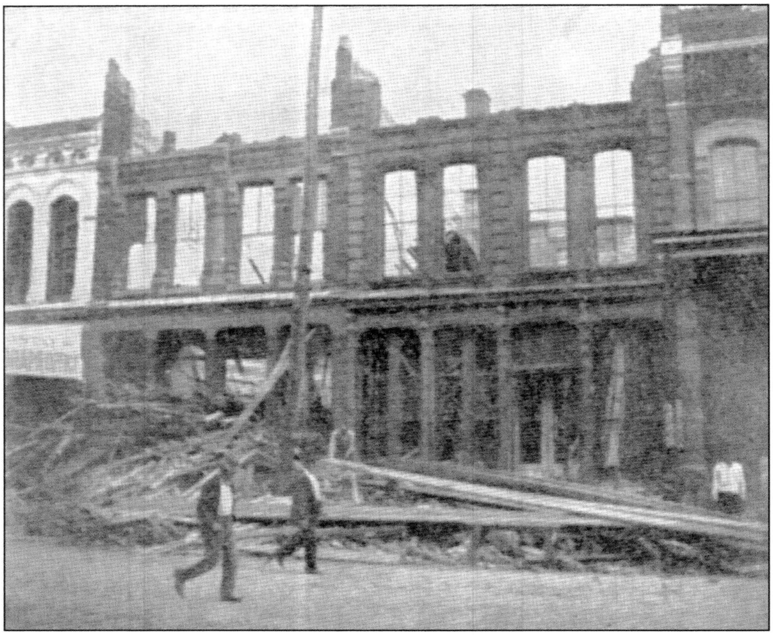

At 2109 Strand, Clara Lang constructed two buildings after the fire of 1877. Originally, 2109 Strand Street was designed by John Moser to be four stories tall and made from pressed brick and artificial stone trim. The 1900 Storm destroyed the upper floors. The cast-iron storefronts were what mostly survived the 1900 Storm. The building functioned as commercial properties for Lang.

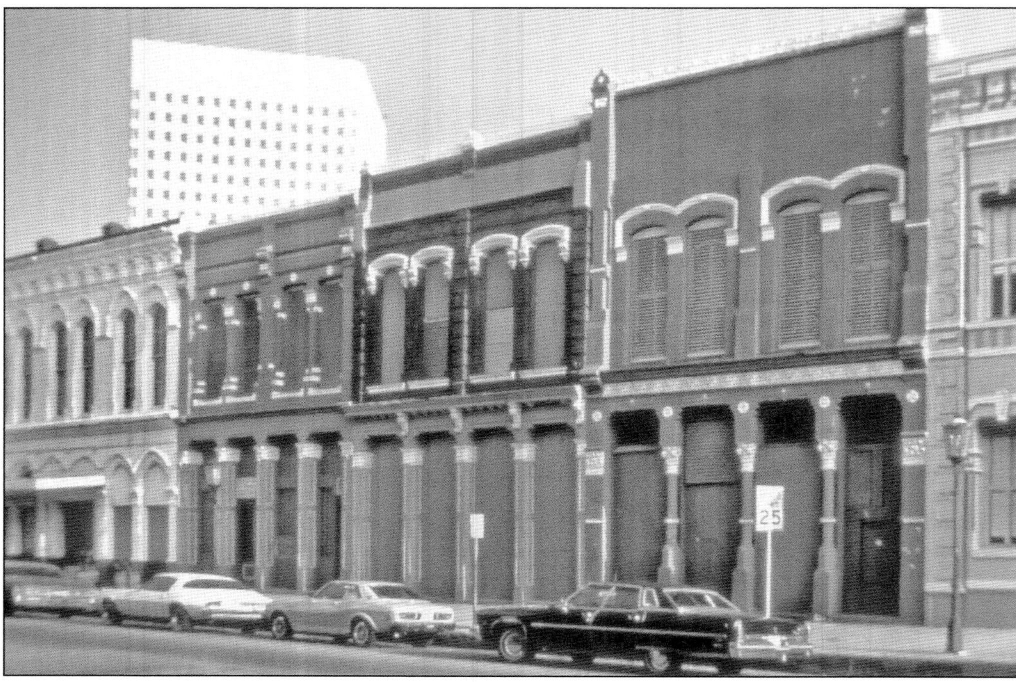

Pictured from left to right are the following four structures: the Schneider, Clara Lang, Brown, and Oppermann Buildings. Lang and Brown both have cast-iron storefronts. Clayton and Lynch designed the Brown Building. It lost one floor in the 1900 Storm. The Oppermann Building was designed for Gustav Oppermann by German, born and trained, architect John Moser. This building lost its decorative cornice, most likely during the 1900 Storm.

The Adoue and Lobit Building was constructed in 1890, with Nicholas Clayton as designer. Like many buildings on the Strand, this building featured a cast-iron storefront, which is still visible today. Although altered, the window fenestration remains. Clayton worked meticulously with details on his buildings, but compared to the W. L. Moody Building on the next block, this one is much more constrained.

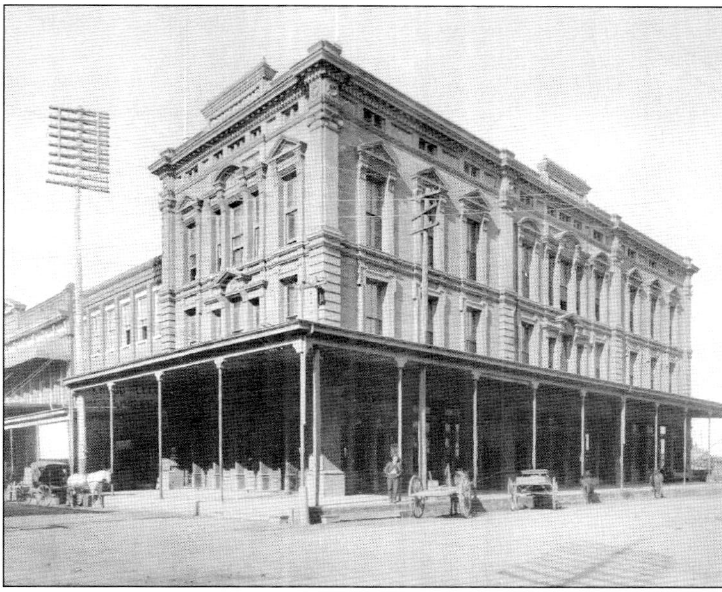

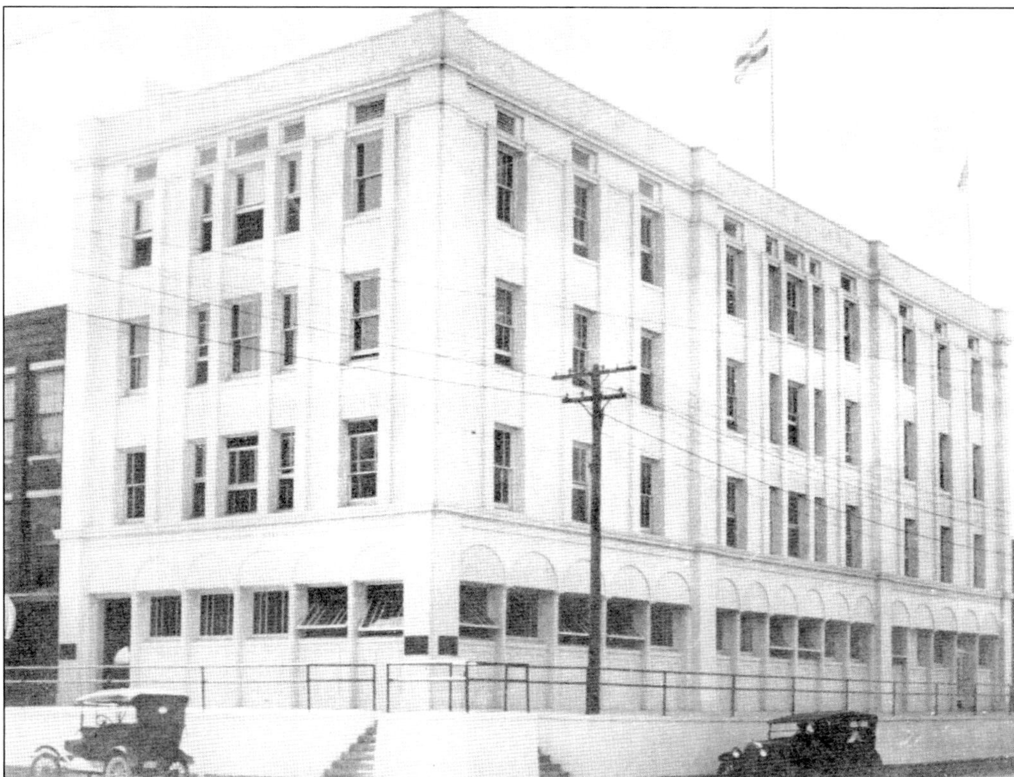

Adoue and Lobit was a private banking firm. Established in 1873, Adoue and Lobit was one of the largest financial operations in Galveston. They did a heavy amount of exchange with Europe in the late 1800s. Jean Baptiste Adoue Sr. was president of the Galveston Oil Mill and was on the board of the Electric Light Company.

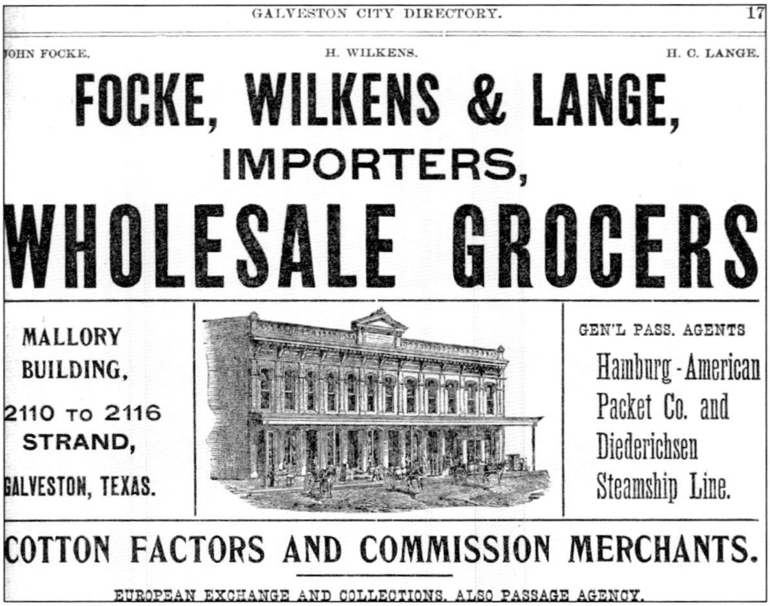
GALVESTON CITY DIRECTORY. 17

JOHN FOCKE. H. WILKENS. H. C. LANGE.

FOCKE, WILKENS & LANGE,

IMPORTERS,

WHOLESALE GROCERS

MALLORY BUILDING,

2110 TO 2116 STRAND,

GALVESTON, TEXAS.

GEN'L PASS. AGENTS

Hamburg-American Packet Co. and Diederichsen Steamship Line.

COTTON FACTORS AND COMMISSION MERCHANTS.

EUROPEAN EXCHANGE AND COLLECTIONS. ALSO PASSAGE AGENCY.

Several grocery houses, which included Moore, Stratton, and Company and Focke and Wilkins, used the Mallory Building as a home for their operations. The Mallory Buildings was one of the first buildings on the Strand to have improvements made after the decline of the 1930s–1960s. The building has a significant structural cast-iron storefront.

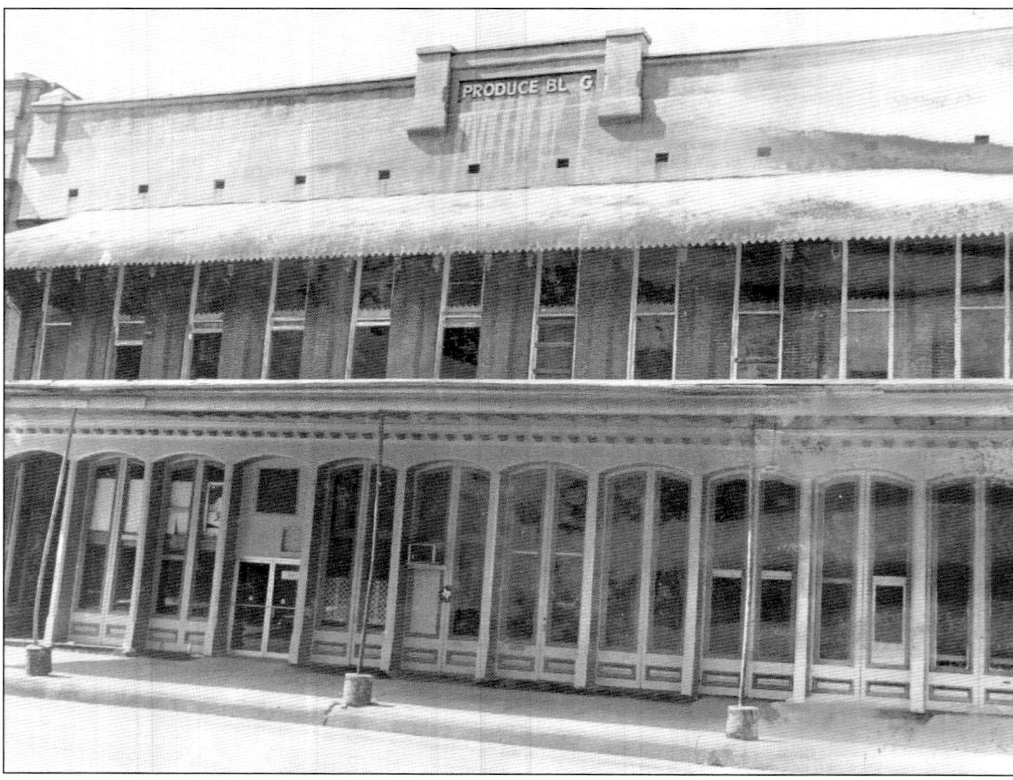

Clyde Mallory was the son of Charles Mallory of the famous Mallory Shipping Line. Clyde Mallory built this building in 1878, replacing the original one that burned in 1877. The building has 12 large double doors that are 14 feet tall, welcoming visitors into the interior space. This building also suffered a fire in 1881 and was repaired the same year.

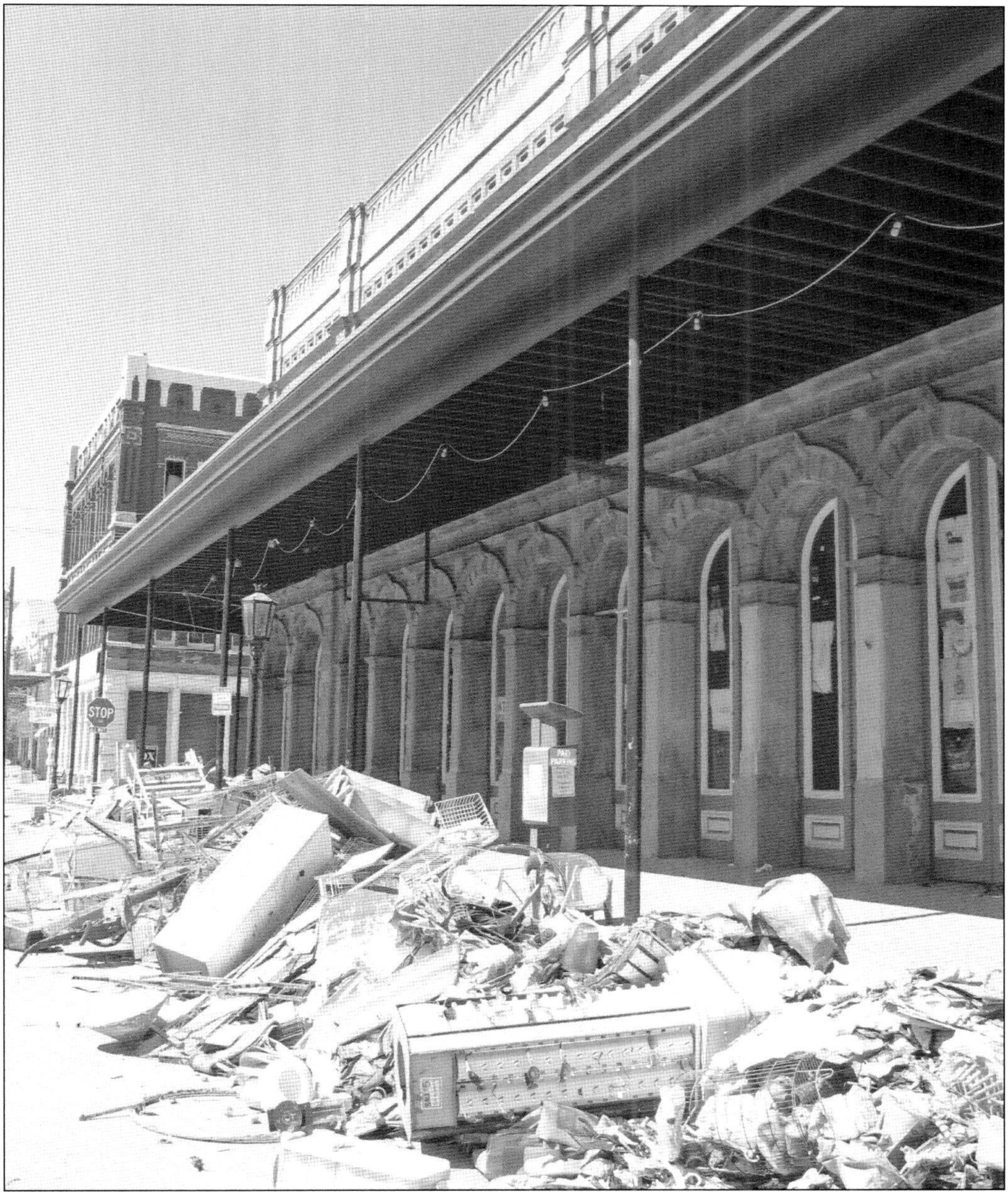

The Strand took the brunt of flooding from Hurricane Ike. Depending on the entrance to the building, most had between 5 and 8 feet of floodwater inside. Cleanup was fast and furious, with most cleaning out their interior spaces with the help of friends and family. Cast-iron storefronts are prolific on the Strand, and these storefronts were listed on the National Trust for Historic Preservation's 11 Most Endangered Historic Places list in 2009. The saltwater and noxious mix that inundated the Strand, left many of the cast-iron storefronts vulnerable to deterioration. Galveston has 36 buildings with cast-iron elements extant. Cast iron was considered a cutting-edge material in the late 1800s, with architects employing cast iron as structural and often decorative elements. Most of the buildings on the Strand have withstood major hurricanes in 1900, 1915, 1943, 1961, 1983, 2005, and now 2008, as well as three great fires.

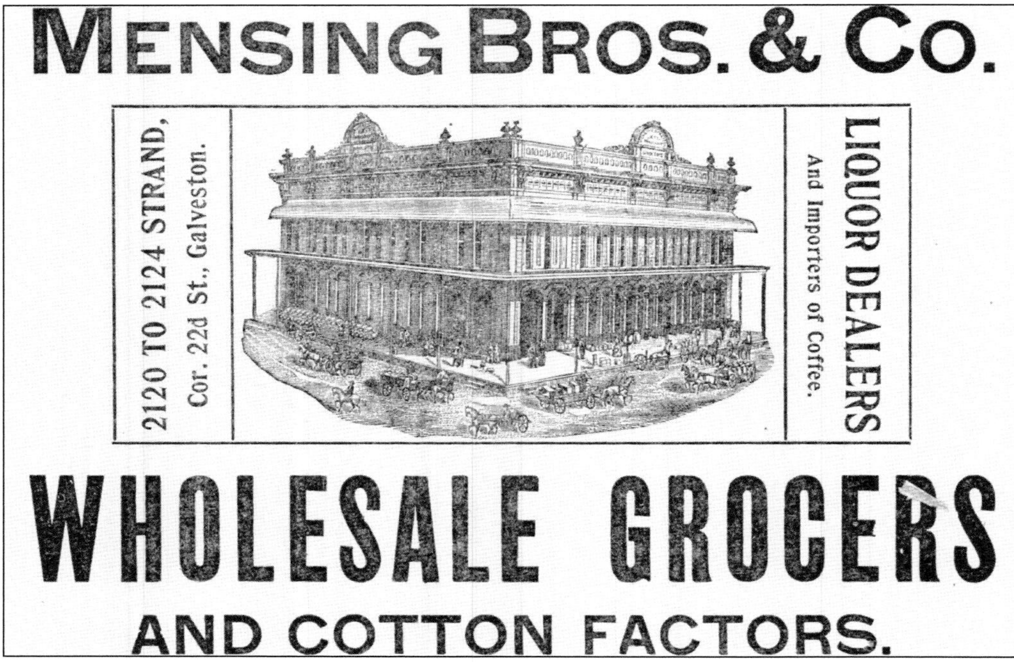

Mensing Brothers and Company was a cotton factor and wholesale grocery business. G. H. Mensing was on the Board of Alderman of the City of Galveston and was the president of the Texas Cotton Press Company. Mensing Brothers handled a very large cotton trade and maintained trade all throughout Texas and Western Louisiana. Gustav H. Mensing, William E. Mensing, and James Moore were the business principles.

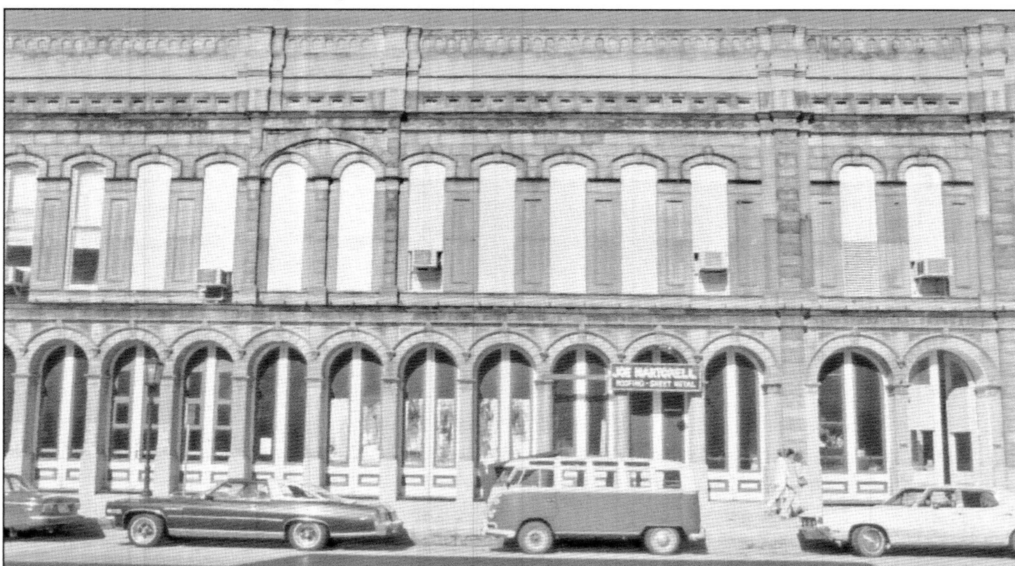
When Moore, Stratton, and Company purchased the northeast corner of Strand and Twenty-second Streets, they paid $32,000 for the two lots in 1881. Only two of the proposed four stories were constructed. The brick building was stuccoed to resemble stonework. This building was constructed in 1882. Unfortunately, the architect is unidentified.

The angled door in the rear of the First National Bank building is a symbol of the Strand's decline in the 1920s. Most banking houses were located on Market Street, which this door is angled towards. Once this building was the location of the oldest bank in Texas and was built as symbol for the strength of the banking industry. In recent years, this building has been home to the Galveston Arts Center and has undergone a major rehabilitation to the cast-iron storefront and other exterior and interior elements.

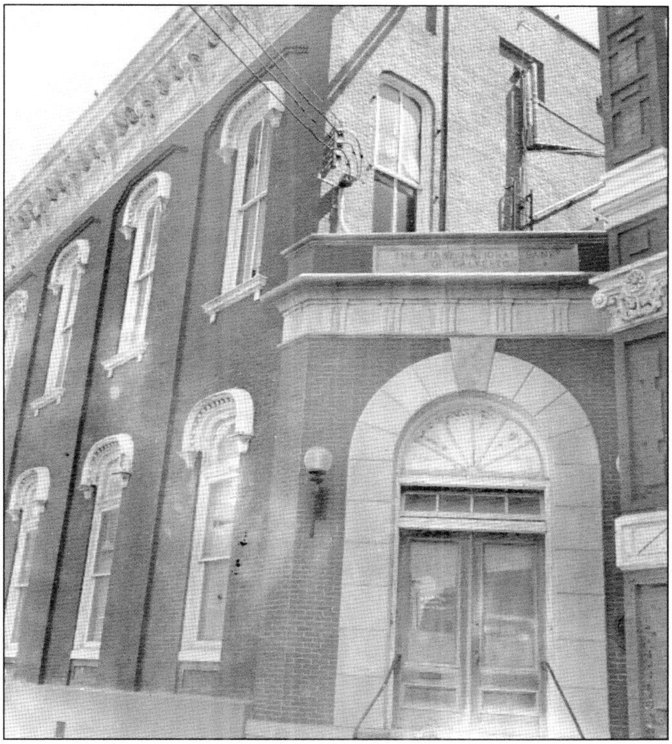

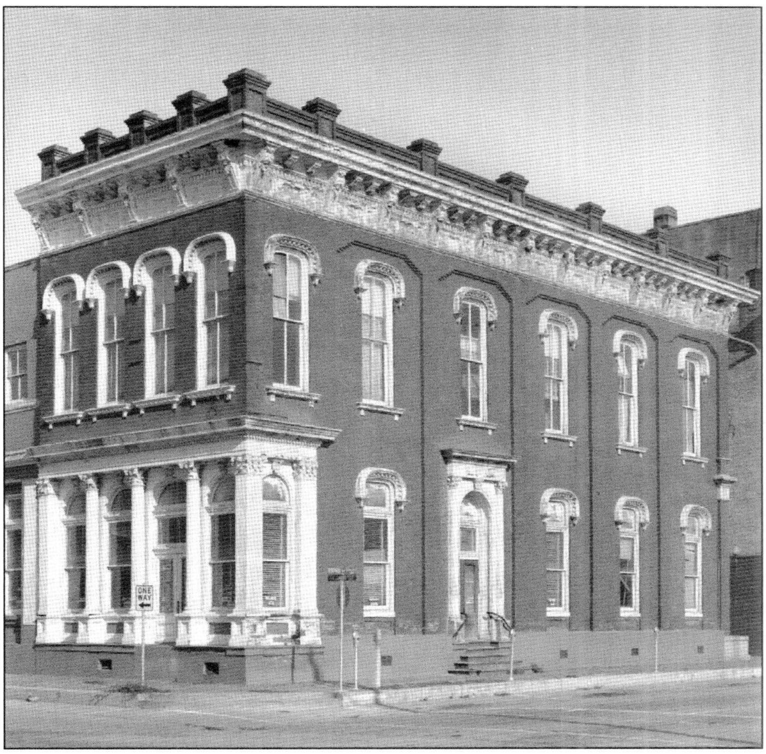

The First National Bank Building at 2127 Strand was built in 1878. The fire of 1877 destroyed the original three-story 1867 building. After the Civil War, like many towns throughout the South and Southwest, Galveston was short on building supplies and materials; it is believed that the brick and ironwork was shipped in from the East.

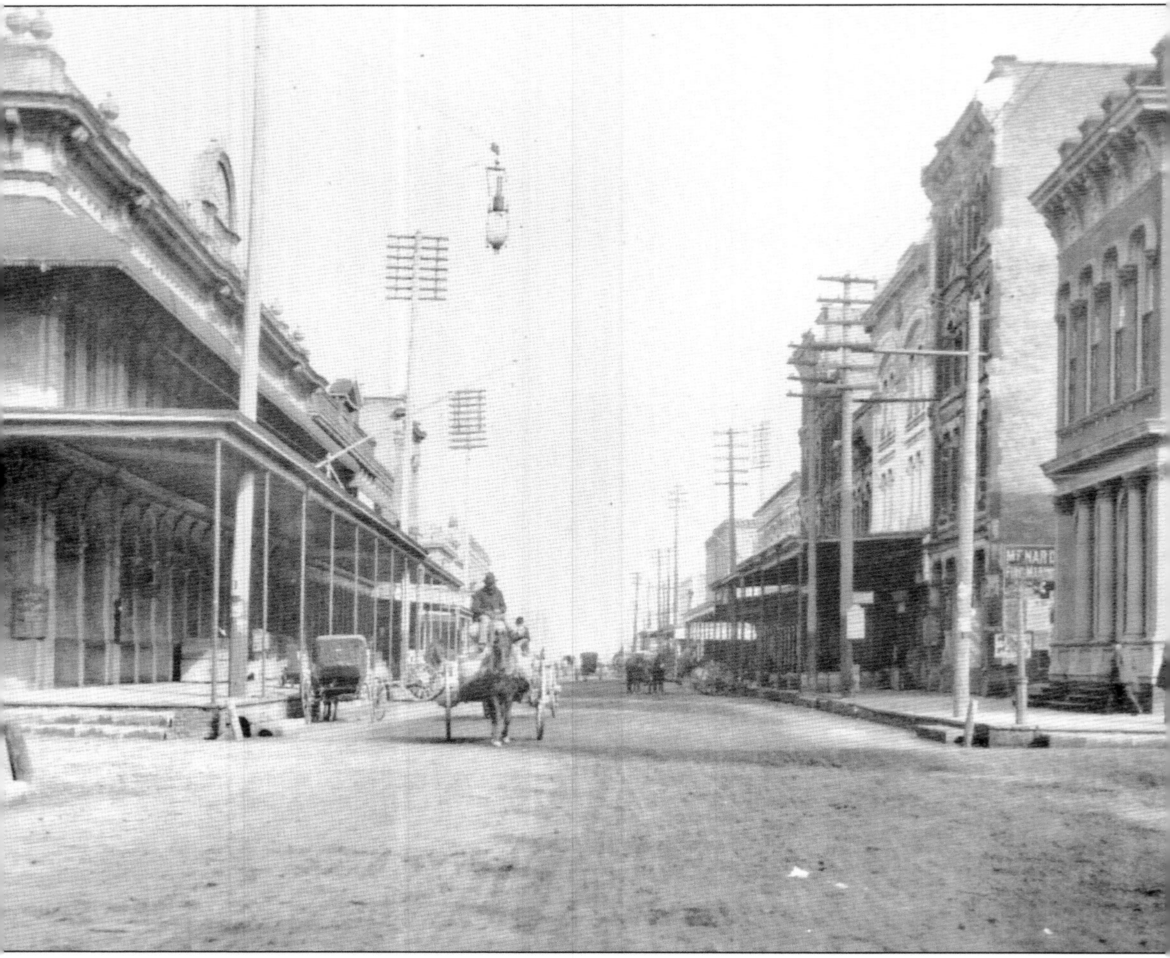

The Strand was called "The Wall Street of the Southwest," because thousands of dollars of wholesale materials were traded, imported, and exported throughout the Southwest through businesses on the Strand. The streets were very low, with high pavements to help facilitate the loading of wagons directly from businesses' front doors. The Strand's most invigorating time began after the Civil War and came to an end with the 1900 Storm. At one time, the Strand had five banks, eight newspapers, steam and sail ship agents, grocers, liquor dealers, and clothing firms. Galveston also was coined as the "Queen City on the Gulf," mainly because all business flowed in and out of the Strand area and its wharves. The commercial area today stands as one of the largest contiguous section of 19th-century commercial buildings in the United States.

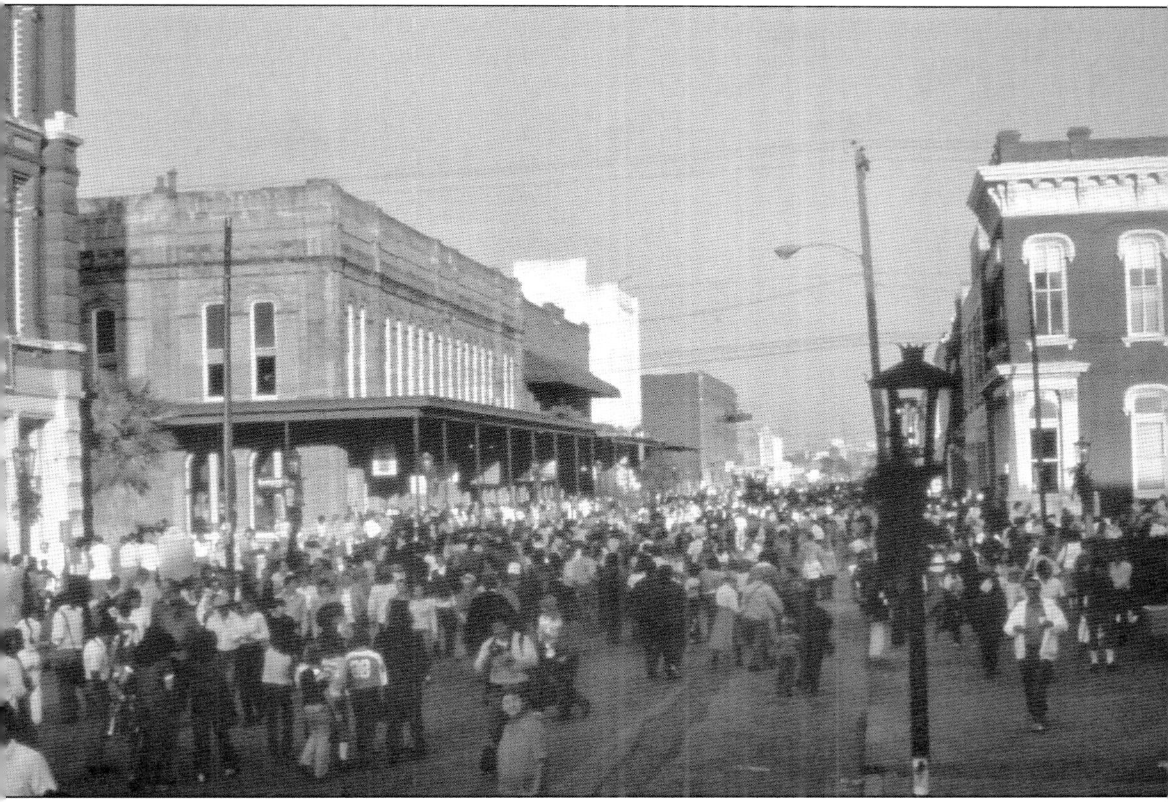

In the 1980s, when this photograph was taken, during Dickens on the Strand, little has changed from the photograph on the previous page taken in 1894. Dickens on the Strand was conceived as an "Evening on the Strand" in 1974 to bring people to downtown. Now in its 37th year, Dickens continues to be a driving force to bring residents of Galveston and tourists to downtown the first weekend of December each year. Dickens on the Strand is a nationally renowned Victorian Christmas festival that celebrates the English roots of the name Strand. Produced by the Galveston Historical Foundation, up to 30,000 people come to take a walk back in time amidst the 19th-century architecture of the Strand and enjoy food, entertainment, crafts, and costumes from a bygone era. Much like in 1974, Dickens in 2008 brought residents and visitors back to the Strand less than four months after Hurricane Ike left the area with up to 13 feet of water.

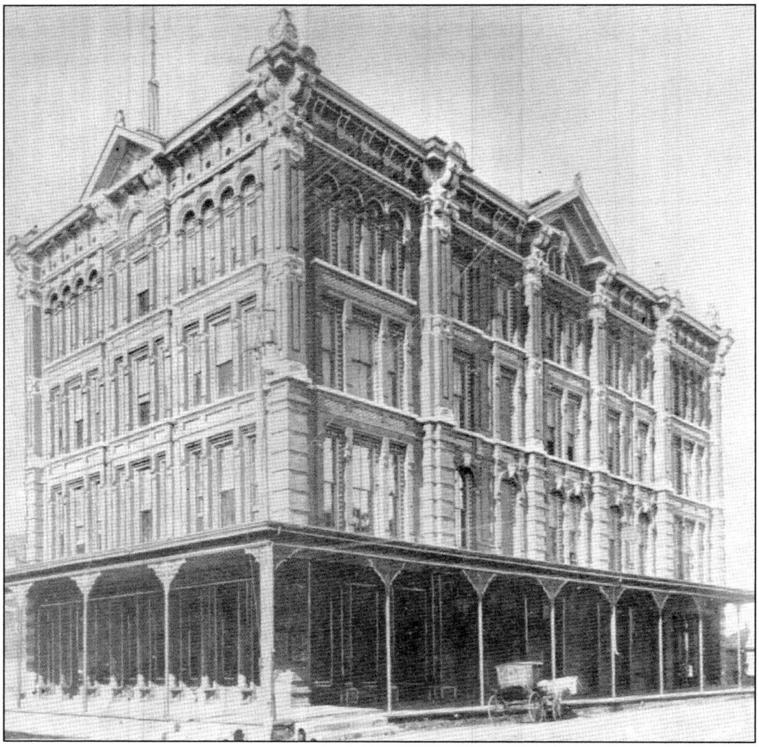

W. L. Moody commissioned Nicholas Clayton to erect a building to house his cotton and banking businesses. Completed in 1883, with an elaborate cast-iron facade, this photograph shows the building before the cornice and the fourth floor were knocked off in the 1900 Storm. Clayton repaired the building after the storm, but the fourth floor was never replaced.

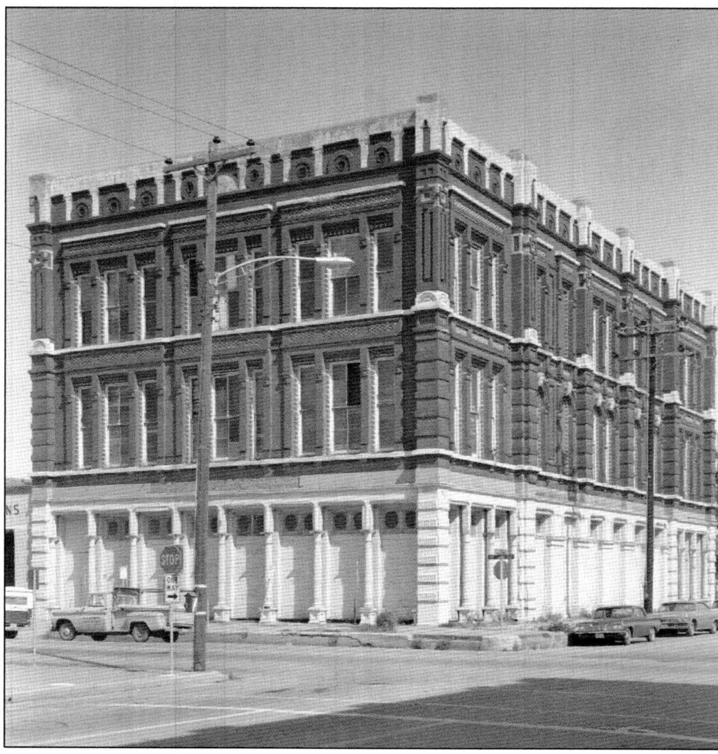

This building shows the delicate way Clayton treated design and paid special attention to details. There are inset panels of tile and different colors of brick showing off the windows. The first floor is decorated with cast-iron columns and brick and terra cotta, which give the building a feeling of depth. The current structure is missing the decorative awning, cornice, and fourth floor. Clayton used both decorative and structural cast iron along the Strand.

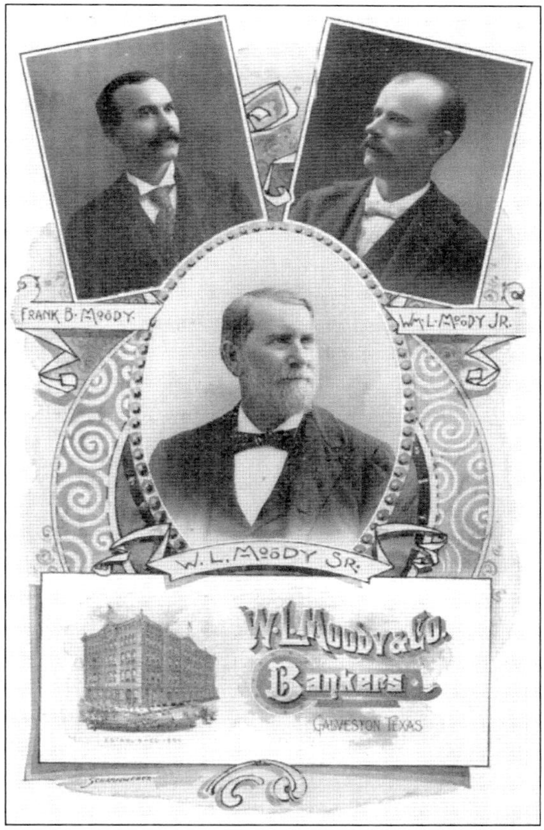

W. L. Moody was president of the Cotton Exchange and was a member of the Legislature of Texas. By 1887, he was a director in the Gulf, Colorado, and Santa Fe railroad, president of the National Bank of Texas, and held director's positions in the Texas Banking and Insurance Company and the Gulf City Cotton Press and Manufacturing Company. Moody came to Texas in 1852 and to Galveston in 1866. He was a graduate of the University of Virginia, Charlottesville, and served for four years in the Confederate Soldiers of America.

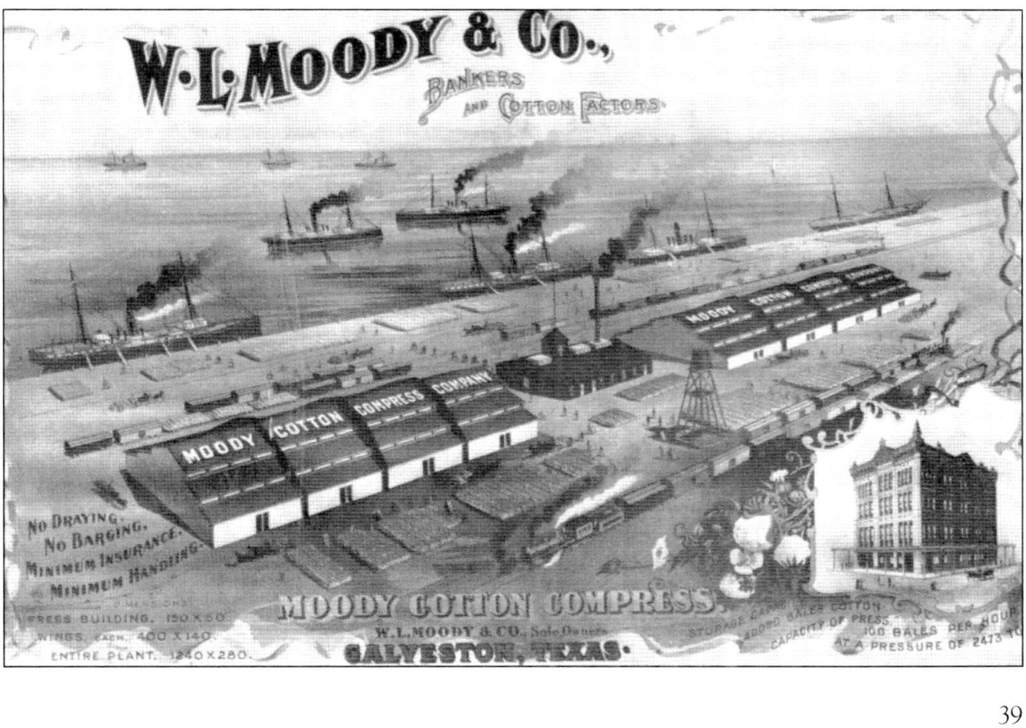

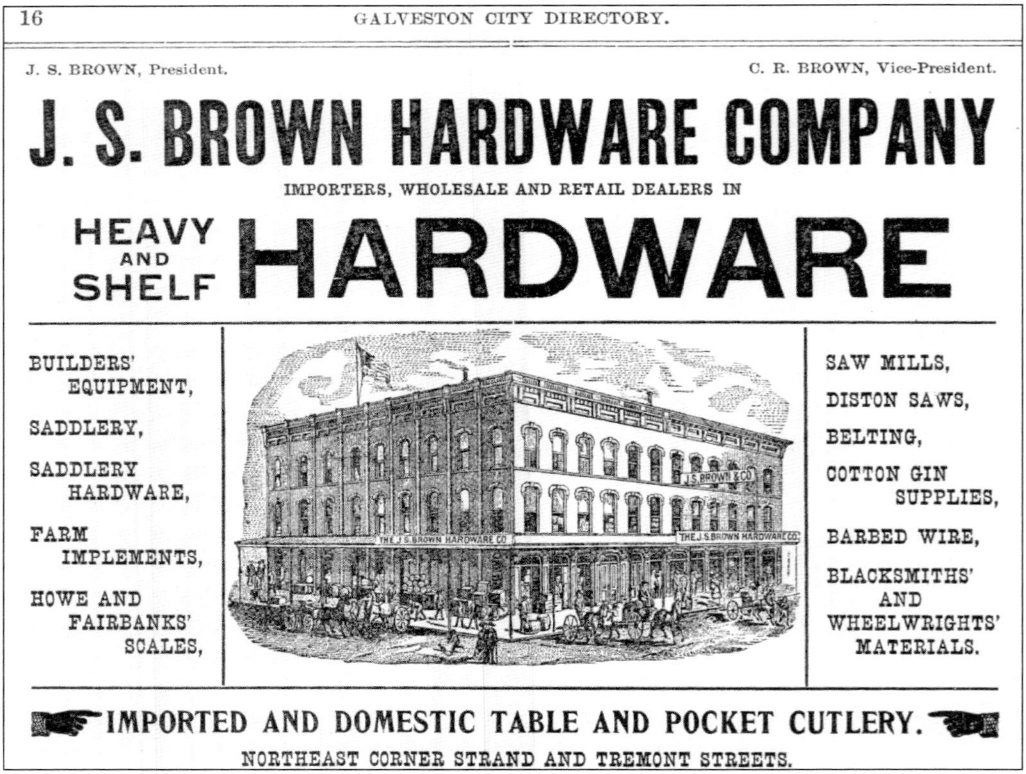

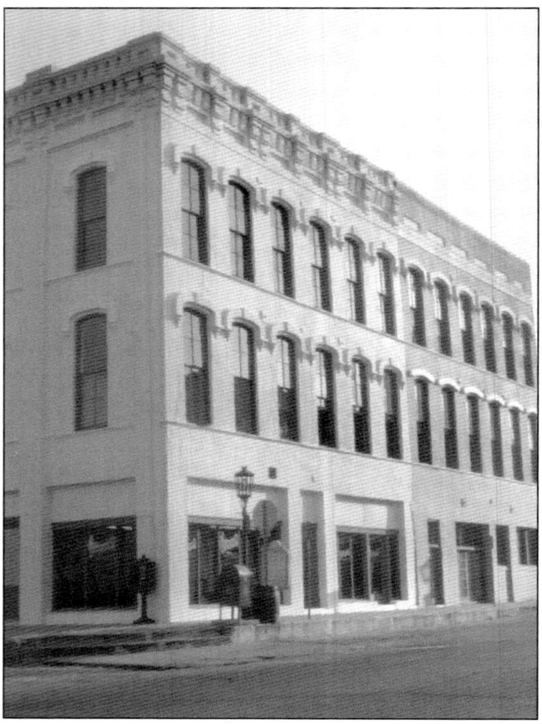

James Moreau Brown arrived from Mississippi in 1843 to Galveston and began one of the first wholesale hardware businesses in Galveston. His son J. S. Brown was vice president of the company. They operated nearly 31,000-square feet of retail space. Parts of this building were destroyed by fire in 1882. James M. Brown was the builder of Ashton Villa (1859) at 2328 Broadway.

This set of buildings at 2218–2228 Strand were constructed in 1870 of local Texas brick at an interim time in Galveston's architectural history. Buildings constructed before 1870 were much more austere in their appearance, with smooth fronts and little to no fancy architectural elements. These structures have elements of a simple front with a more elaborate cornice.

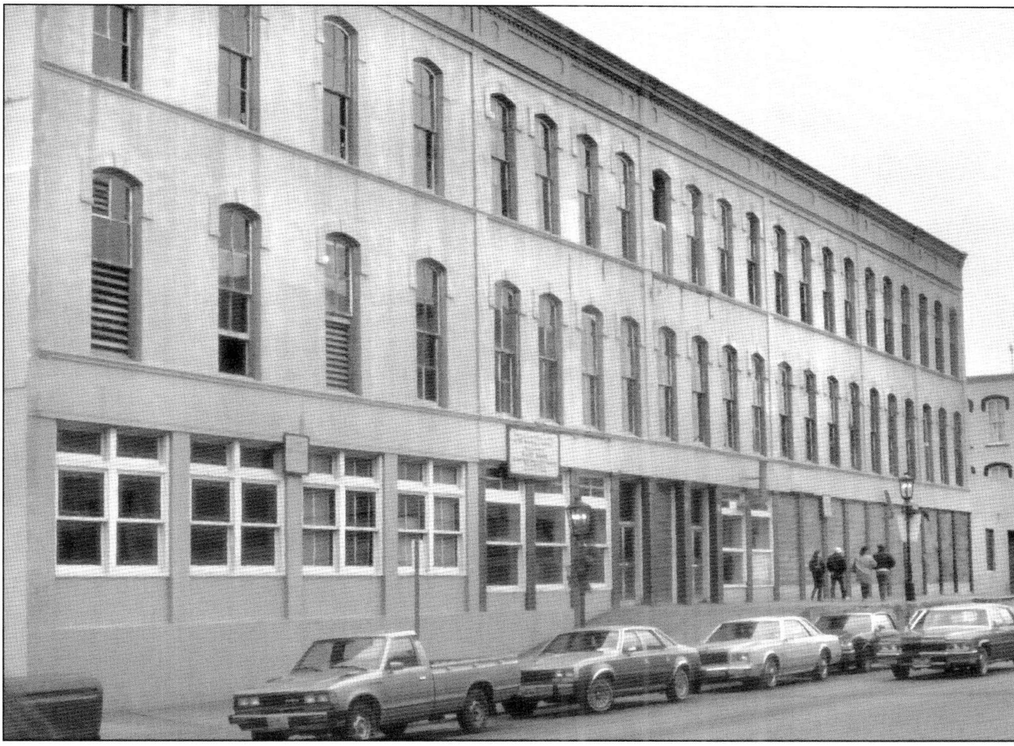

Revitalized in 1987, this block is actually four separate buildings. The six bays closest to Twenty-third Street originally belonged to the Berlocher Building, the next four to the Henry Runge building, the next eight to the T. W. House Building, with the final four belonging to the E. W. Wood Building. The first three were destroyed in the fire of February 24, 1870. The E. S. Wood Building (1858) was only partially damaged.

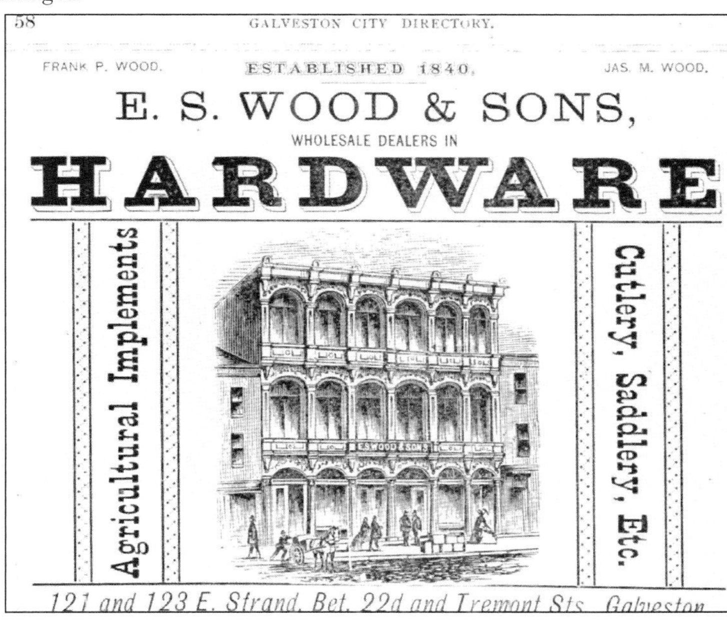

This etching from a *Galveston City Directory* shows an image of what the full cast-iron storefront of the E. S. Wood Building looked like. Sanson and Farrand of Philadelphia manufactured this cast-iron storefront. E. S. Wood was a leading hardware merchant of the Southwest. This building also had an elaborate cornice and is the second oldest structure on the Strand.

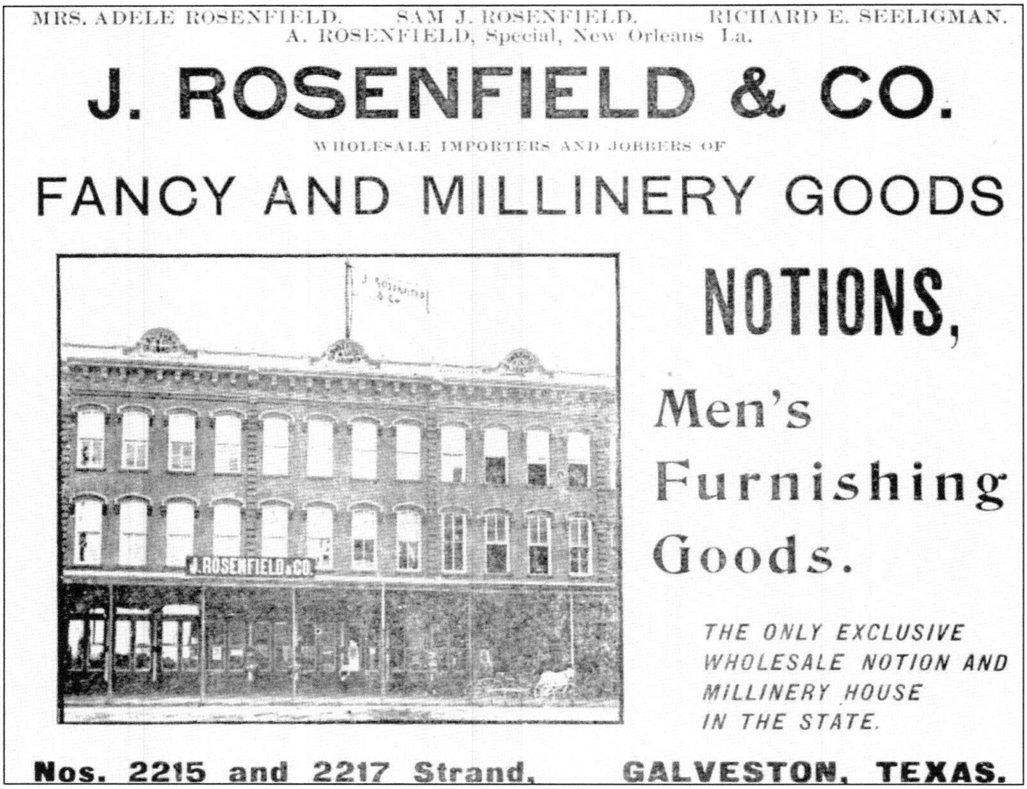

In a stark comparison to the decline of this block on the previous page, and before, the Blum Hardware Company turned these four buildings into one, making this block of the Strand highly ornamented. Shops on the Strand changed hands often, with the floor plans allowing for multiple uses.

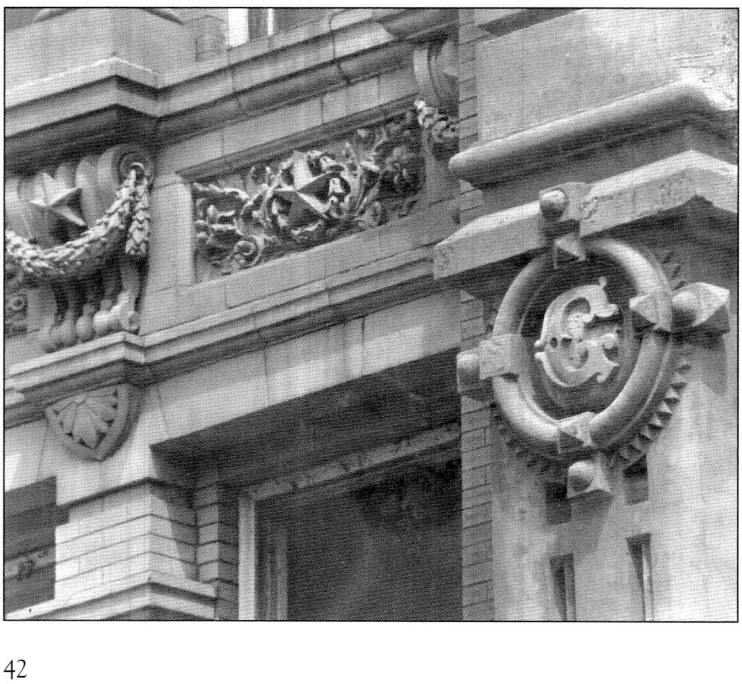

The detail Clayton used on the Greenleve Block is evident in this close up of the details, including a "G" for Greenleve and the five-point star, typically a sign for the State of Texas. The intricately carved design was layered with cast-iron supports to give this building superior massing. It cost $65,000 to build the Greenleve block.

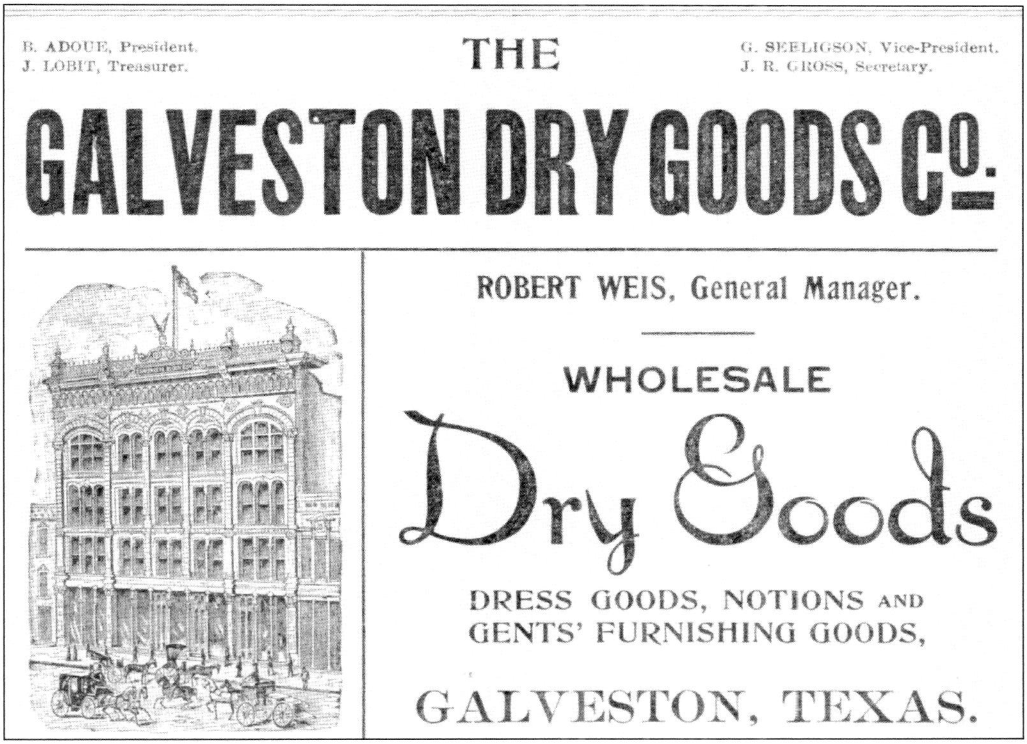

This etching from a *Galveston City Directory* shows the full fourth floor and cornice and the many details of the building. Parts of the cornice were lost in the 1900 Storm. Greenleve and Company erected this building in 1881–1882, and the building is considered one of Clayton's most elaborate works downtown.

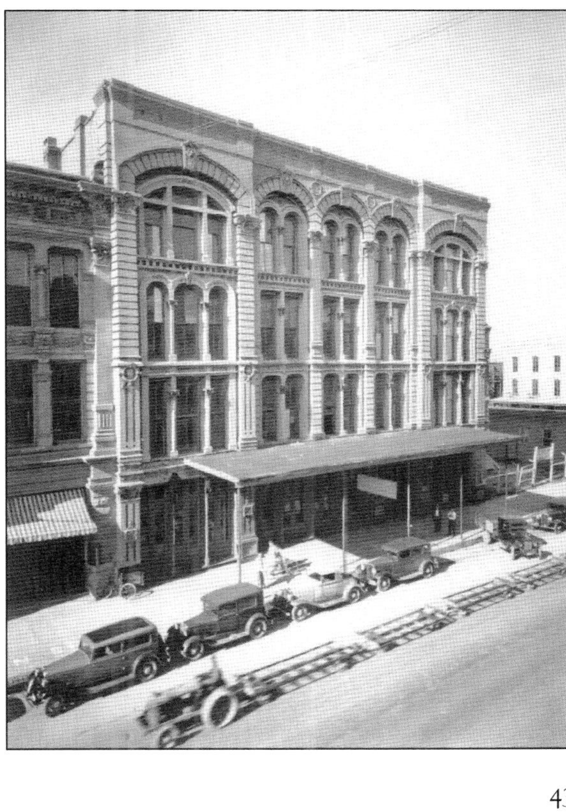

It was not hurricane or tornado that caused the Greenleve, Block, and Company Building to lose its top floor in 1953, it was demolition. The owners at the time were to said to have no use for the top floor. The building appears to have an unfinished look, but its historic photograph on the previous image shows the detail that architect Nicolas Clayton took with its elaborate cornice. (Courtesy of the Dolph Briscoe Center for American History, The University of Texas at Austin.)

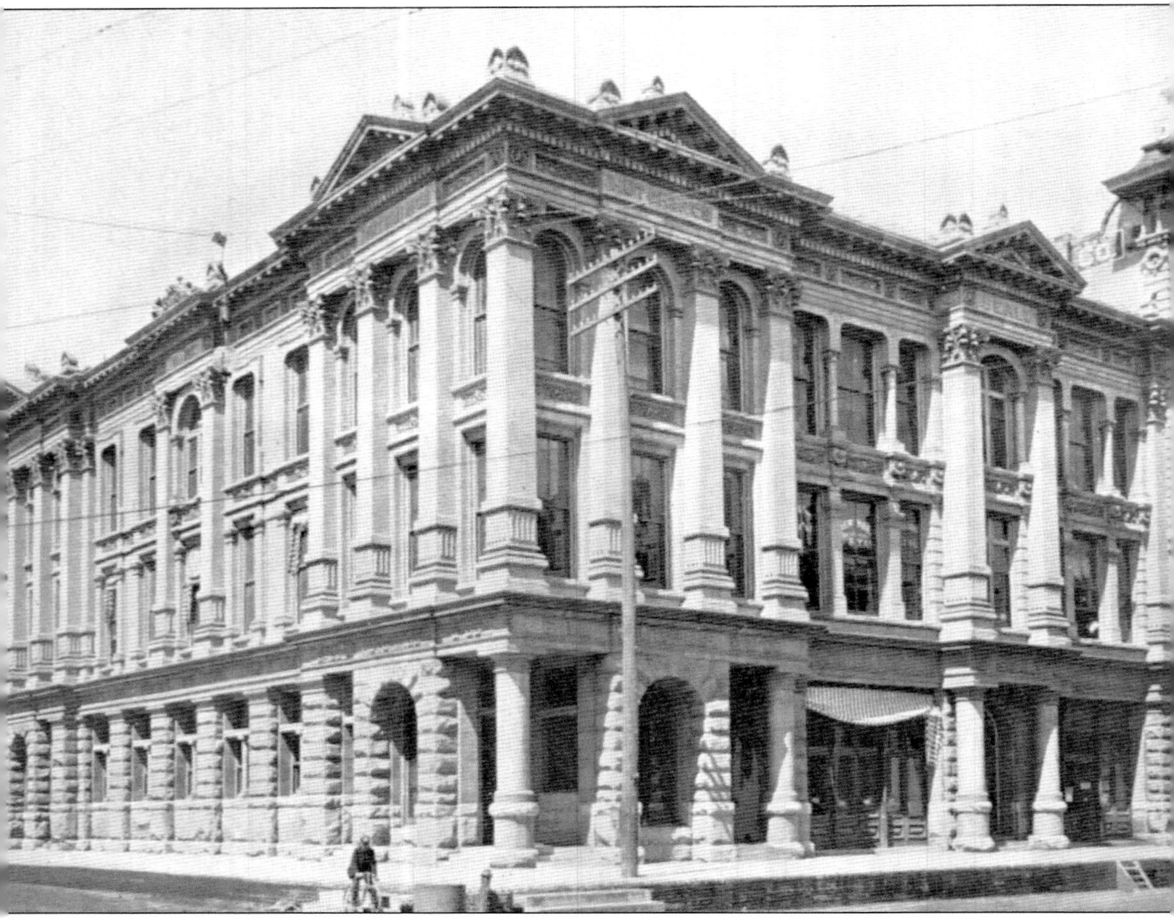

The Ball, Hutchings, and Sealy Building, located along 2326–2328 Strand, was constructed between 1895 and 1896 with Nicholas Clayton as architect. One of the last buildings built before the 1900 Storm, this building used a new form of construction technique; terra-cotta encased in steel. Clayton used Classical architecture as his inspiration for this bold design. Many architects were taking inspiration from Classical styles, but Nicholas Clayton was unable to give up his passion for Victorian styling, as this building shows influences of both. Harry Devlin was the general contractor for the construction, and the estimated value of the buildings was $110,000. Clayton's original designs called for a much larger building, the final result being smaller but with additional detail. This building was used as a warehouse after the bank moved out in 1975.

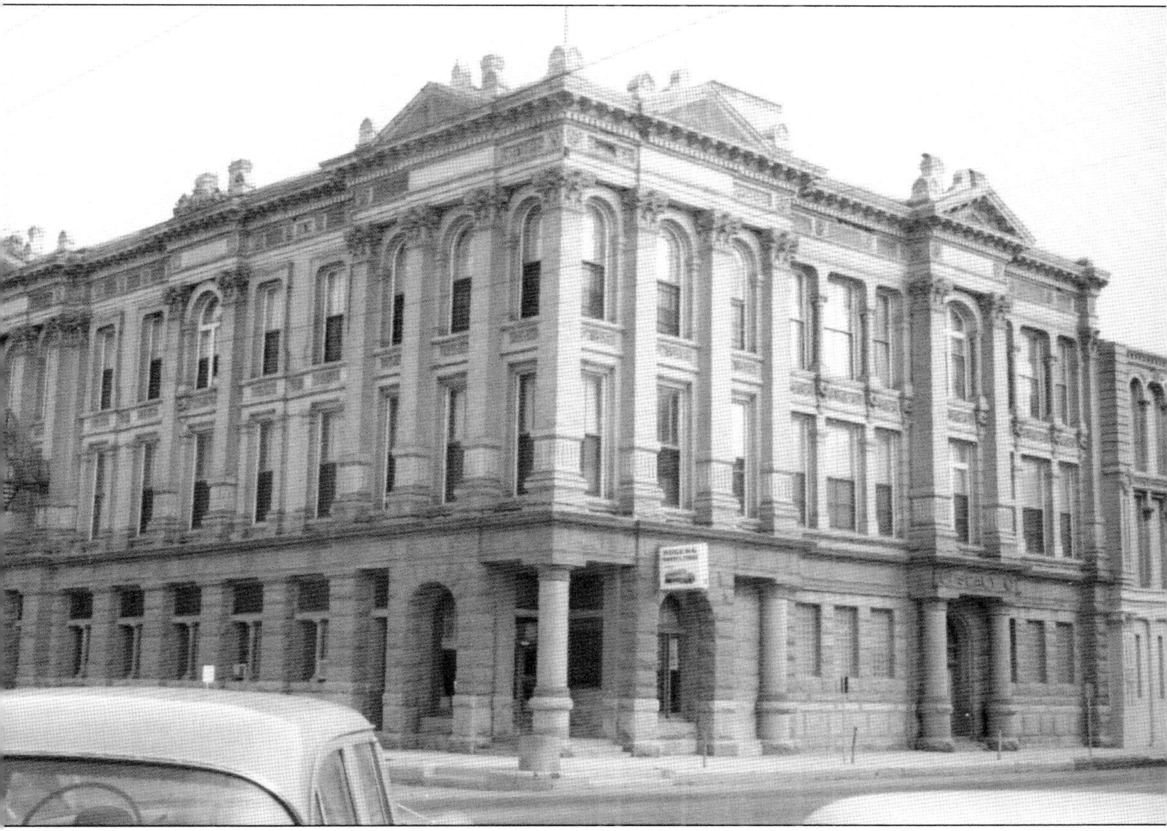

This building was constructed in the Renaissance Revival style and served as a bank and office building for the Ball, Hutchings, and Sealy Company. In 1897, the Ball, Hutchings, and Sealy Company became the Hutchings Sealy Company. Built in 1870, the first structure that George Ball, John H. Hutchings, and John Sealy built was a modest three-story building, combined with another structure next door, encompassing up the newly formed banking company. They demolished the original 1856 and 1870 structures in July 1895 to build this new larger building. Hutchings, Sealy, and Company stayed at this address until 1935. Like many banking houses, this organization moved to Market Street in the 1930s. (Courtesy of the Library of Congress, Prints and Photographs Division, Historic American Buildings Survey.)

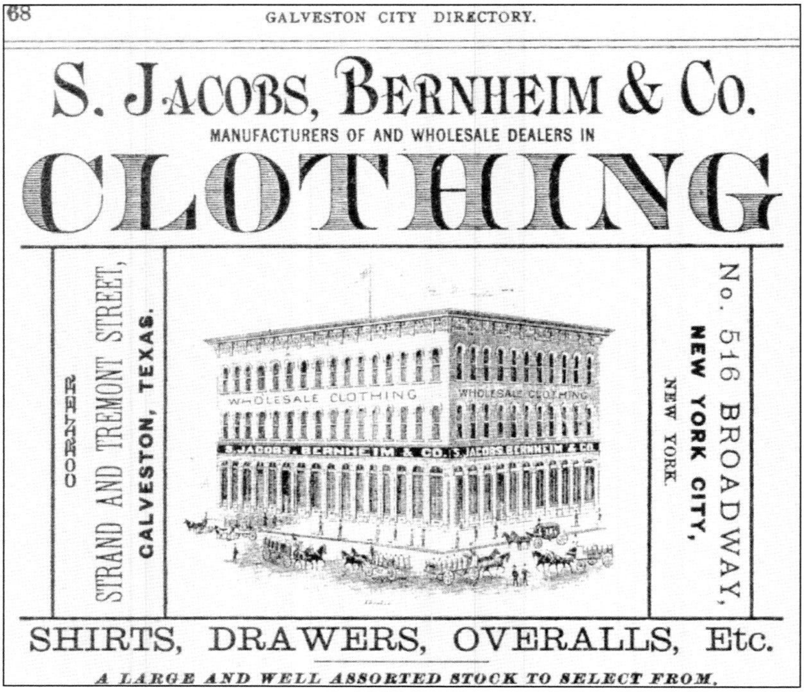

The T. J. League Building was constructed in 1872 on the site of the start of one of Galveston's wildest fires, the Moro Castle Saloon fire of 1869. This building has cast-iron and glass storefronts along the Twenty-third and Strand sides. The upper floor windows have cast-iron decorative elements, and Houston brick was used in the construction.

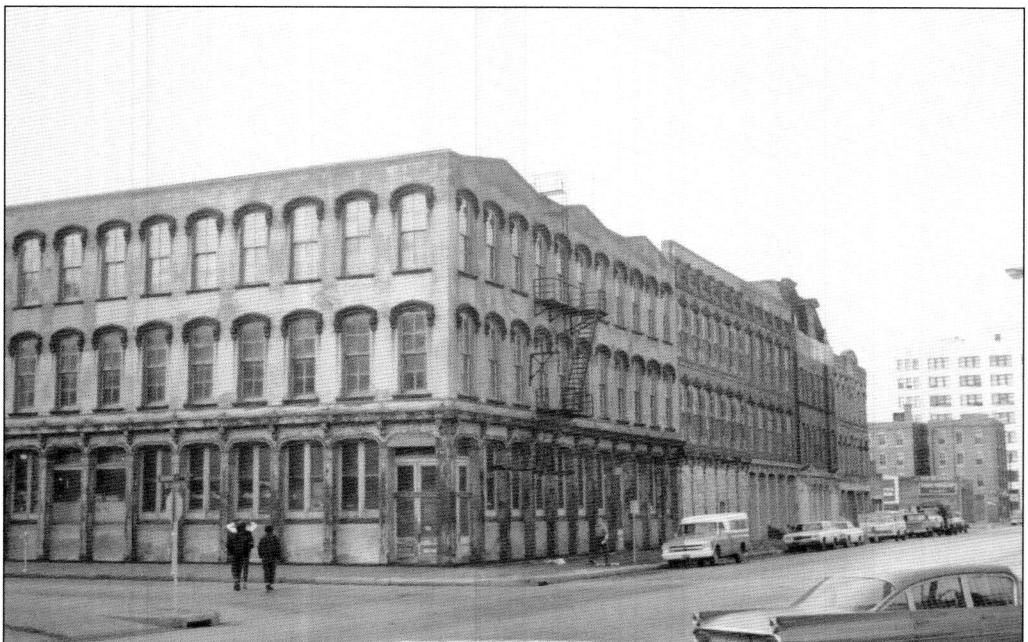

With its revolving fund, Galveston Historical Foundation bought the T. J. League Building in 1975 to save the building from further decay. Then purchased by Cynthia and George Mitchell, the new owners worked with San Antonio architects Ford, Powell, and Carson to rehabilitate the building and were thankfully able to raise the first-floor interior spaces to mitigate future flooding.

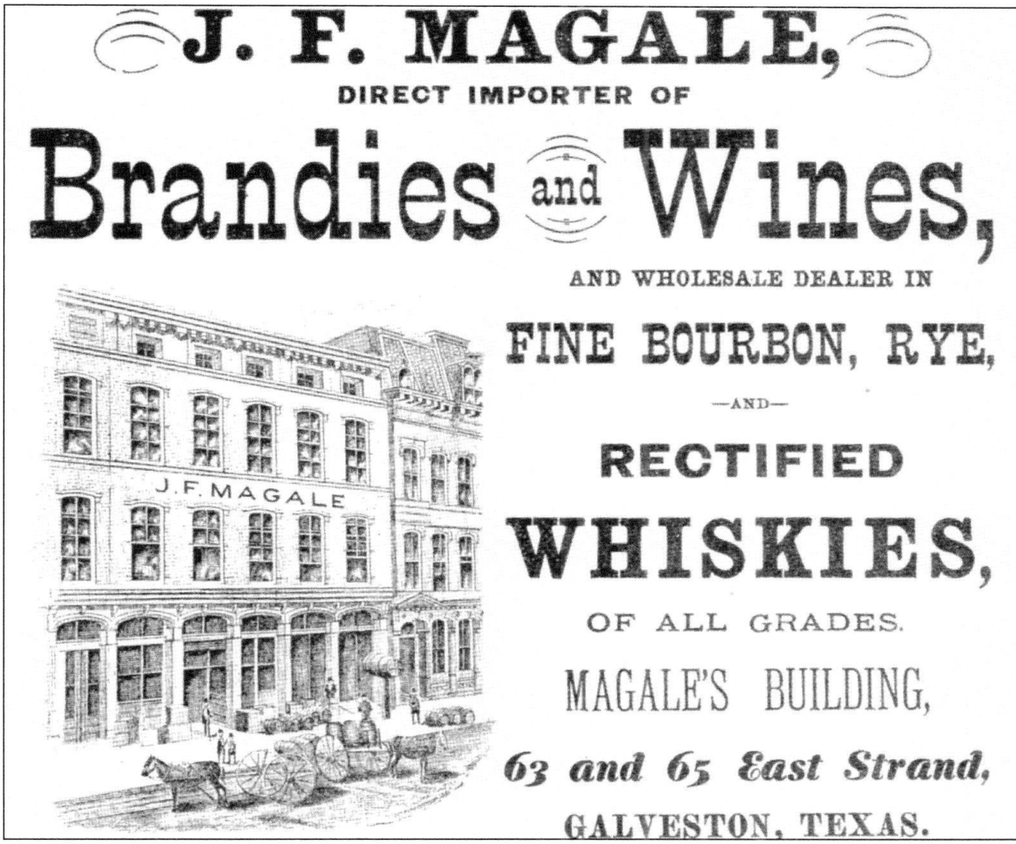

J. F. Magale was a wholesale liquor and cigar distributor; his successors were W. S. Davidson and S. J. Flanagan. Magale established himself in Galveston in the 1860s and began his liquor trade. This business had connections with the Kentucky distillers and was lucky enough to get bourbon and other liquors from there.

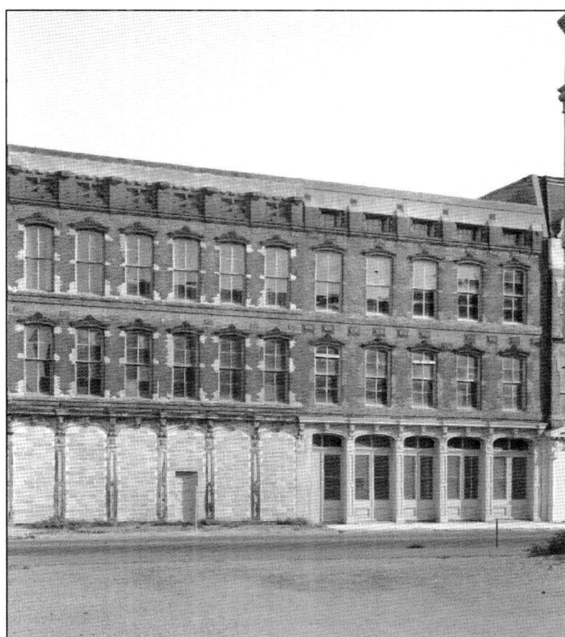

Rosenberg Building is located at 2309–2311 Strand and was built in 1870 and designed by P. N. Comegys for Henry Rosenberg. It is similar in design to its neighbor to the west, the J. F. Magale Building, also built in 1870 by Henry Rosenberg. Both were constructed after the fire in 1869 and have cast-iron storefronts and are constructed of brick. They look like one building, but are really two separate structures.

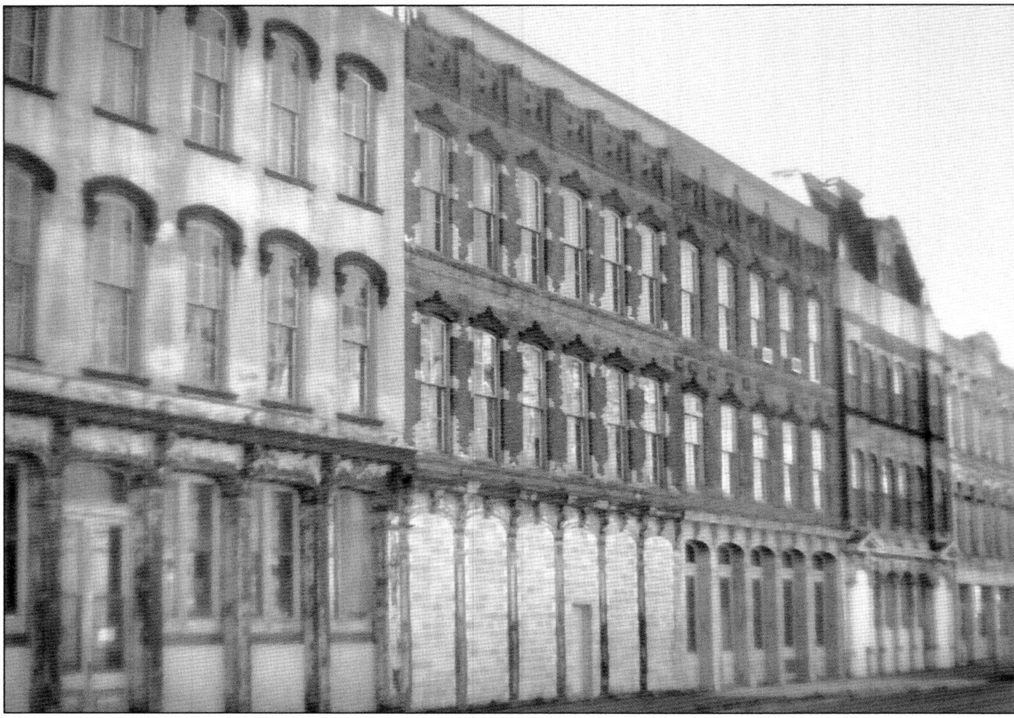

As this photograph shows, the Strand was in serious decline in the late 1970s and early 1980s. Many buildings were boarded, up and there were limited visitors and locals coming downtown. The T. J. League, Rosenberg, Magale, and Merchants Mutual Buildings all have elaborate cast-iron storefronts and were all in a much deteriorated state that is before real estate investors purchased the buildings and completed renovations, converting many into condominiums.

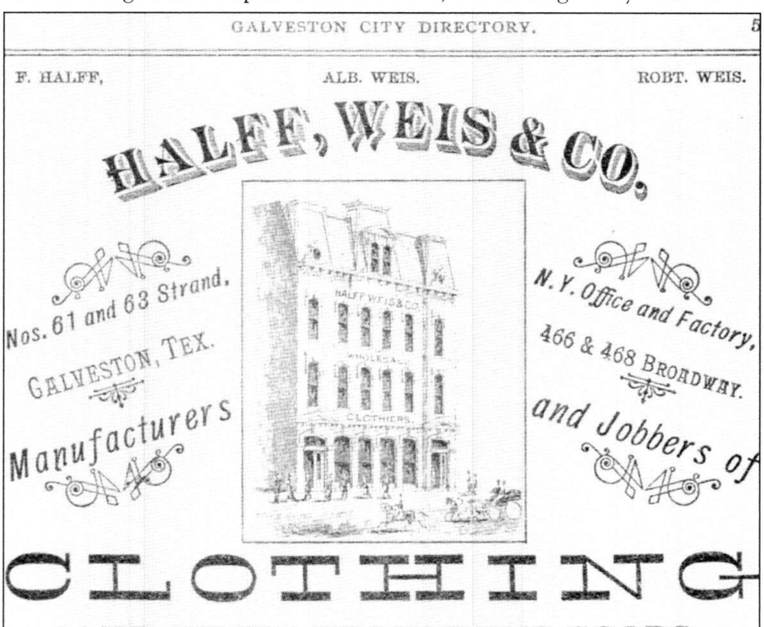

Founded in 1872, a wholesale clothing house, Halff, Weis, and Company shared the Merchants Mutual Building in 1874. The firm had an office, and its factory was in New York City at 466-468 Broadway. Felix Halff and Albert Weis were the founders with Robert Weis a member of the company. The Weis brothers were natives of Germany, and in 1885, the firm was reorganized as the Weis Brothers.

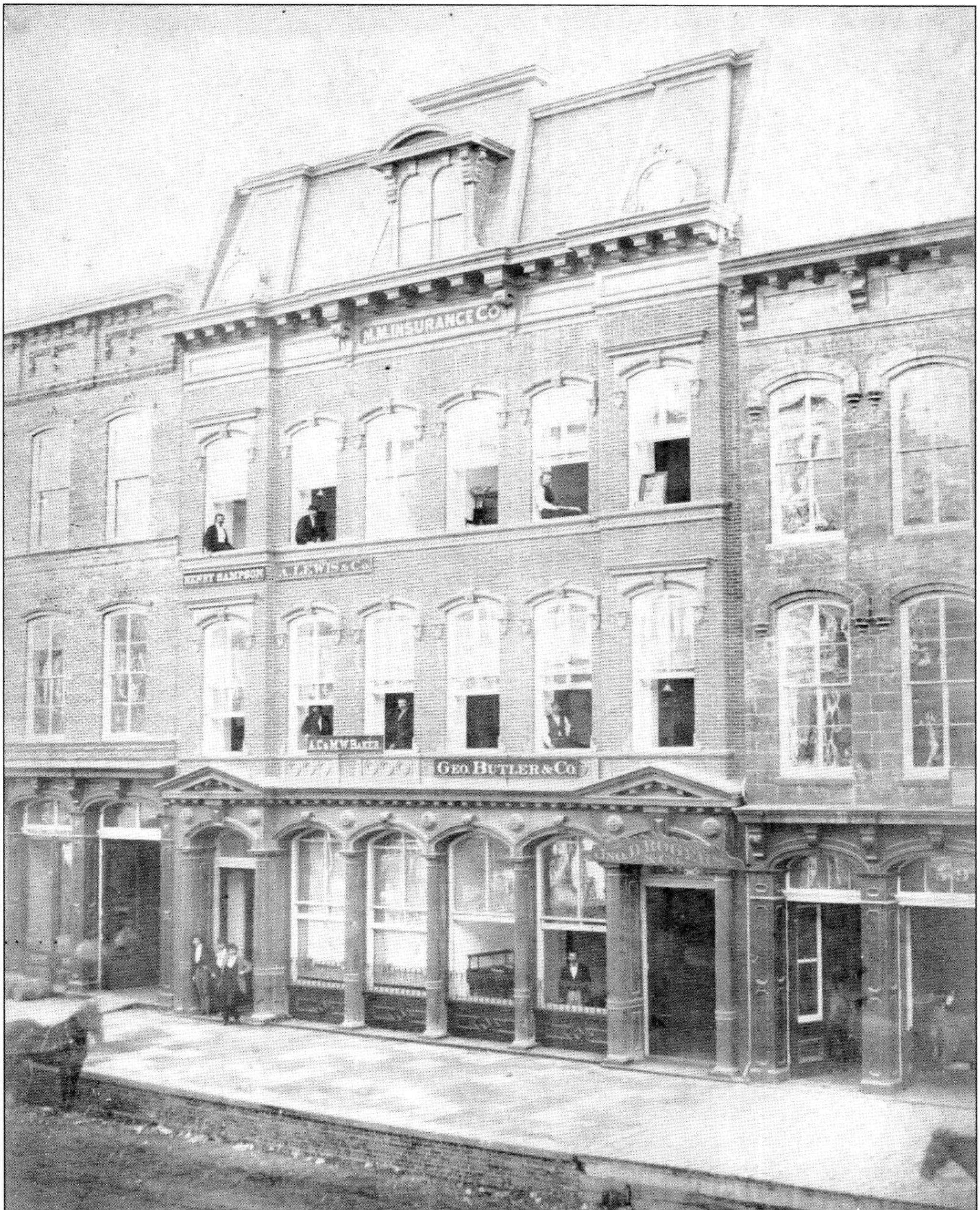

Donald N. Mckenzie and Fritz Weinherner, rebuilt this structure in 1870. Merchants Mutual ceased operations, and I. Lovenberg and Halff, Weis, and Company purchased the building in 1881. The building is three-and-one-half stories in height with a six-bay facade. This historic photograph, as well as the photograph on the next page, shows a sharp contrast in the condition of the building and gives photographic evidence of the decline of the Strand. A headline in the *Galveston County Daily News* even called the street "Raggedy Ole Strand" in 1963. (Photograph courtesy of the Rosenberg Library, Galveston, Texas.)

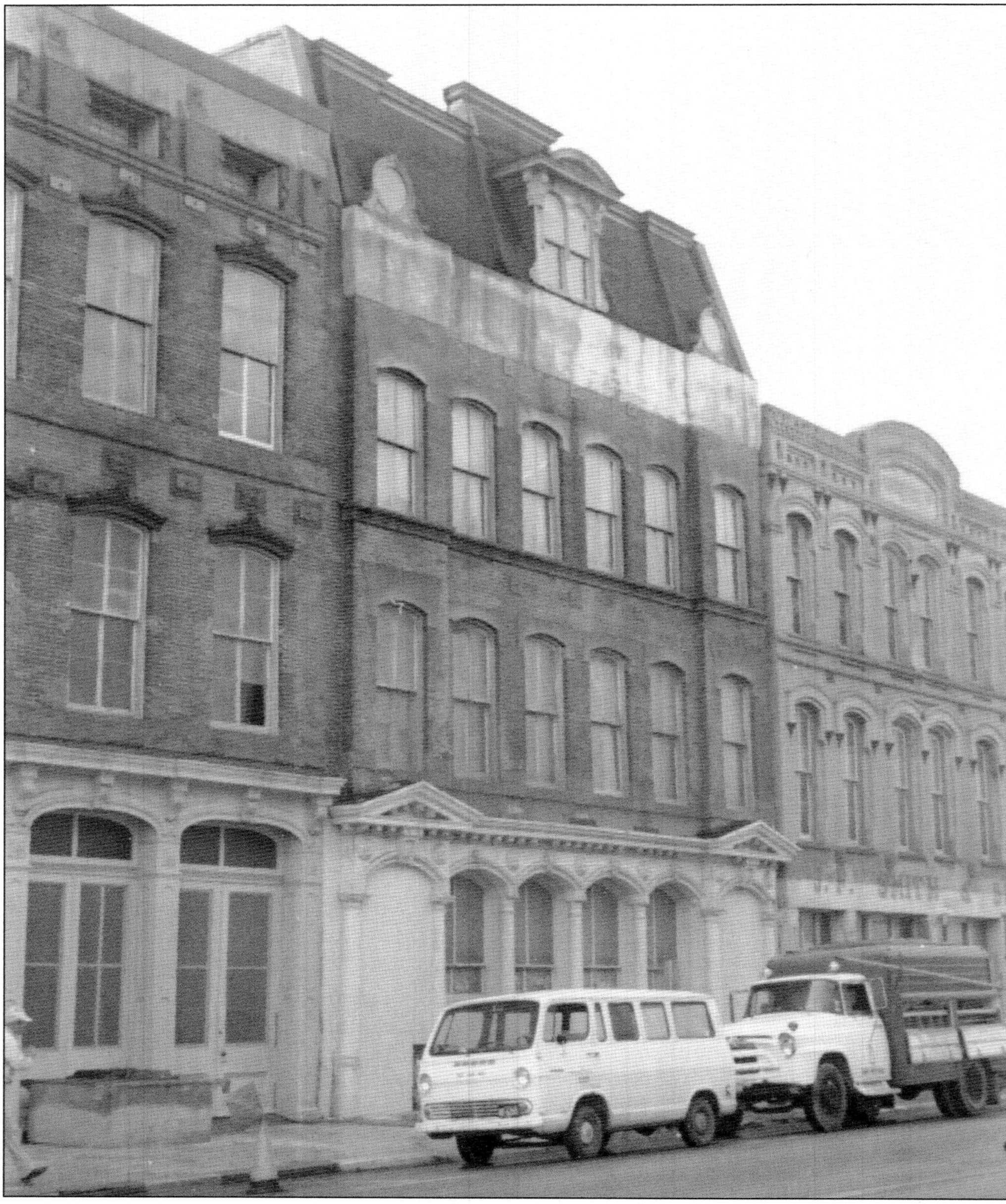

The Merchants Mutual Insurance Building was constructed for the first time in 1869. A few months later, it was burned in the fire that took most of this block. This building has cast-iron structural elements on the front facade and is known for its French-style Mansard Roof. The building at one time even had water tanks on the attic level to supply water closets and washstands. Reconstructed in 1870 as replica of what was just completed, architect P. N. Comegys used French influences in his design, including the mansard roof, which was a first for Galveston, and the "bull's-eye" window on the third floor. Second Empire is an architectural style that reached its height of popularity between 1865 and 1880. It was named for the "French" elements in style during the Second French Empire. Many public buildings were designed in this style to project a stately feeling.

Taken in 1915, this photograph of the 1877 Bolton Estate Building shows a much simpler ornamentation pattern, which can still be seen today. A building that is not photographed as often, as its neighbors to the east. The Bolton Building was designed by Nicholas Clayton, and in 1976, a restored cornice was reconstructed. (Courtesy of the Galveston County Historical Museum, Galveston, Texas.)

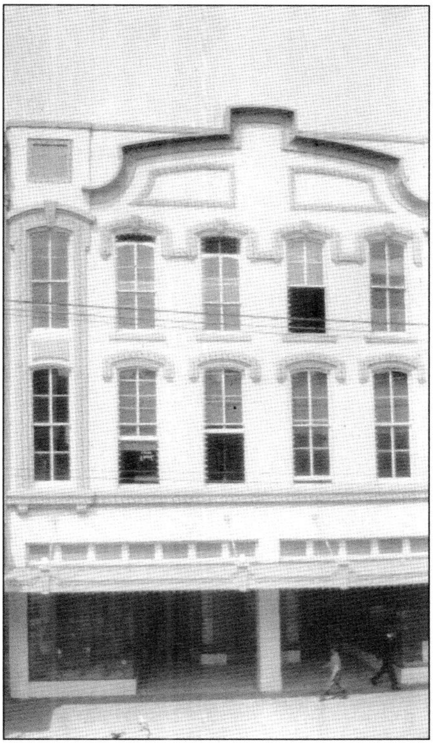

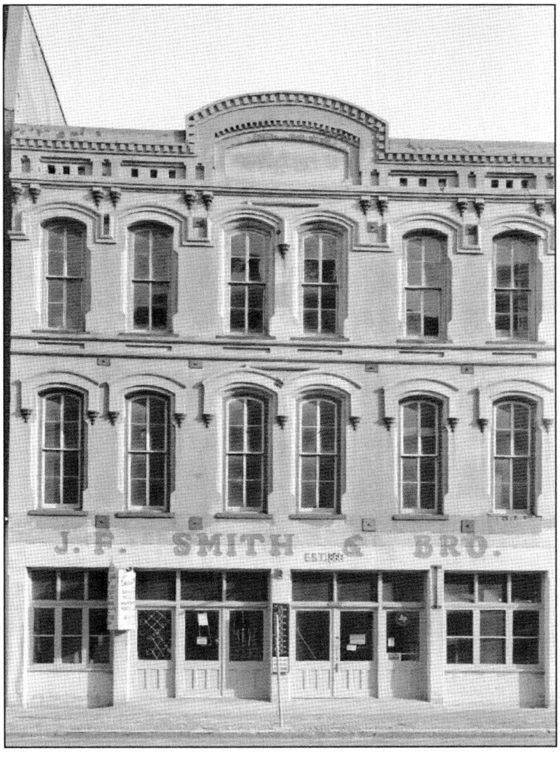

At one time, this building had a cast-iron storefront, and the original building also burned in the Moro Castle fire. The building was commissioned by Colonel Bolton and was leased out for years to J. F. Smith and E. A. Smith Brothers Hardware. (Courtesy of the Library of Congress, Prints and Photographs Division, Historic American Buildings Survey.)

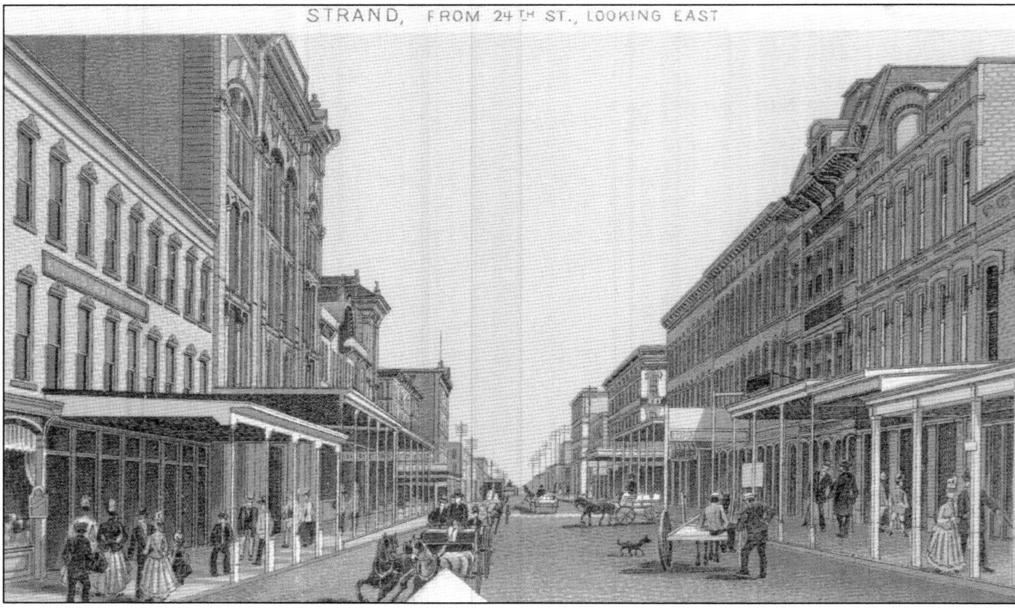

This image, taken from an 1888 *Souvenir Book of Galveston*, shows a view from Twenty-fourth and Strand. The building to the left was the original Ball, Hutchings, and Sealy Building. In 1896, it was demolished for the current building standing today. The 1857 building was similar to other pre-Civil War structures in the area, including the Hendley Building a few blocks to the east.

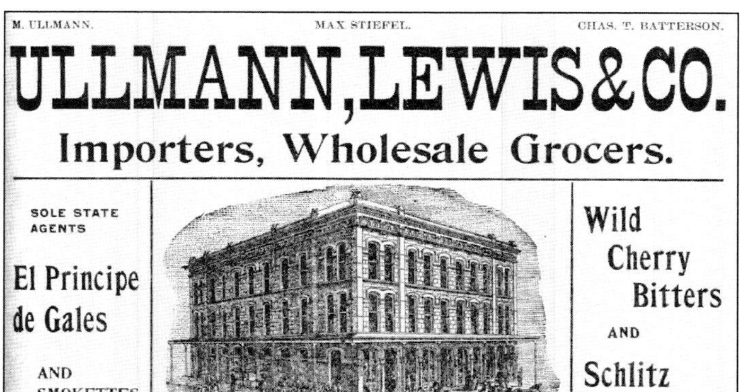

Ullmann, Lewis, and Company was a wholesale grocer and liquor dealer. It occupied the southeast corner of Twenty-fourth and Strand. The store also sold cigars, which included the "La Belle Creole," the "Common Sense," and "Diamond" brands. It had 25 employees. This building is no longer standing; it was almost completely destroyed by the 1943 hurricane. It was built by Brian M. McDonnell in 1870.

Wallis, Landes, and Company was a wholesale grocer, liquor dealer, cotton factor, and importer. In 1877, Wallis and Landes had transactions in excess of $2 million per year. This company carried a full line of groceries, liquors, tobaccos, and woodenware. J. E. Wallis held several ranking positions in Galveston with banks, real estate, oil, and railroad companies. H. A. Landes was a director in the Texas Land and Loan Company and the Galveston Real Estate and Loan Company. Landes's house still stands at 1604 Postoffice Street.

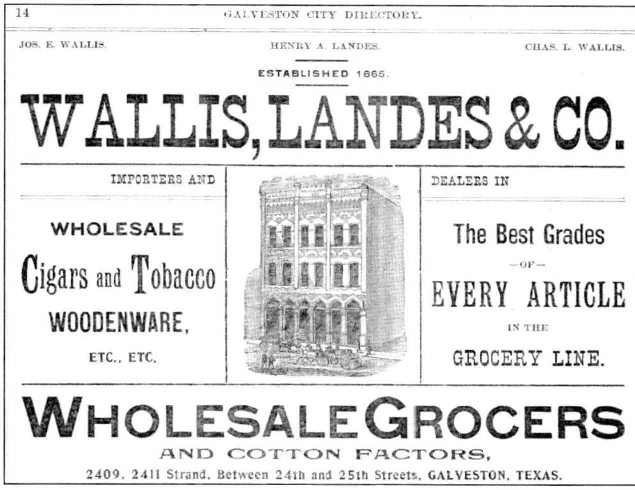

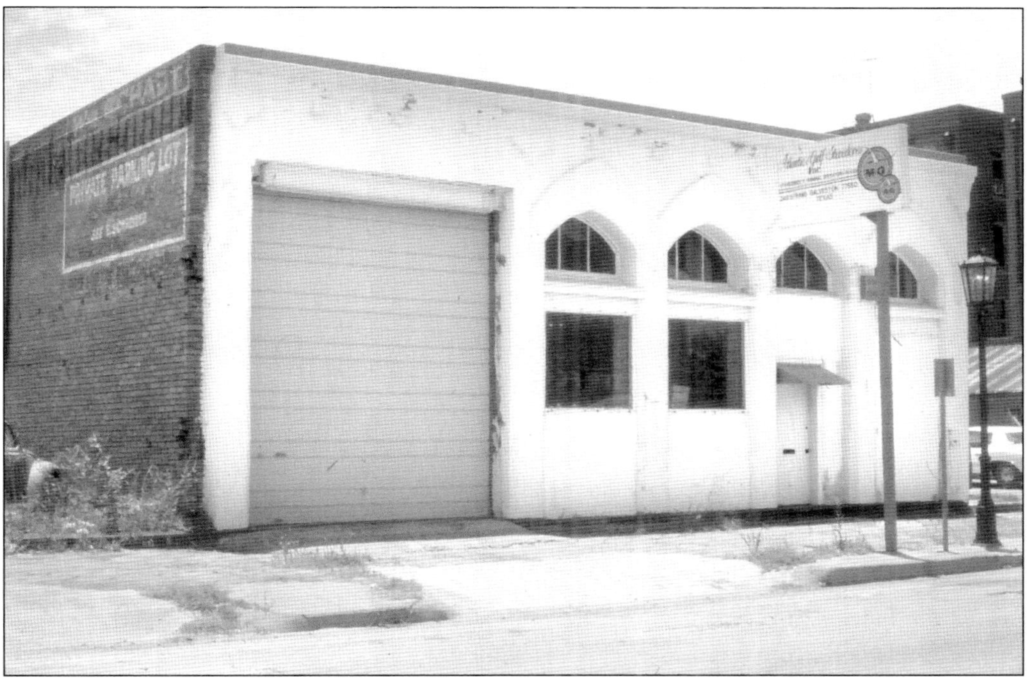

This photograph shows what remained of the Wallis, Landes, and Company Building in the early 1990s. The building was constructed in 1877 by Clayton and Lynch. Once a three-story building, all that remains is the Victorian Gothic level windows. Typical for buildings in Galveston, the upper floors were lost in one of the many hurricanes, and the standing floors were salvaged with business continuing operation. Wallis, Landes, and Company lost its upper floors in the 1943 hurricane and resulting tornadoes.

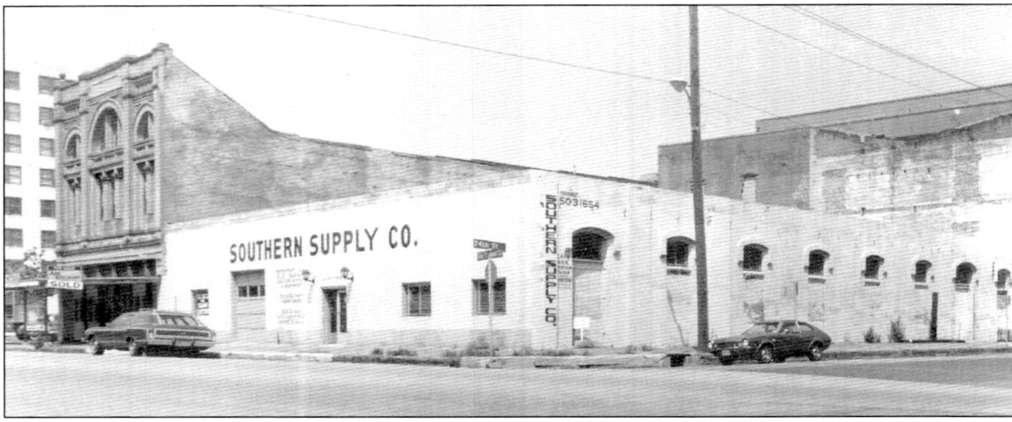

Once a three-story building for the Wills Brothers wholesale shop, this building took up an entire city block of Twenty-fourth and Strand when it was built in 1869. Additions were completed in 1875. Fire in 1975 burned most of the building, and what remains of the building is shown in the photograph. Since, the building has once again undergone rehabilitation, and in 2010, a restaurant occupies it.

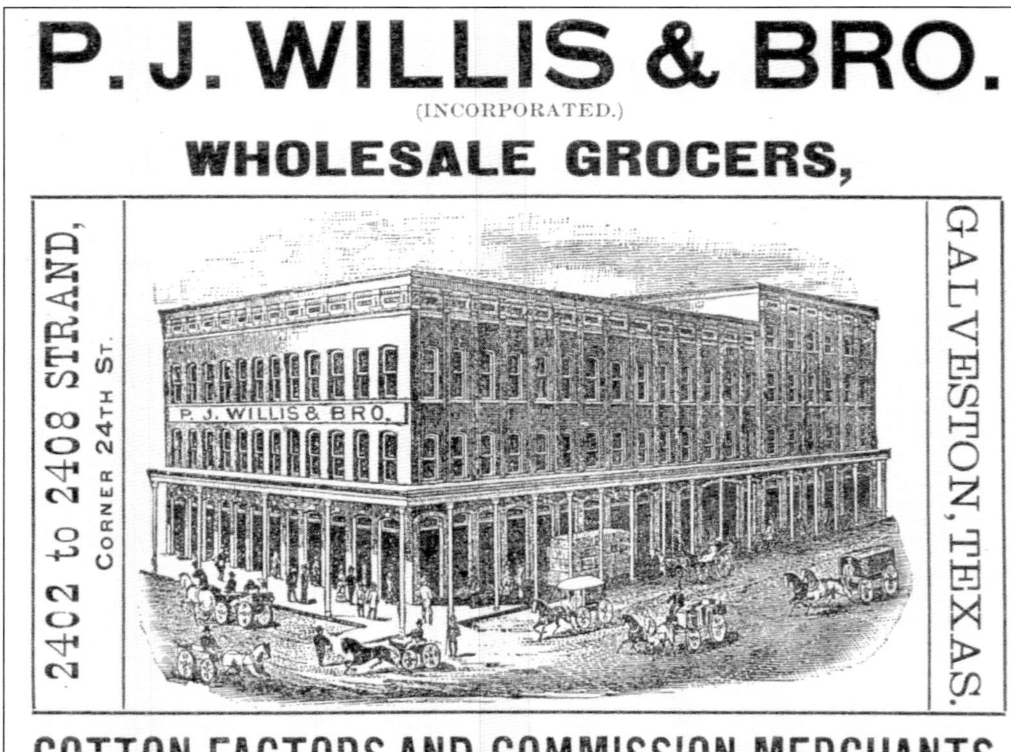

P. J. Willis and R. S. Willis came to Galveston from Maryland in 1837. They were wholesale dealers in groceries, dry goods, boots, shoes, hats, and dresses. They traded actively with Texas, Louisiana, and Mexico. In 1877, the building had a steam elevator and had a railroad track running into the rear of the structure to facilitate trade. Many of the employees of Willis Brothers settled along Thirty-fifth Street.

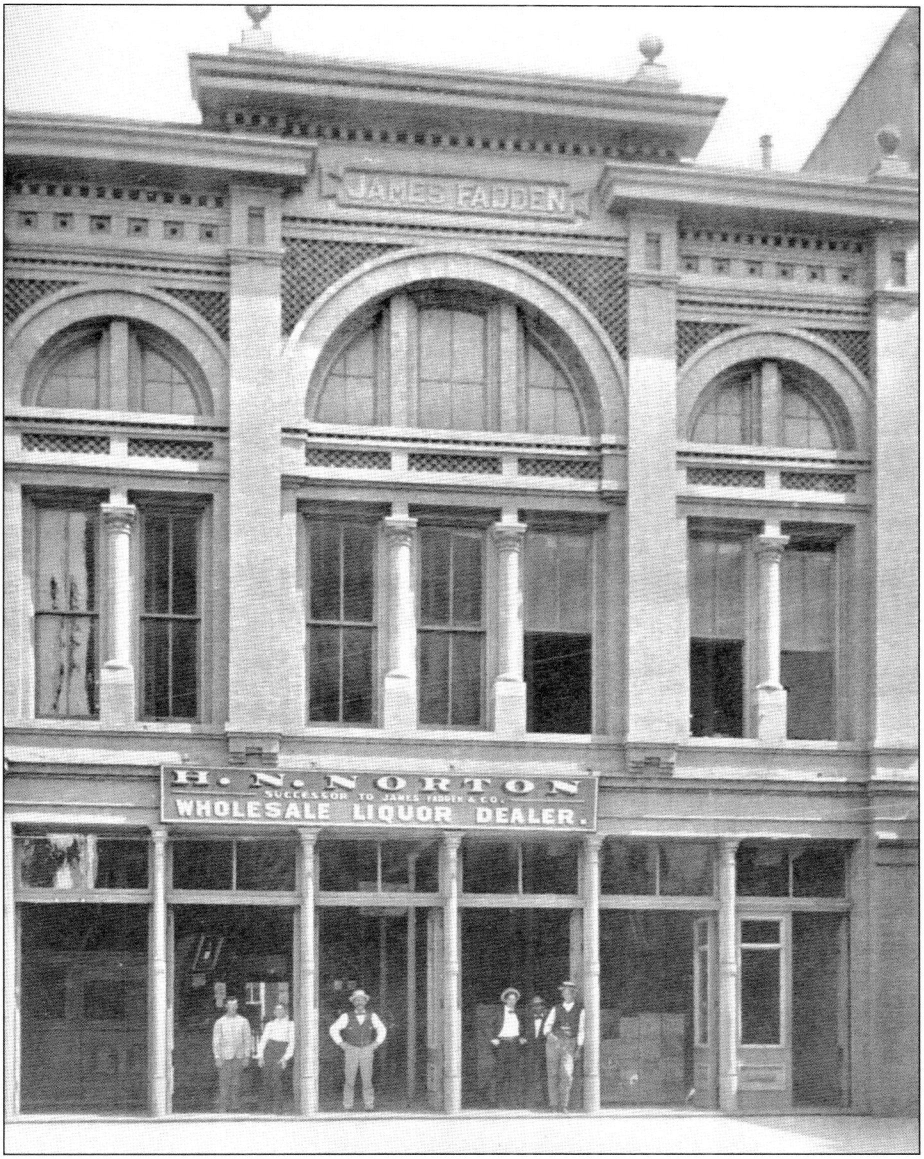

Of more modest scale than some of Nicholas Clayton's other buildings in downtown Galveston, the James Fadden Building fit well in scale with the wholesale, liquor, wine, and cigar business housed here. Completed in 1898 at 2410–2412 Strand, this building is an understated stand out. The building was constructed for $7,500 and has a simple cast-iron storefront. James Fadden died shortly after the completion of this building, and his widow Rosa Fadden operated the firm until H. N. Norton took over the business in 1900. The brick curb in front of the Fadden Building is original. Cast iron in Galveston was imported from Philadelphia, Baltimore, New Orleans, and a local firm, Lee Iron Works. Cast-iron fronts in Galveston are mostly decorative veneer, bolted onto the brick facades. Over 44 percent of the buildings in the Strand/Mechanic National Historic Landmark District have cast-iron elements. There are more than 10 other structures in the downtown area with cast-iron elements. Cast-iron storefronts were introduced in Galveston in 1856.

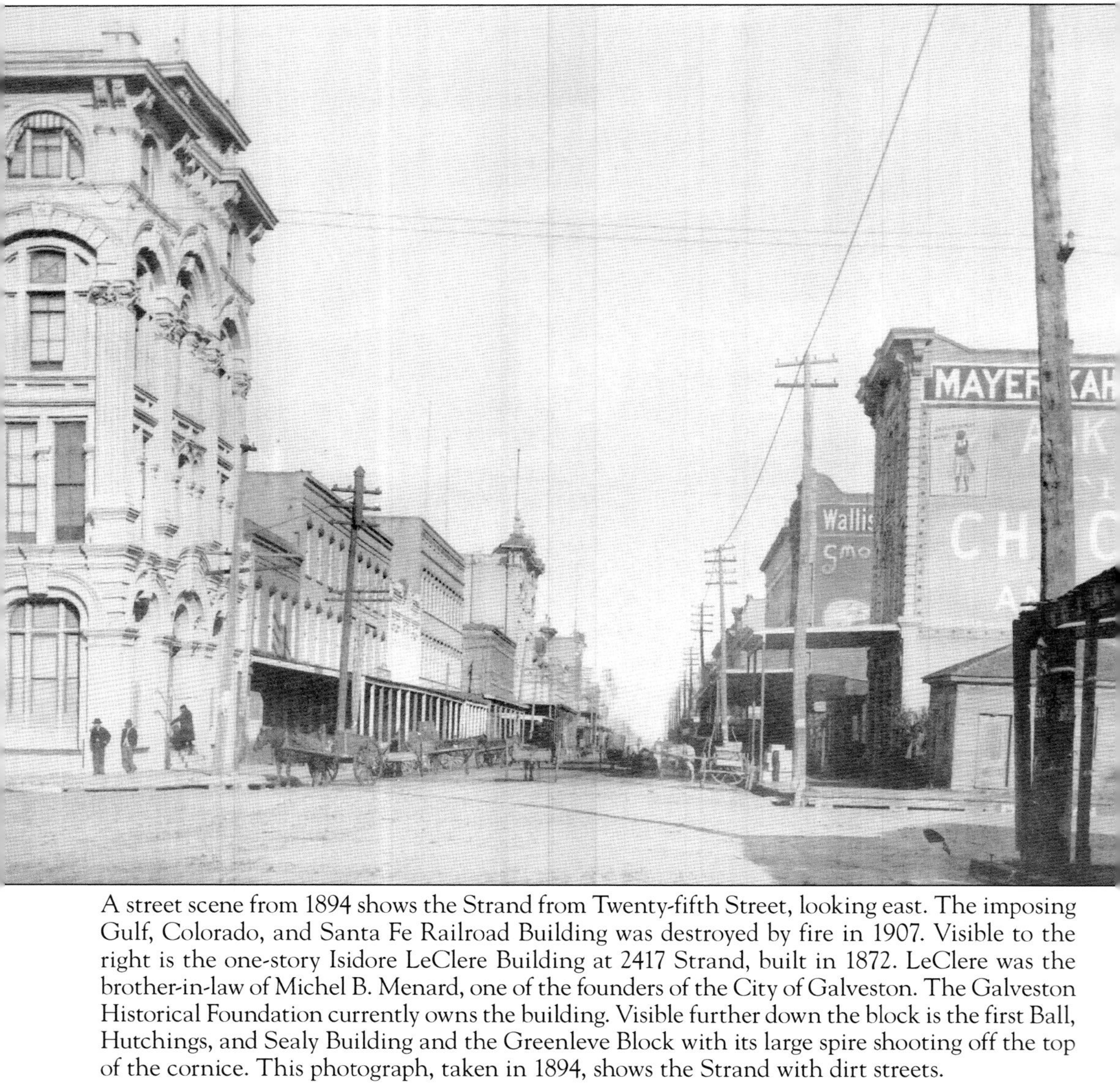

A street scene from 1894 shows the Strand from Twenty-fifth Street, looking east. The imposing Gulf, Colorado, and Santa Fe Railroad Building was destroyed by fire in 1907. Visible to the right is the one-story Isidore LeClere Building at 2417 Strand, built in 1872. LeClere was the brother-in-law of Michel B. Menard, one of the founders of the City of Galveston. The Galveston Historical Foundation currently owns the building. Visible further down the block is the first Ball, Hutchings, and Sealy Building and the Greenleve Block with its large spire shooting off the top of the cornice. This photograph, taken in 1894, shows the Strand with dirt streets.

Three

Avenue C, Ships Mechanic Row

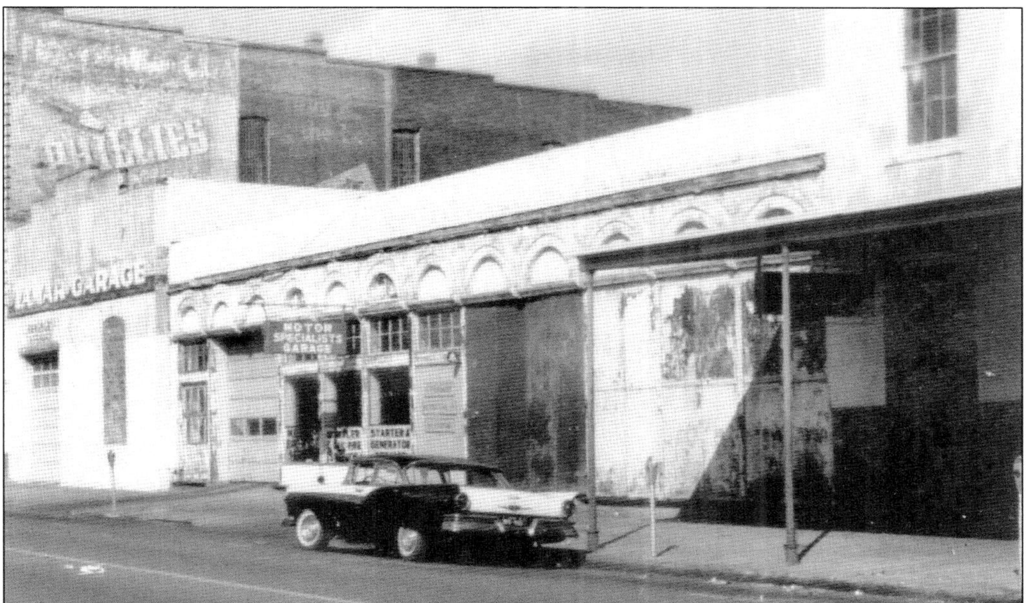

Ships Mechanic Row, or as it is most commonly known as Mechanic, has many distinguished structures but has not retained the same amount of integrity as its neighboring street Strand. Many buildings on Mechanic Row were used to house merchants with shipping interests. This photograph is of the Mechanic Street Warehouse, built in 1888. Its most notable features are the interior supports and barrel vaulted brick ceilings. This building is owned by the Galveston Historical Foundation.

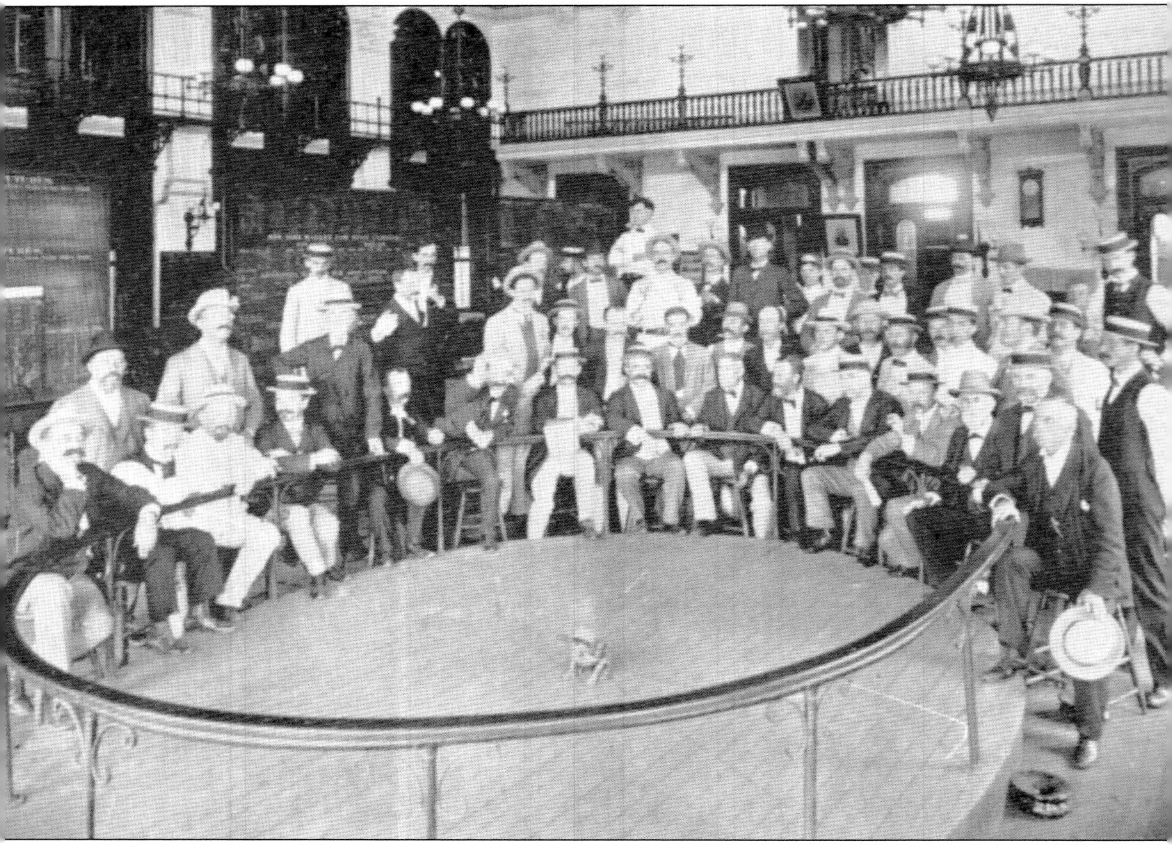

Col. W. L. Moody called the meeting to order to form the Galveston Cotton Exchange. Colonel Moody nominated J. Frederich for chairman and E. S. Flint as secretary of the new organization, and both men were unanimously elected. There was some discussion as to the rules and bylaws, and the membership roll was opened. Another meeting was held on April 27, 1873, and a committee was appointed to draft rules and bylaws. At the meeting on May 6, 1873, it was announced that 20 members had been secured, and the Galveston Cotton Exchange was organized. At a meeting on the May 24, 1873, the first election of permanent officers was held and W. H. Sellers was chosen for president, W. K. McAlpin as vice president, and M. Quin as treasurer. The Exchange made a significant difference in the way cotton was traded, allowing for maximum return on investment. The impact was felt as far away as Chicago.

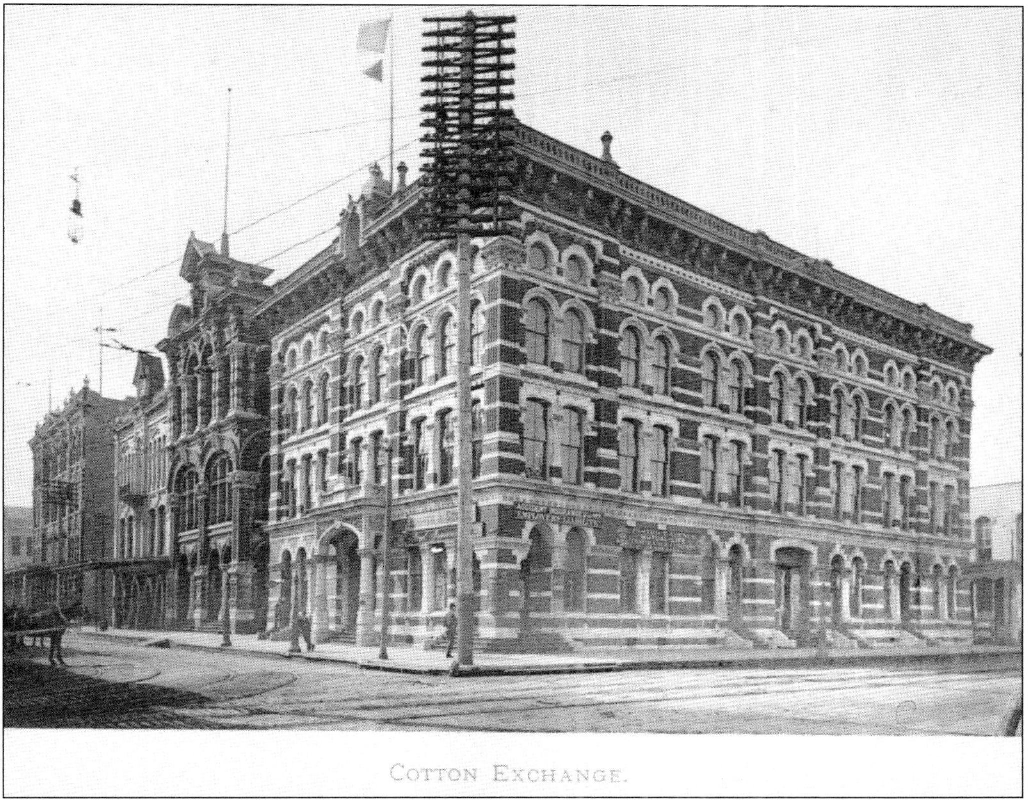

The original Galveston Cotton Exchange Building was built in 1879 and was designed by John Moser. The Galveston Cotton Exchange organization was the first of its kind in Texas and needed a large building to accommodate all of the trade occurring in Galveston. Fortunes reversed, and the building was demolished for a smaller structure in 1938.

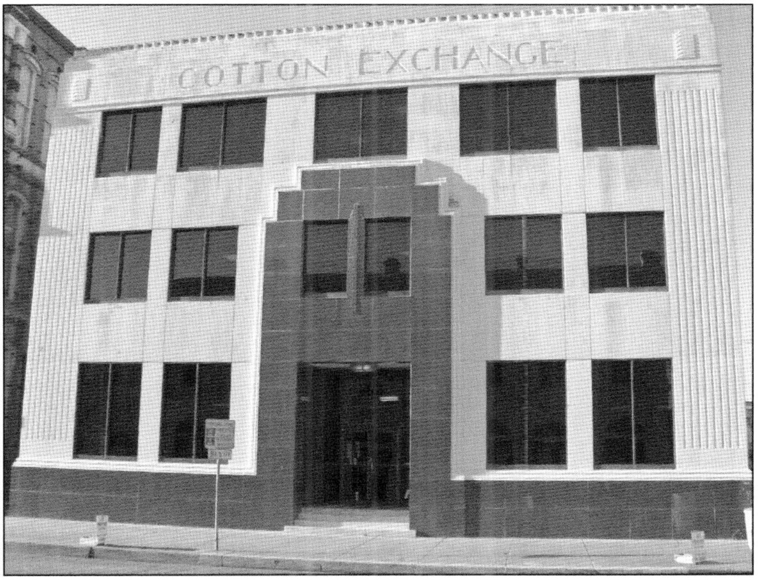

One of the only art deco buildings in downtown Galveston, the Galveston Cotton Exchange and Board of Trade Building at 2102 Ships Mechanic Row was constructed in 1940 with architect Ben Milam as designer. Built with polished granite exterior, this building looks like an outcast on Ships Mechanic Row, but its exterior is an example of Galveston's changing architectural tastes.

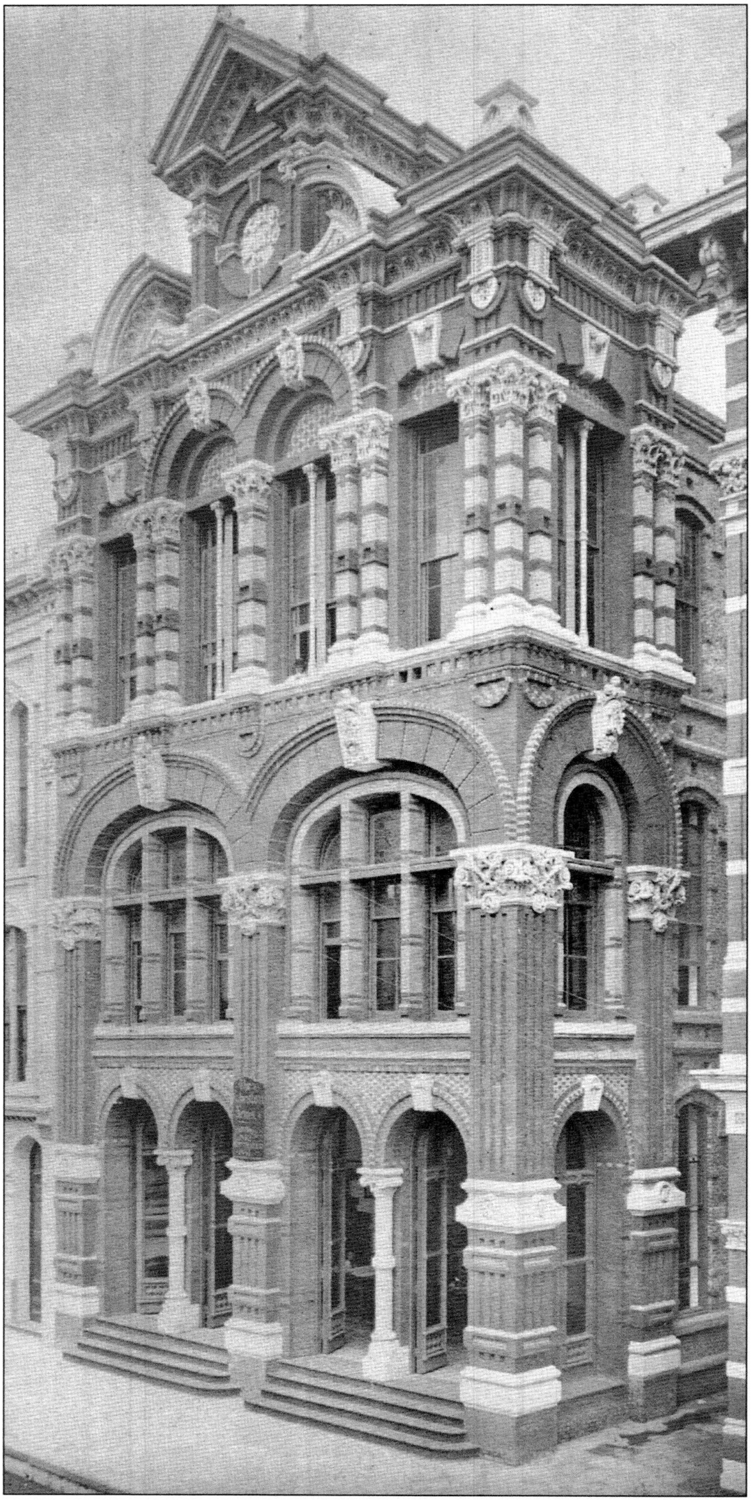

The Galveston Daily News Building is thought by many to be one of Nicholas Clayton's masterpieces. Built in 1884 for the newspaper, the iron and brick caged building contained offices and production facilities for the *Galveston Daily News*. The building is located at 2108 Ships Mechanic Row. (Courtesy of the Rosenberg Library, Galveston, Texas.)

The *Galveston Daily News* is the oldest surviving newspaper in Texas, founded in 1842. The newspaper reached prominence when Alfred H. Belo took over the newspaper in 1875. A. H. Belo also started the *Dallas Morning News*. The Belo Corporation (still in existence today) ran the newspaper until 1923, when W. L. Moody purchased it. At one time, Galveston had over 15 newspapers.

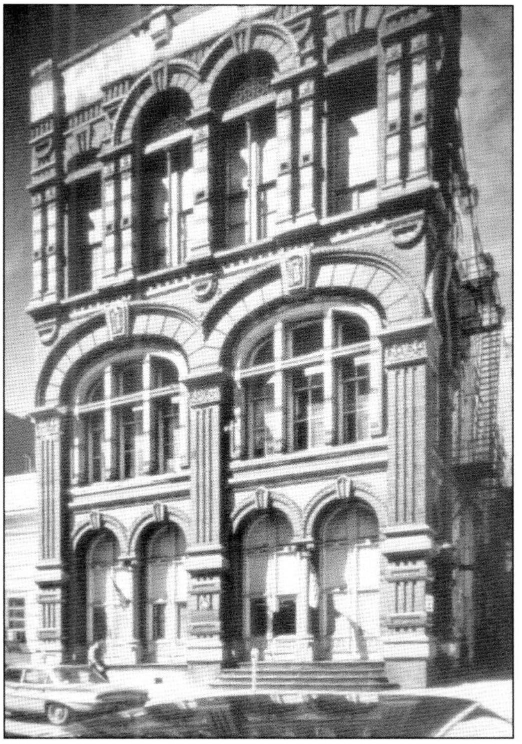

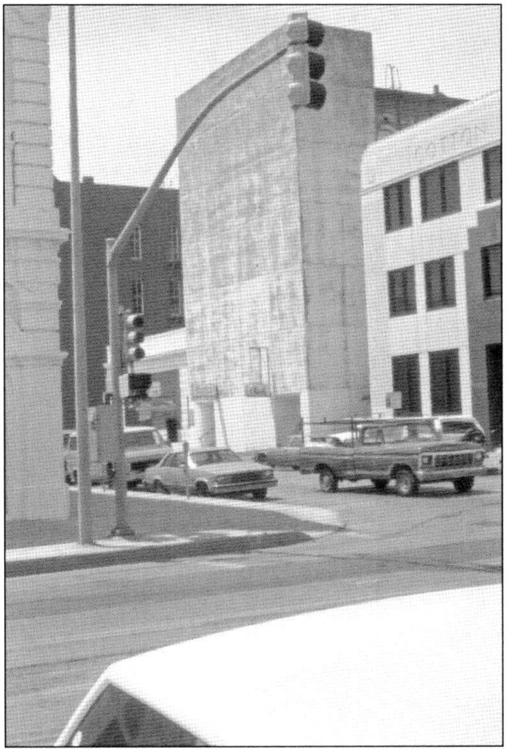

Like many buildings in the middle of the 20th century, the Galveston Daily News Building was swathed in a facade cover. Facade covers were used to cover up a building's original elements to give it a modern touch. These covers were put in place to give new life to old buildings. The facade cover for the Galveston Daily News Building was removed between 1995 and 1996, showing once again the graceful styling of Nicholas Clayton.

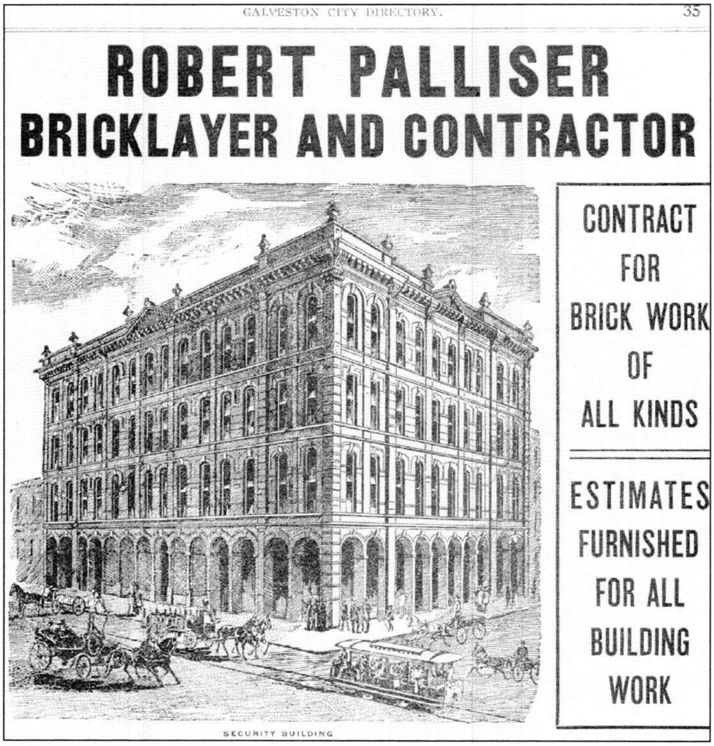

This building was erected in 1882 for Kauffman and Runge. The brick is Philadelphia pressed brick and has many substantial architectural features. It was designed by Houston architect Eugene T. Heiner. Heiner had the ability to design a much larger building in Galveston than he did in Houston. The building was designed in a Victorian version of the Italian Renaissance.

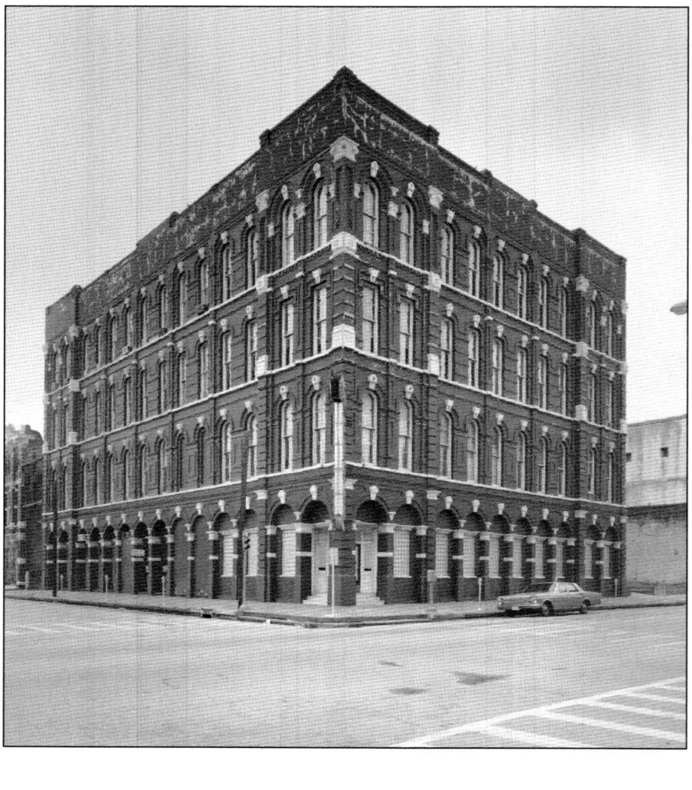

This photograph shows the Kauffman and Runge Building in 1967, without its restored cornice. In 1977, the Stewart Title Company, commercial inhabitants of the building since 1905, used Galveston architect David V. Barker to reconstruct the cornice. This building was also modified in 1905 by Charles W. Bulger to turn the building into offices for lawyer Maco Stewart. Bulger added a central court to the interior of the building. (Courtesy of the Library of Congress, Prints and Photographs Division, Historic American Buildings Survey.)

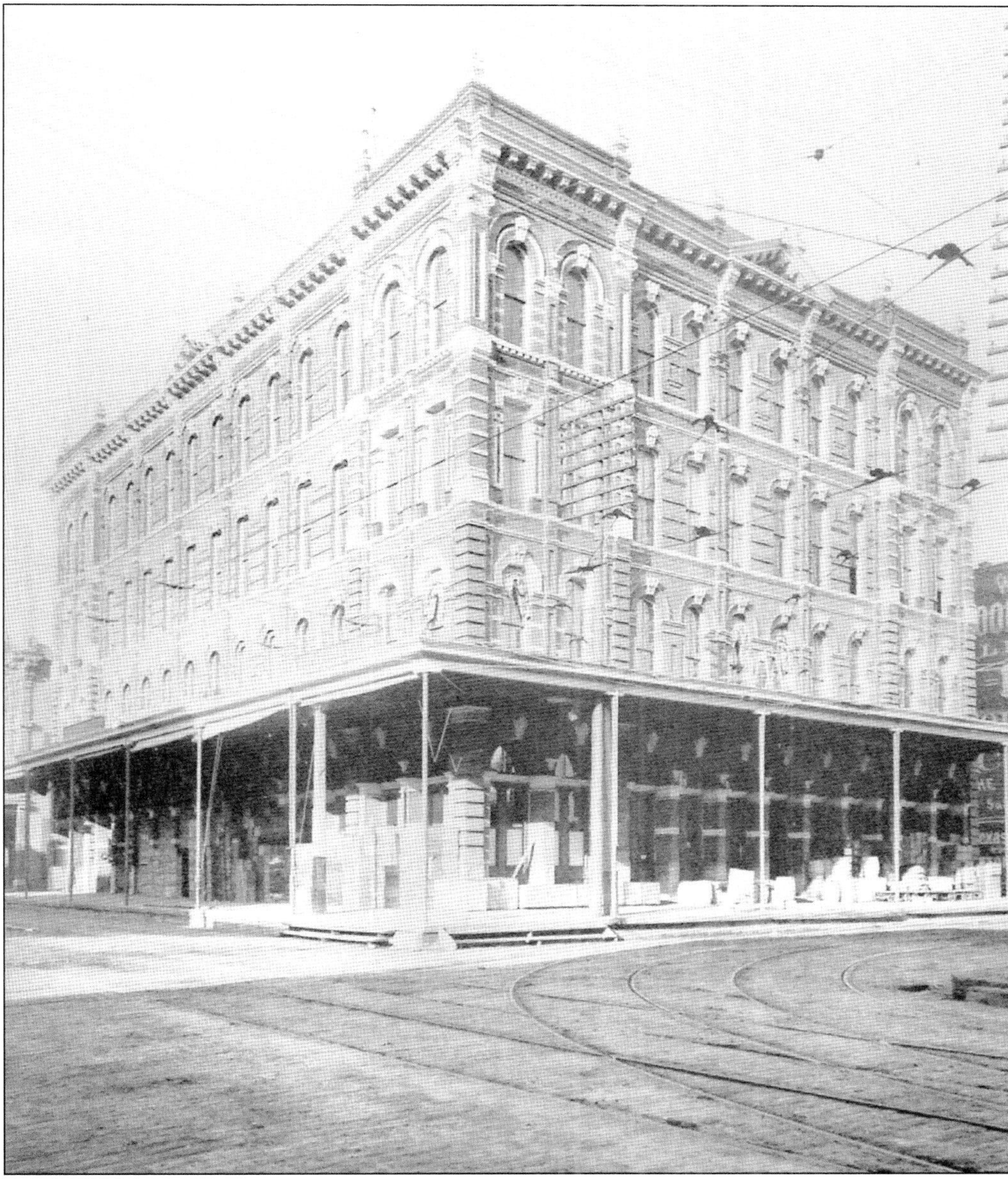

Julius Kauffman and Julius Runge were known as importers of coffee and liquors. In the year 1887, Kauffman and Runge imported more coffee than any other business in Galveston. They were also known for having a great cotton exporting business. Their trade of groceries reached only Texas patrons, but the trade of cotton reached to Mexico, England, France, Germany, and Russia. In the late 1880s, Kauffman and Runge held a strong role in helping immigrants settle in Galveston. Julius Kauffman was the Austrian counsel to the Port of Galveston, and Mr. Runge was a representative of Germany and was the Treasurer for the City of Galveston in 1887. Mr. Runge was also held two terms as Alderman and was the Chairman of the Finance Committee for the City of Galveston. The combination of civic duty, import, export, and ties to immigration all aided in helping make Galveston a leading port in the 1880s. Even with all of this, Kauffman and Runge went bankrupt in 1887.

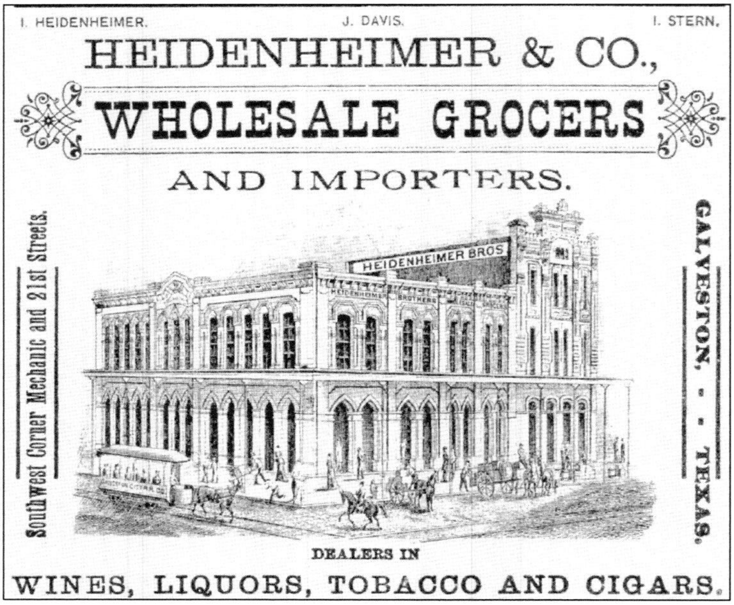

Isaac Heidenheimer came to Galveston from Virginia City, Montana, to open a business. He held interests in other businesses that imported coffee and salt. He also owned a flour mill and a sugar plantation. Heidenheimer and Company dealt with groceries, liquor, tobacco, and cigars and imported coffee and sardines.

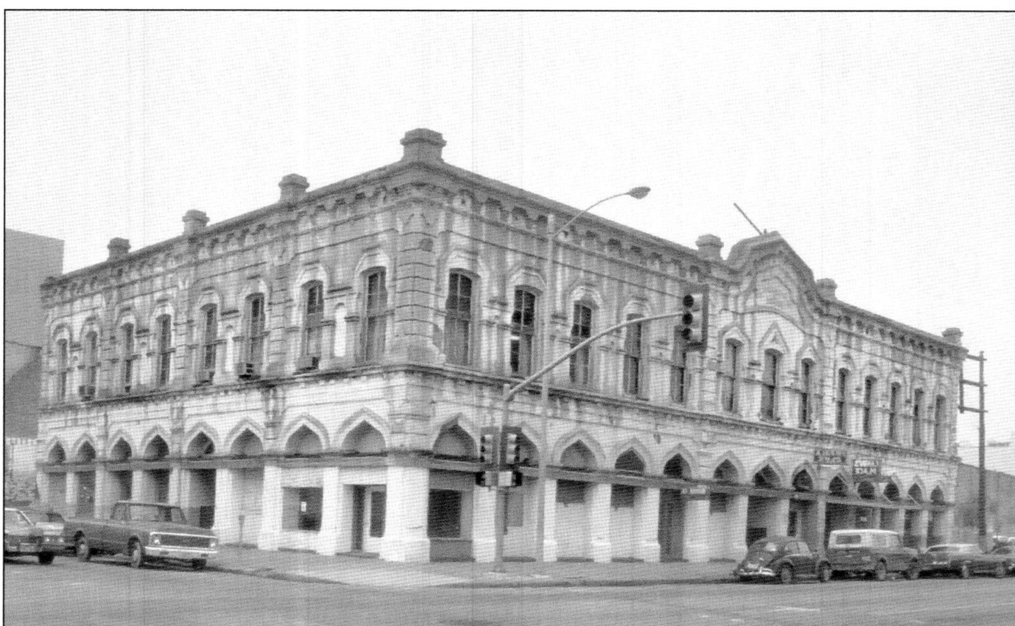

The Heidenheimer and Company Building was constructed in 1875 at the corner of Twenty-first and Ships Mechanic Row. The architect for the building is unknown. This building has a Victorian Gothic feel, and the brick has stucco applied on the surface. This photograph, taken in the early 1980s, shows the building before renovation by the Mitchell family.

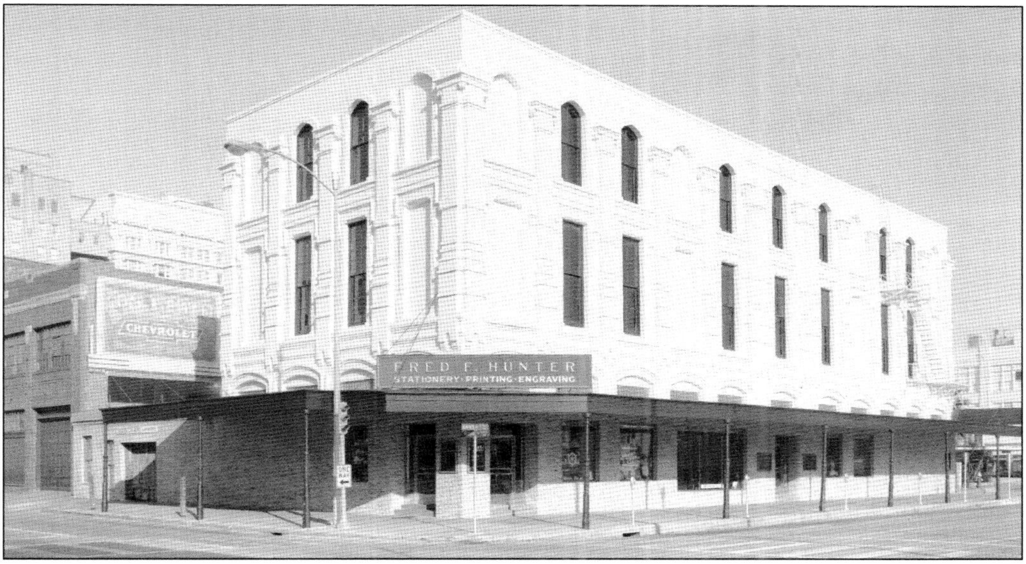

On the corner of Twenty-second and Ships Mechanic Row is the H. Marwitz and Company Building, erected in 1878 and designed by John Moser. Sampson Heidenheimer built several buildings on this block as rental properties. This building has lost its original cornice. (Courtesy of the Library of Congress, Prints and Photographs Division, Historic American Buildings Survey.)

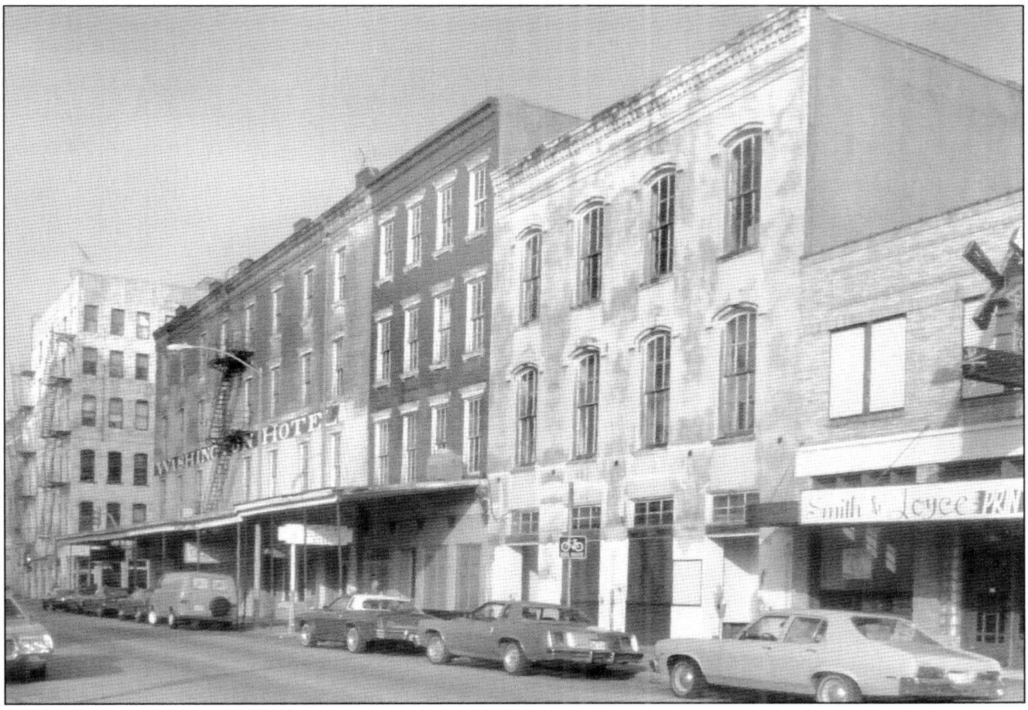

This photograph, taken in the late 1970s, shows the decline of Ships Mechanic Row. This entire block, which included the Reyermershoffer's Sons Building (1877), the investment building (1873), the Davie Building (1860), and Washington Hotel (1873), was in disrepair. By 2010, three of the buildings had undergone rehabilitation.

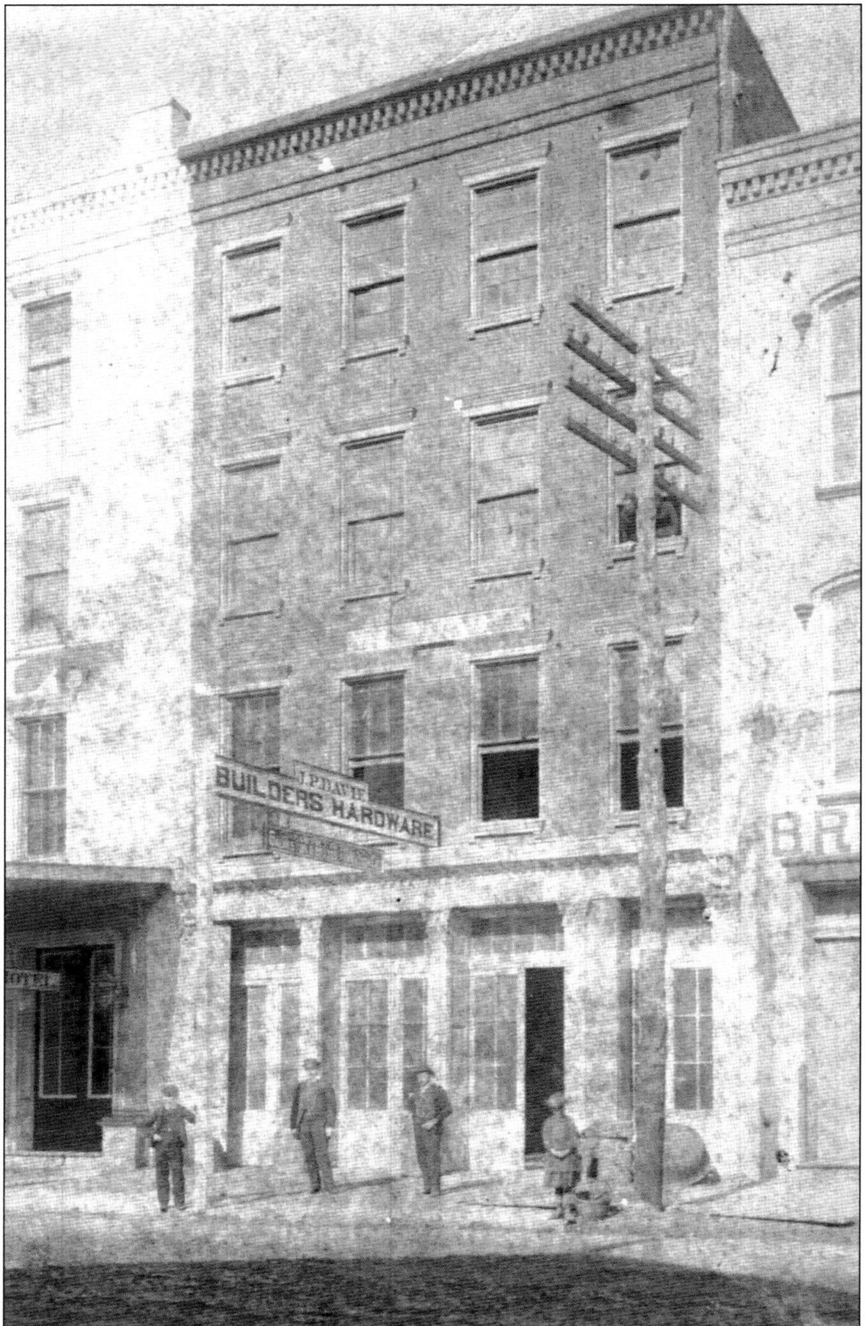

The Davie Building at 2220 Ships Mechanic Row was constructed in 1860 and is typical of the conservative architecture style of Galveston in the 1850s and early 1860s. The Davie Building has cast-iron details and small cast-iron columns on the first floor. This is an understated building today, but in 1860, this four-story building would have been quite a standout, as much smaller neighbors surrounded it. (Courtesy of the Rosenberg Library, Galveston, Texas.)

The original Washington Hotel was built by John P. Davie in 1873. It was a simple, four-story hotel. The building had red brick that was covered in white stucco with iron windowsills and iron lintels. For many years, this site was operated as a hotel, which was originally known as the Cosmopolitan Hotel.

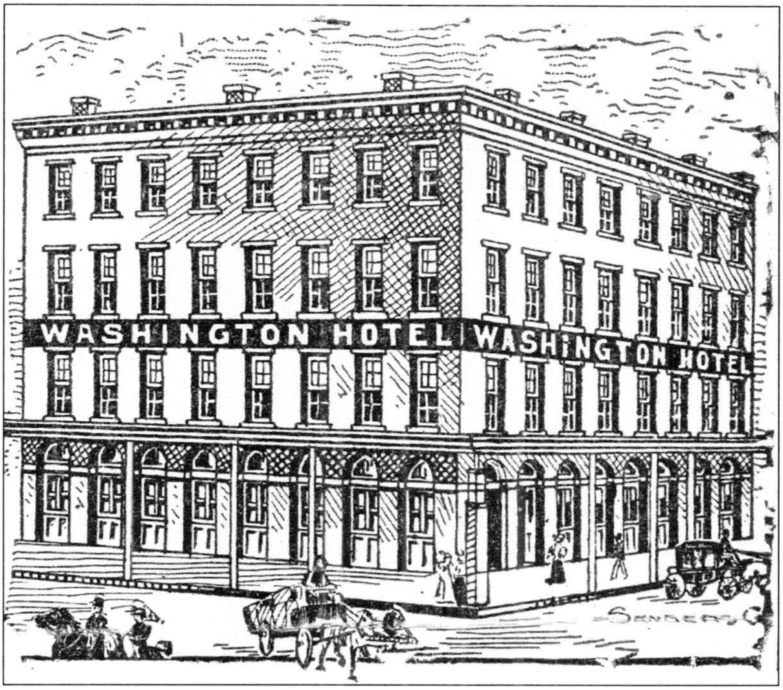

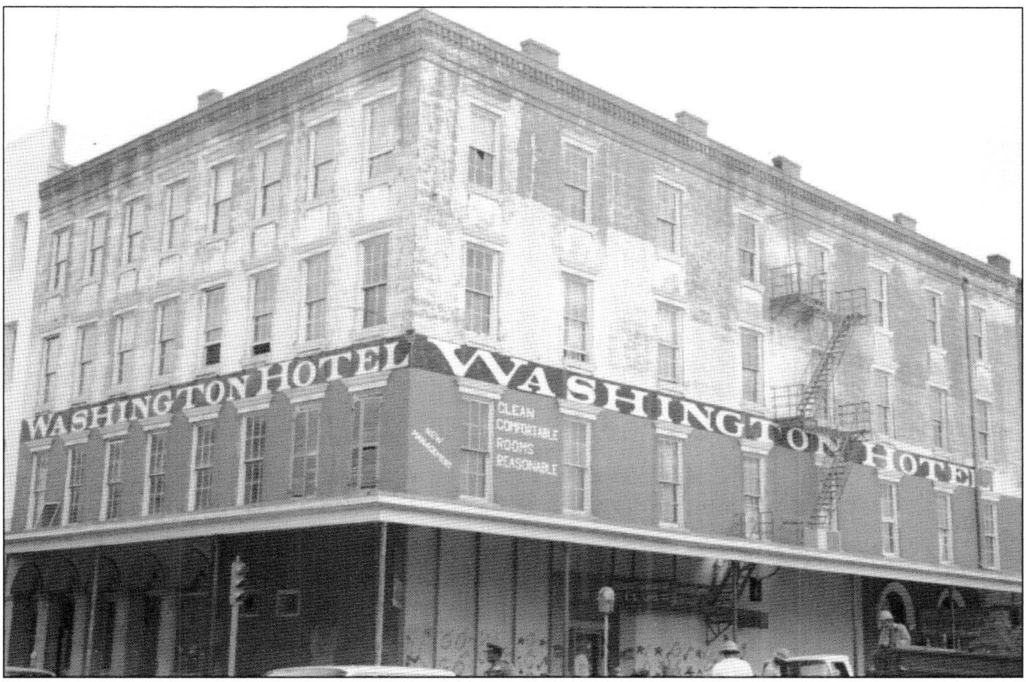

During Hurricane Alicia in 1983, an electrical fire caused the original Washington Hotel to burn down. The Mitchell family purchased the building, and it was in the beginning stages of rehabilitation. Ford, Powell, and Carson already had plans for the building drawn, and the building was reconstructed.

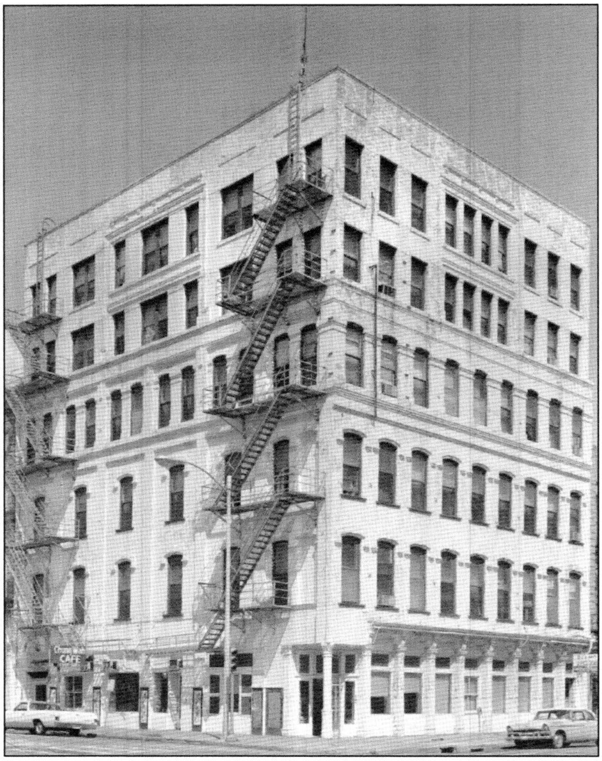

This photograph taken in 1967 shows the McDonnell Building on the northwest corner of Ships Mechanic Row and Twenty-third, with its two additions. Originally, this building was constructed with three floors with additions coming in 1907 and 1909. In 1990, the top two floors were removed. (Courtesy of the Library of Congress, Prints and Photographs Division, Historic American Buildings Survey.)

The Mistrot Brothers dry goods enterprise lasted until 1908. In the 1900 Storm, the Mistrot Brothers lost between $20,000 to $25,000 worth of goods and merchandise. The store in Galveston was the distribution point for 25 stores throughout Texas.

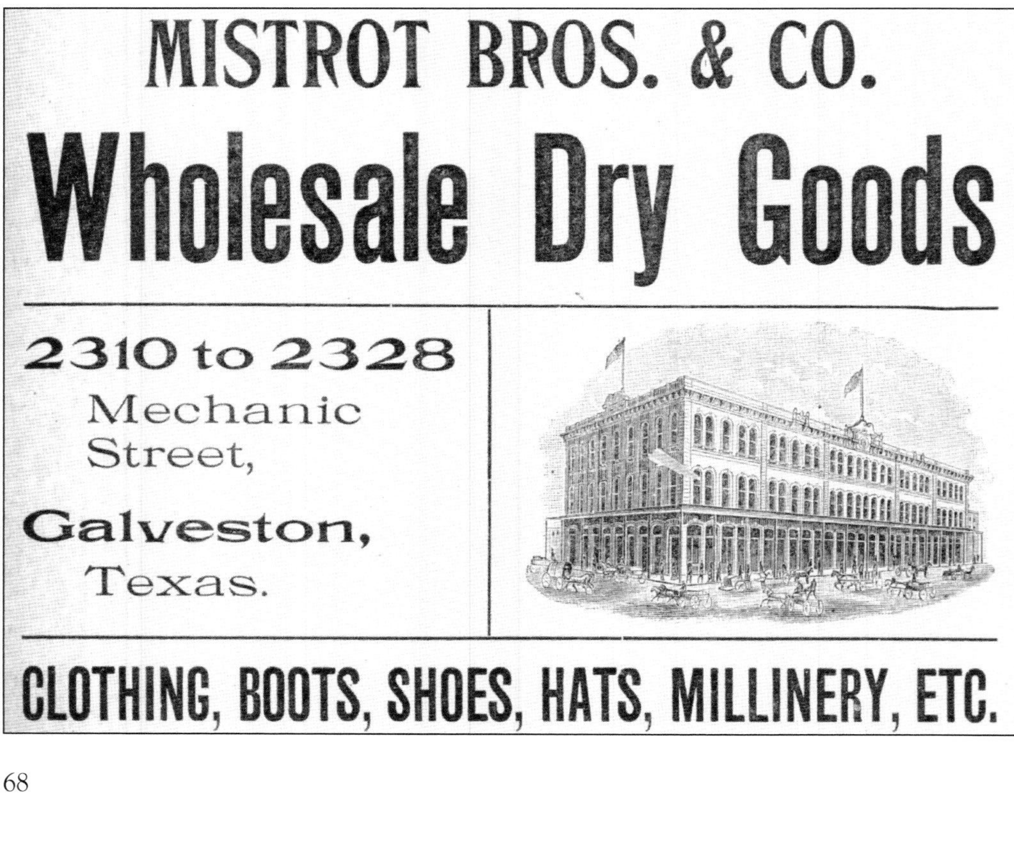

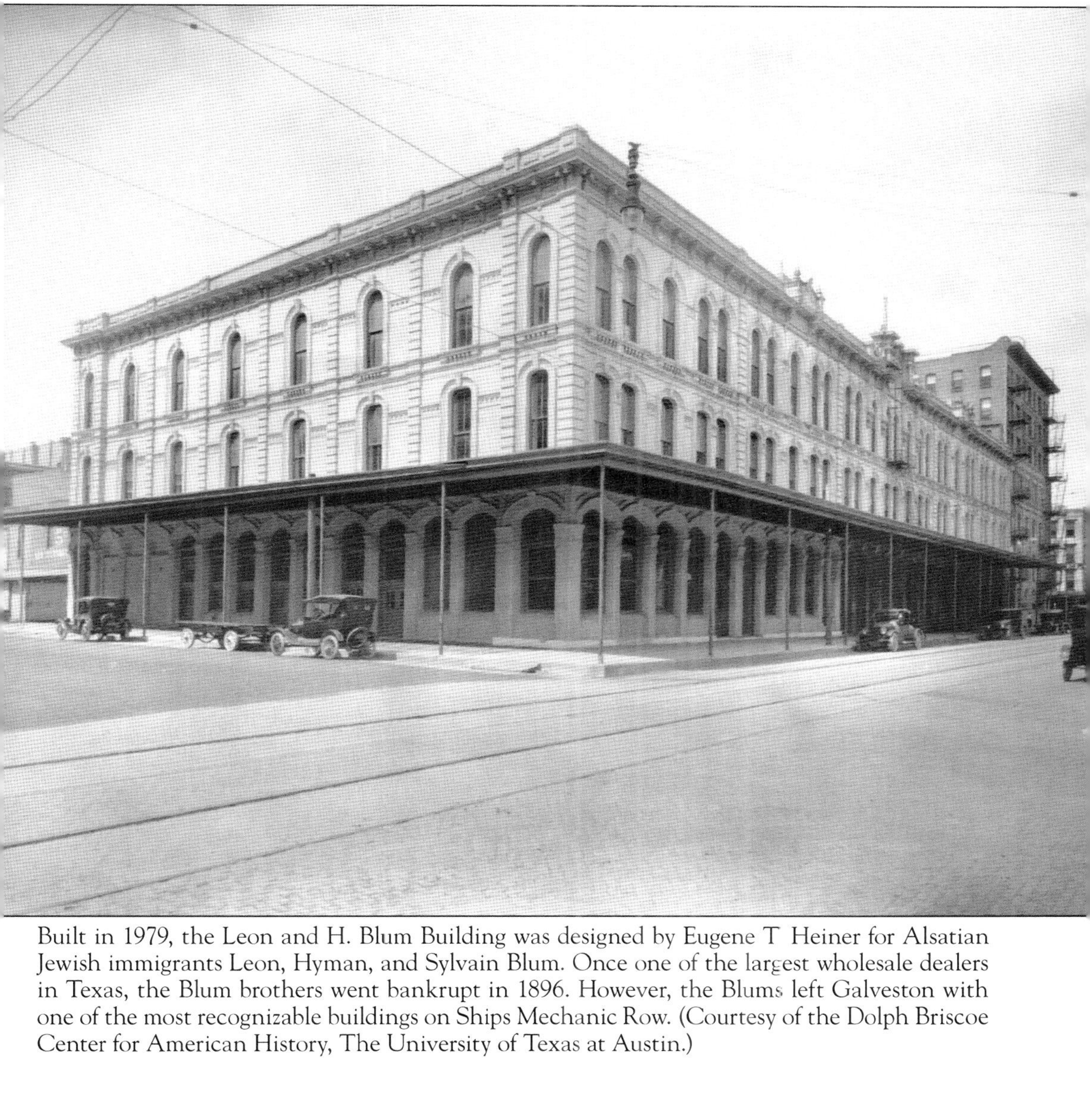

Built in 1979, the Leon and H. Blum Building was designed by Eugene T Heiner for Alsatian Jewish immigrants Leon, Hyman, and Sylvain Blum. Once one of the largest wholesale dealers in Texas, the Blum brothers went bankrupt in 1896. However, the Blums left Galveston with one of the most recognizable buildings on Ships Mechanic Row. (Courtesy of the Dolph Briscoe Center for American History, The University of Texas at Austin.)

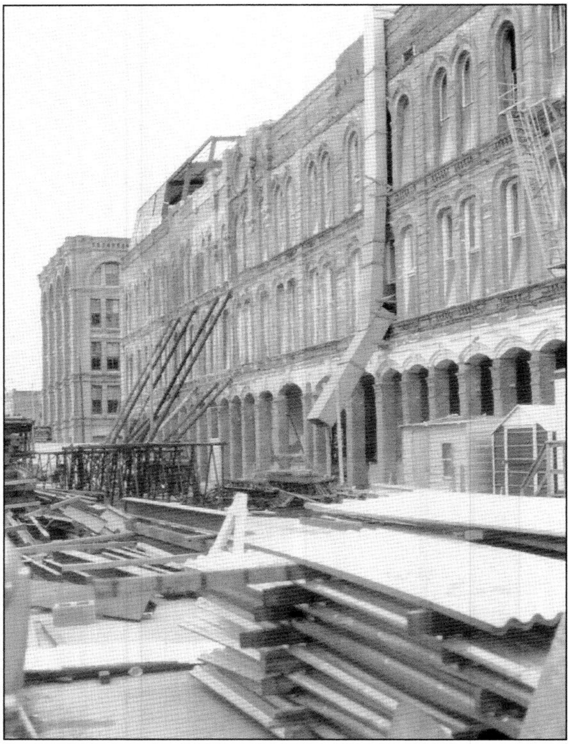

In 1981, Cynthia and George Mitchell purchased the Blum Building and began an extensive renovation with Ford, Powell, and Carson and interior designer Ann Miller Gray to turn this building into the Tremont House Hotel. This was the first major hotel to be in downtown Galveston in about 60 years. The Mitchells named the hotel after the Old Tremont Hotel that was demolished in 1928.

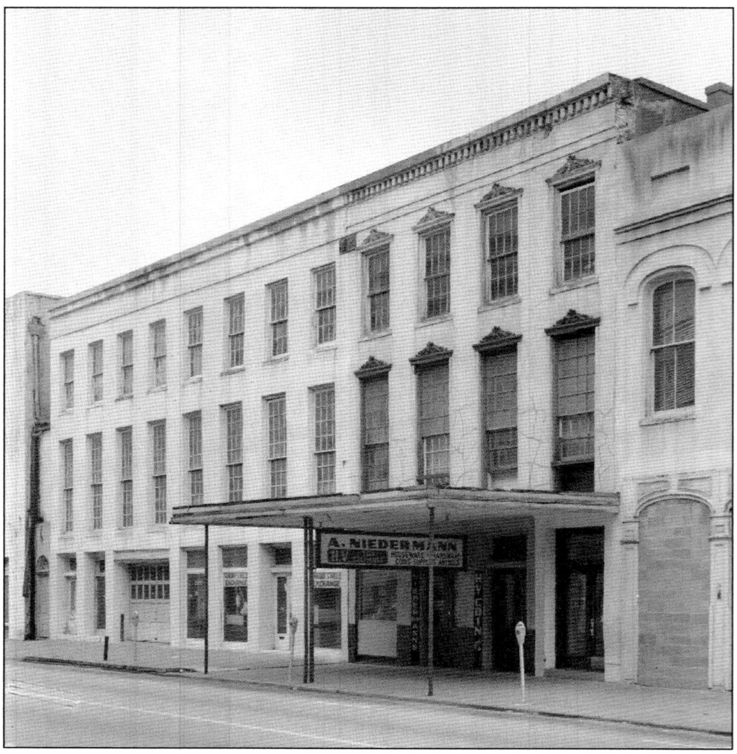

One of the oldest buildings in the Strand Mechanic National Historic Landmark District is the John Berlocher Building constructed in 1858 and 1859. One of the most noticeable elements is the 16-pane-over-16-pane windows and their cast-iron accent elements. This building is very typical for the time, sharing similarities with the Hendley, Pix, and Davie Buildings. (Courtesy of the Library of Congress, Prints and Photographs Division, Historic American Buildings Survey.)

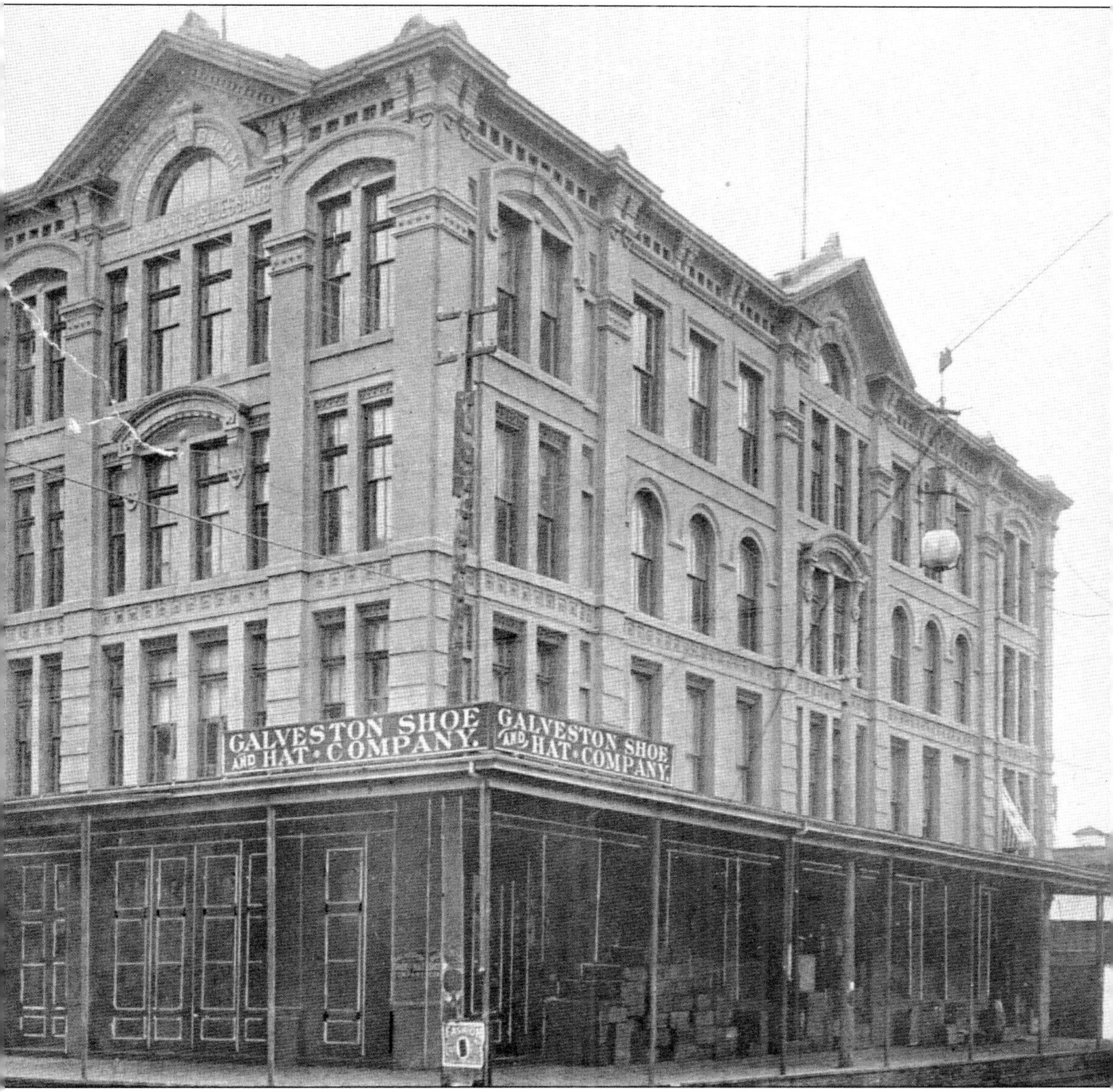

With Nicholas Clayton as architect, the Marx and Blum Building was constructed in 1890. This building also was done in Clayton's signature style of classical detail. The 1900 Storm took the top three floors from the building, and in 1904, the Mistrot brothers involved architect Charles W. Bulger to help with the reconstruction.

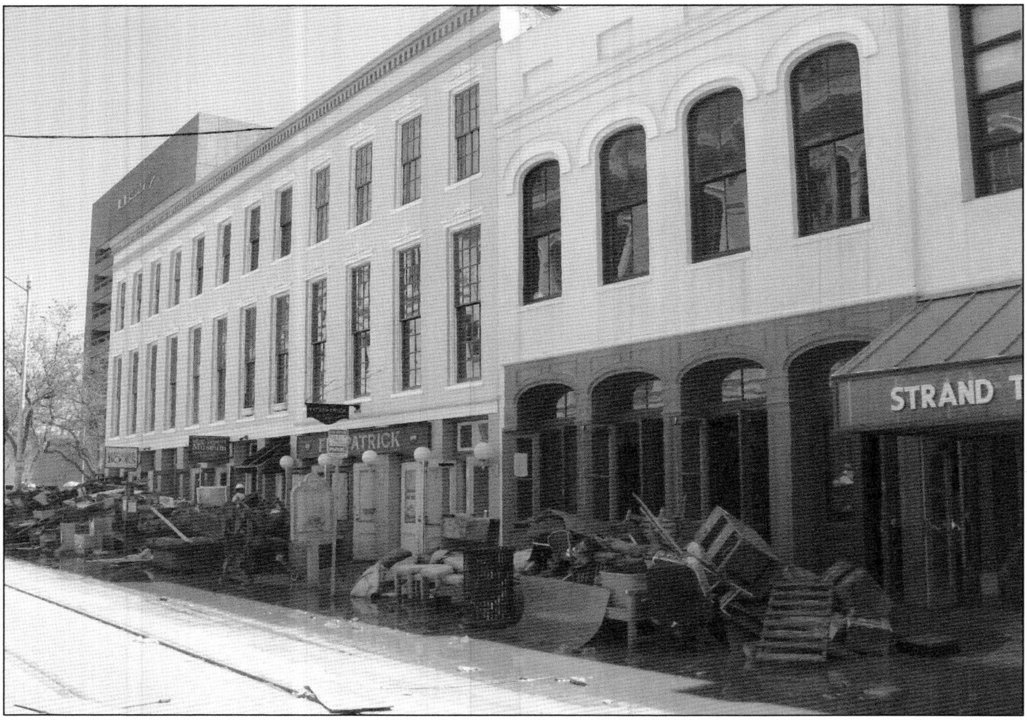

The storm surge of Hurricane Ike left Ships Mechanic Row with up to 10 feet of water. Many of the merchants along the block were left with their stock and furnishings ruined. Unlike many other hurricanes to hit Galveston Island with high winds, the floodwaters from the bay caused building damage. This photograph also shows the 1870 John Berlocher Building, designed by P. N. Comegys.

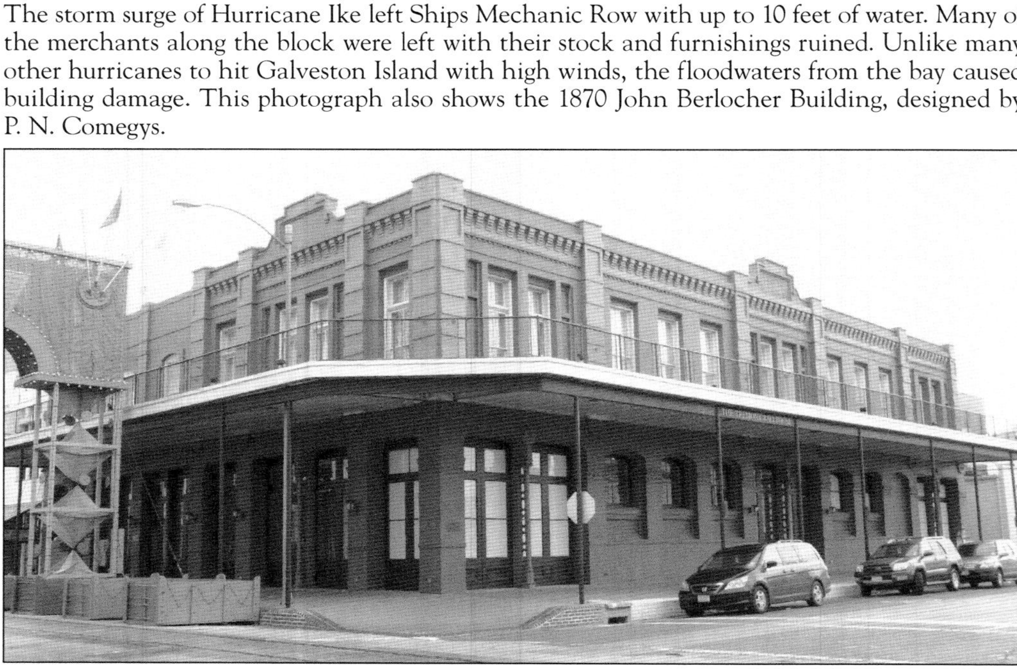

Like many buildings in the Strand Mechanic National Landmark District, the one-story remnants of the Marx and Blum Building were in a serious state of decline. It was only 1995 when this building was restored. It functions as a meeting and event space for the Tremont House Hotel, located across the street. The two stories that are left are a reminder of the once grand four-story building.

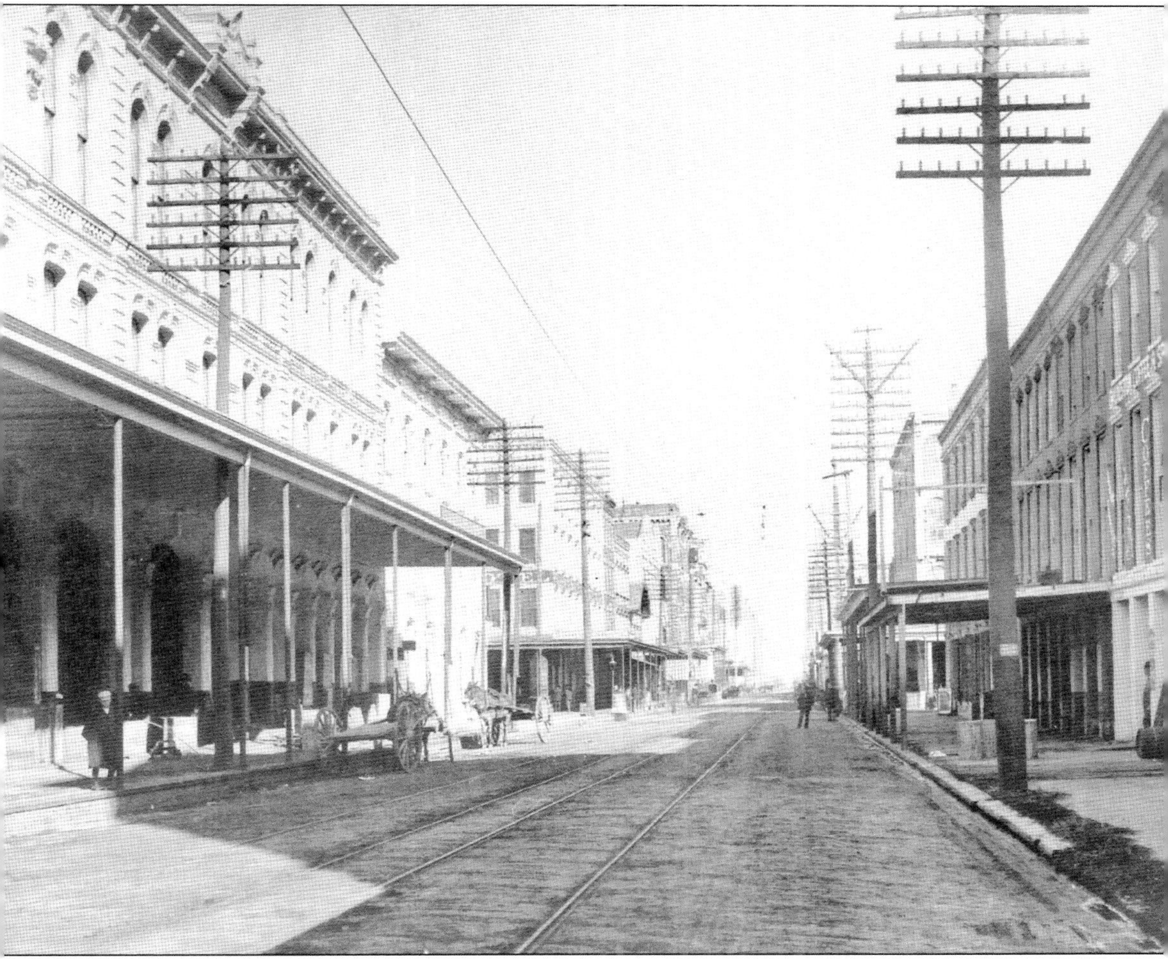

Taking a look east on Twenty-fourth and Ships Mechanic Row, the Leon and Blum Building is on the left, followed by the Washington Hotel, with the Berlocher Buildings to the right. This photograph from 1894 shows the trolley tracks with the dirt and sand soil of the downtown streets. Galveston was and still is a very windy city; it was not uncommon for first floors to be built up some to keep the dirt from filling the interiors. This photograph also shows the sidewalk canopies.

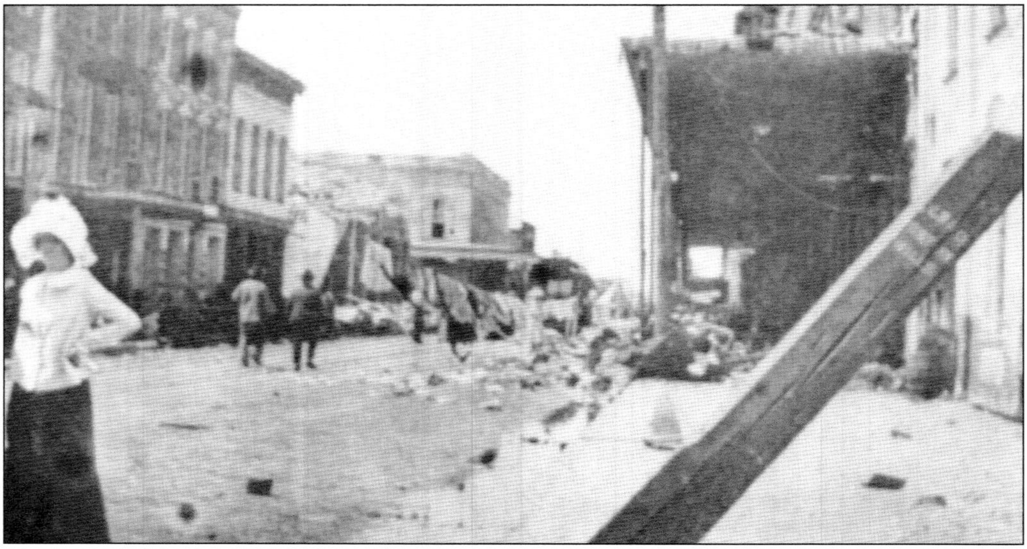

This remarkable photograph shows the aftermath of the 1900 Storm on Ships Mechanic Row, and the ruins of the Marx and Blum Building in the background. This vantage point is from the sidewalk in front of the Leon and Blum Building, now the Tremont House Hotel. The Berlocher Buildings and the Seeligson and Company, the Moore, and the McKinney Buildings are shown to the left.

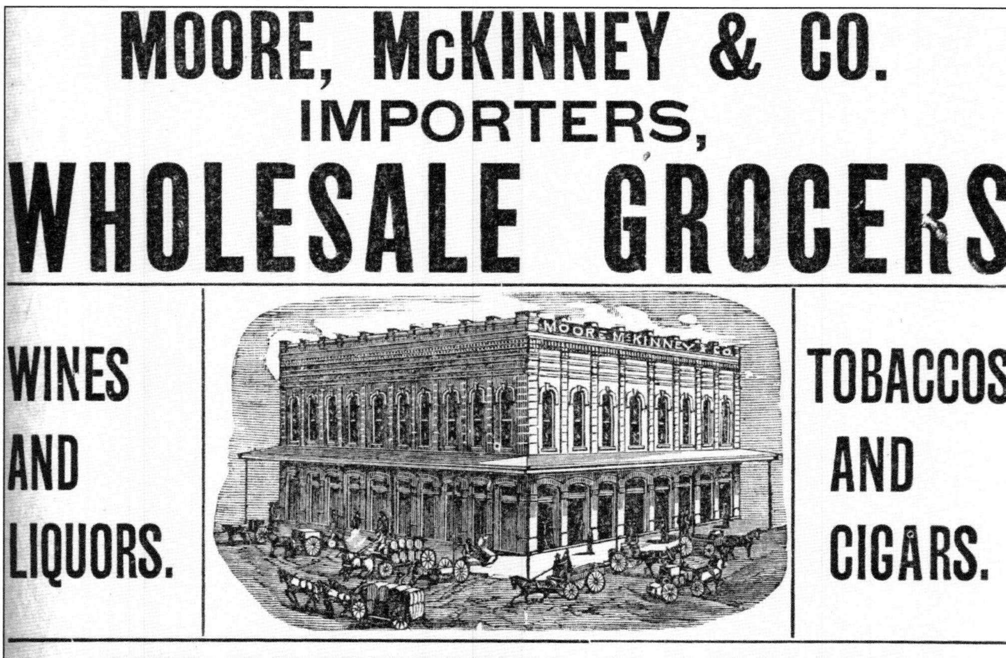

In the 1887 *Industries of Galveston*, this building is called the Seeligson and Company Building and is noted as the "Company" being L. S. McKinney and Max Maas. Liberty S. McKinney and James Moore became the proprietors of Moore, McKinney and Company at the southwest corner of Twenty-fourth and Ships Mechanic Row. Although this commercial building no longer stands, the Liberty McKinney House, built in 1888, is extant at 926 Winnie.

Clarke and Courts was formed after Robert Clarke bought out Samuel Burke to form a company with Miles Strickland, named Strickland and Clarke. George M. Courts was already a wholesale stationary salesman and went into partnership with Robert Clarke in 1879. In 1887, another re-organization led Clark and Courts into being a business.

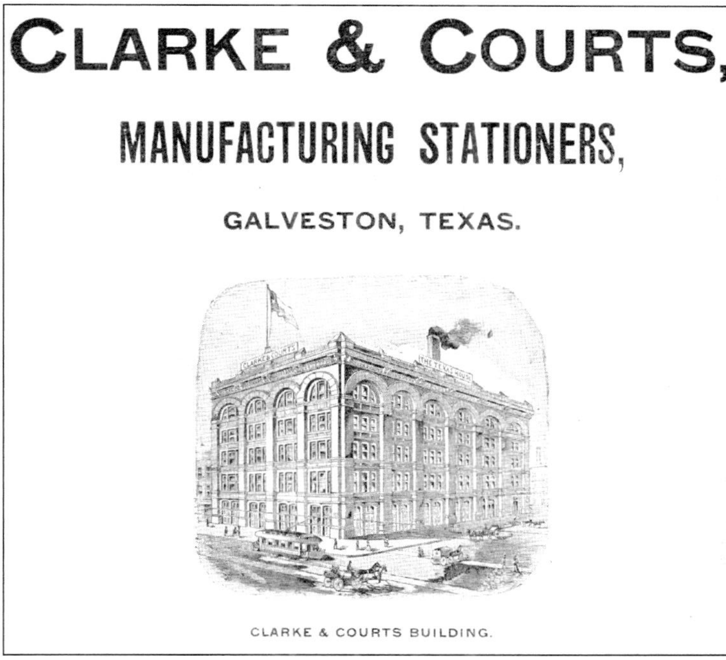

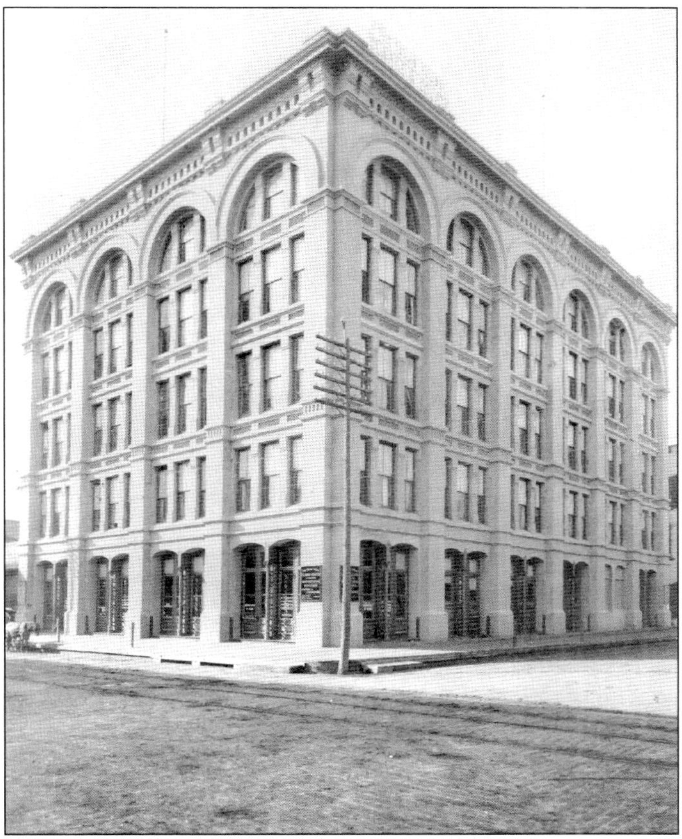

Built by Nicholas Clayton in 1890 for Robert Clarke and George M. Courts to hold their production of printed forms, government documents and bank checks, Clarke and Courts at five stories was the tallest building in Galveston until 1900. This building was constructed more for production rather than as an office building, which might be the reason for its lack of ornamentation.

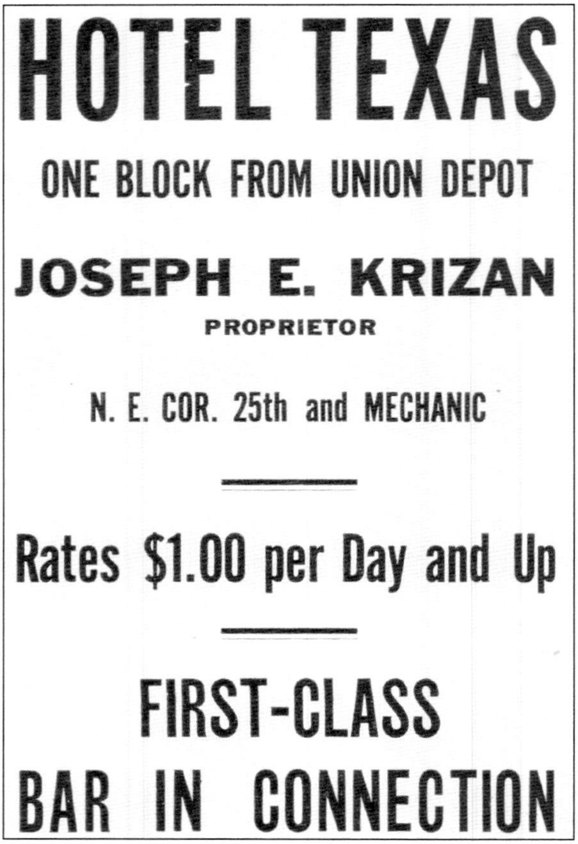

The Hotel Texas operated for a short time in the Sergeant Building in the early 1900s at 2422–2428 Ships Mechanic Row. This hotel targeted immigrants looking for an affordable place to stay before boarding trains, traveling to the interior of Texas. Many small hotels downtown catered to the immigrant class.

The Sergeant Building was constructed around 1874 and was used as a warehouse for Leon Blum and Company. The building has changed hands numerous times and the uses have been many, ranging from a warehouse, to a hotel, mechanic shop, and now condominiums. What has not changed is the stucco-faced brick, which makes a delightful pattern down both Twenty-fifth and Ships Mechanic Rows.

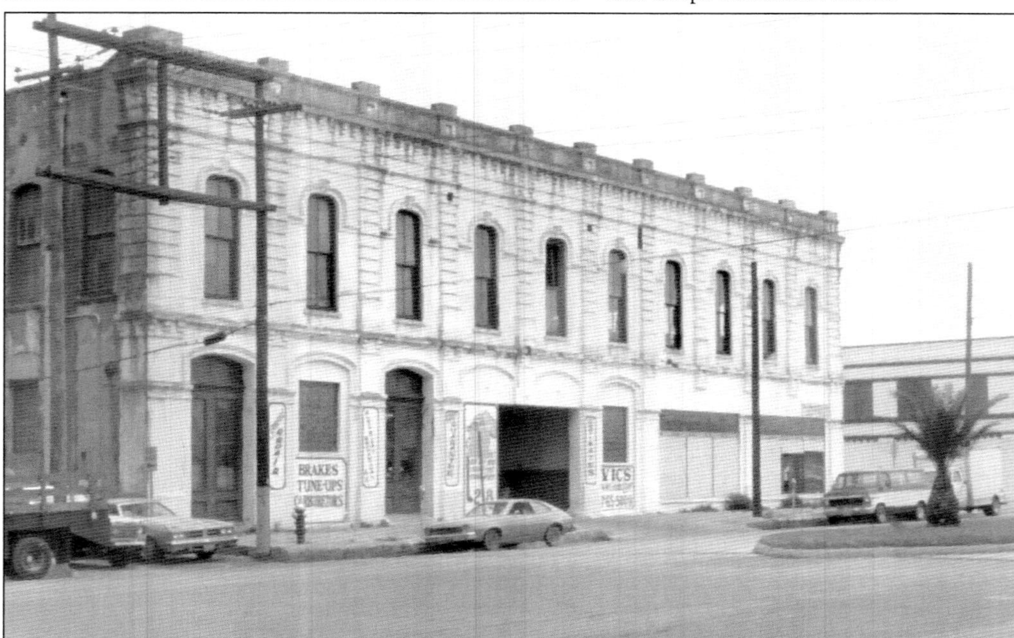

Four

Avenue D, Market

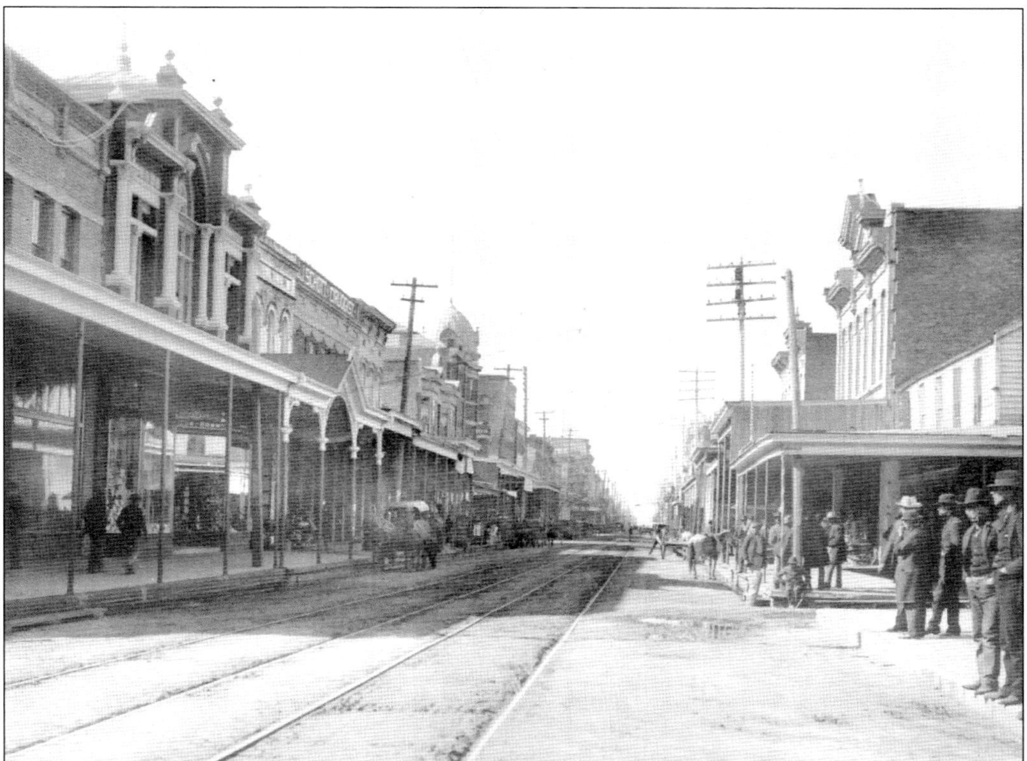

Market Street in the early 20th century was known for having banks and theaters. In the last of the 19th century, the Strand was the center of banking and commerce—a man's street. Market was a street more women frequented. Due to its proximity to the Galveston City Market, located on the first floor of city hall, Market Street had many stores that sold clothing, groceries, and household goods. The photograph shows Market Street, looking west from Twentieth Street.

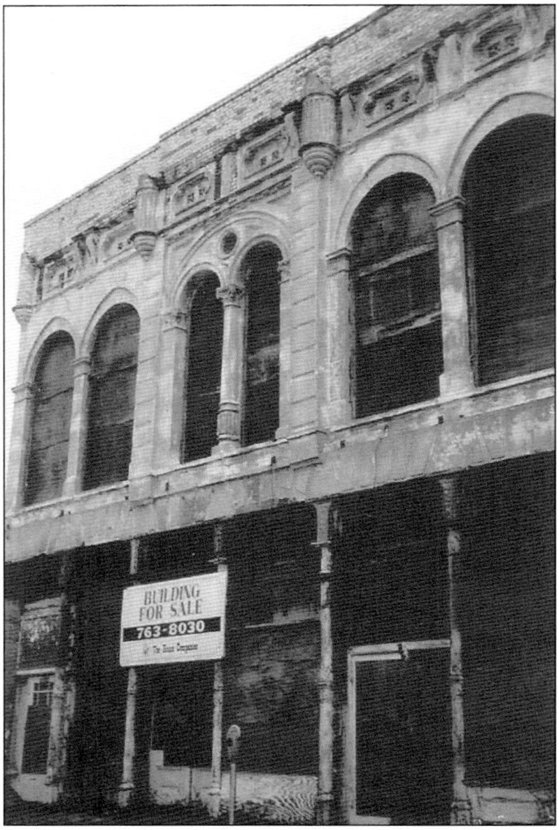

The Wegner Brothers Building was built in 1889. The Wegner brothers sold groceries and liquors. The building has a striking cast-iron structural storefront. This photograph was taken before the building was rehabilitated in 1995.

In 1888, Nicholas Clayton designed the Catholic Building, located at 402-410 Twentieth (Corner of Market and Postoffice) Streets. The building was built for the Catholic Church to provide rental income on the first floor and meeting space and services on the second floor. The Catholic Building was rehabilitated in 1987.

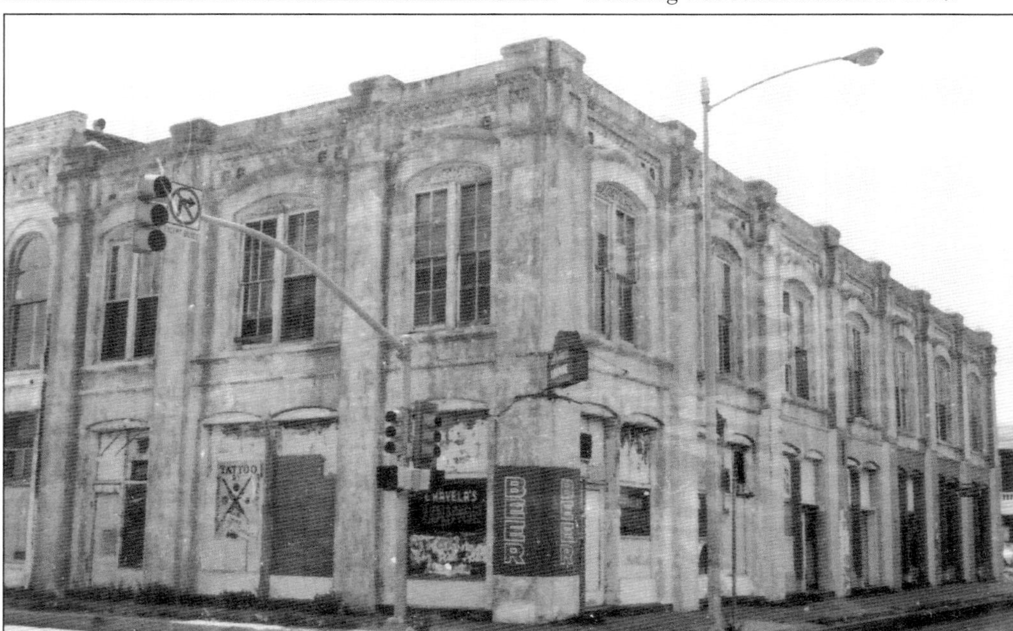

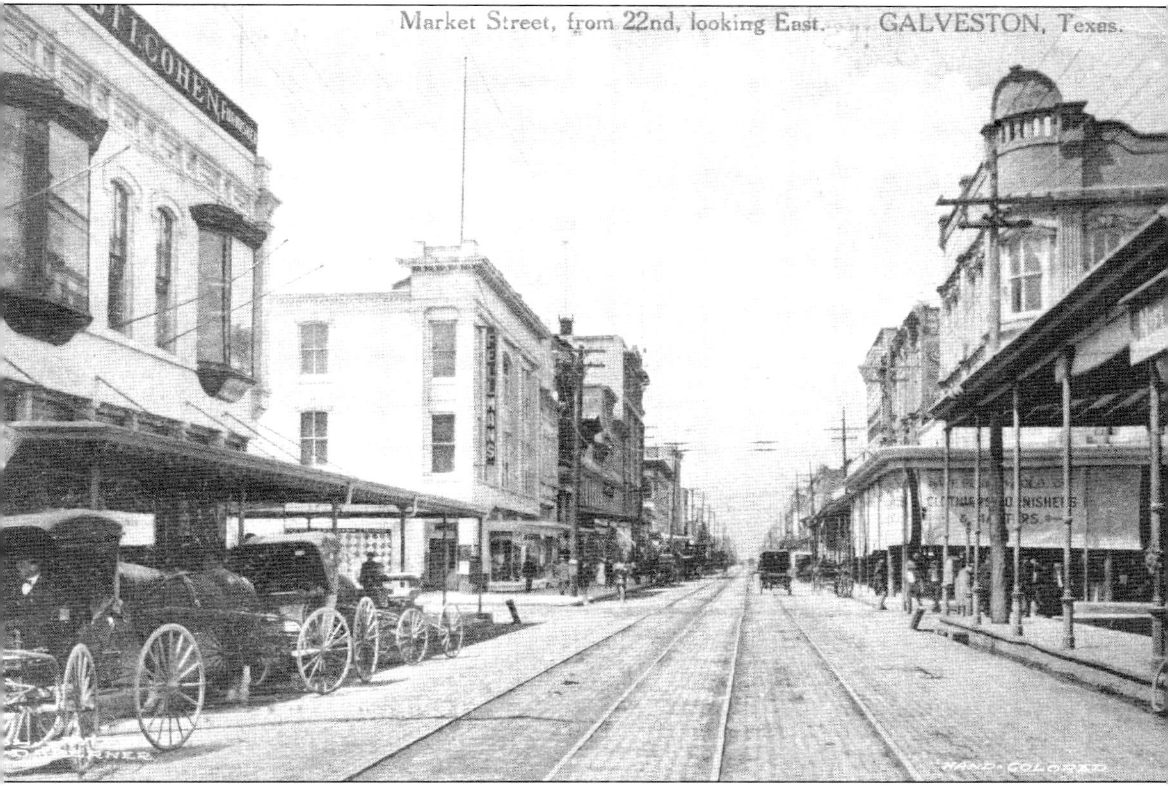

This street scene is incorrectly marked "Market from Twenty-second looking east," the view is actually looking west. This picture was taken in the early 1900s. The Fellman's Department Store eventually moved a block over to Twenty-second and Postoffice, and at this site, the 1925 United States National Bank Building is located. The Cohen Brothers Furniture Store is the first building on the left. Most of the buildings in this scene are no longer standing, but what is noticeable is that first floor balconies that extend out to the sidewalk flank the buildings. Galveston weather in the summer can be hot, humid, windy, and often dusty. Canopies would have provided extra shade to cool down the businesses, especially those carrying perishable items like many of the stores in the photograph.

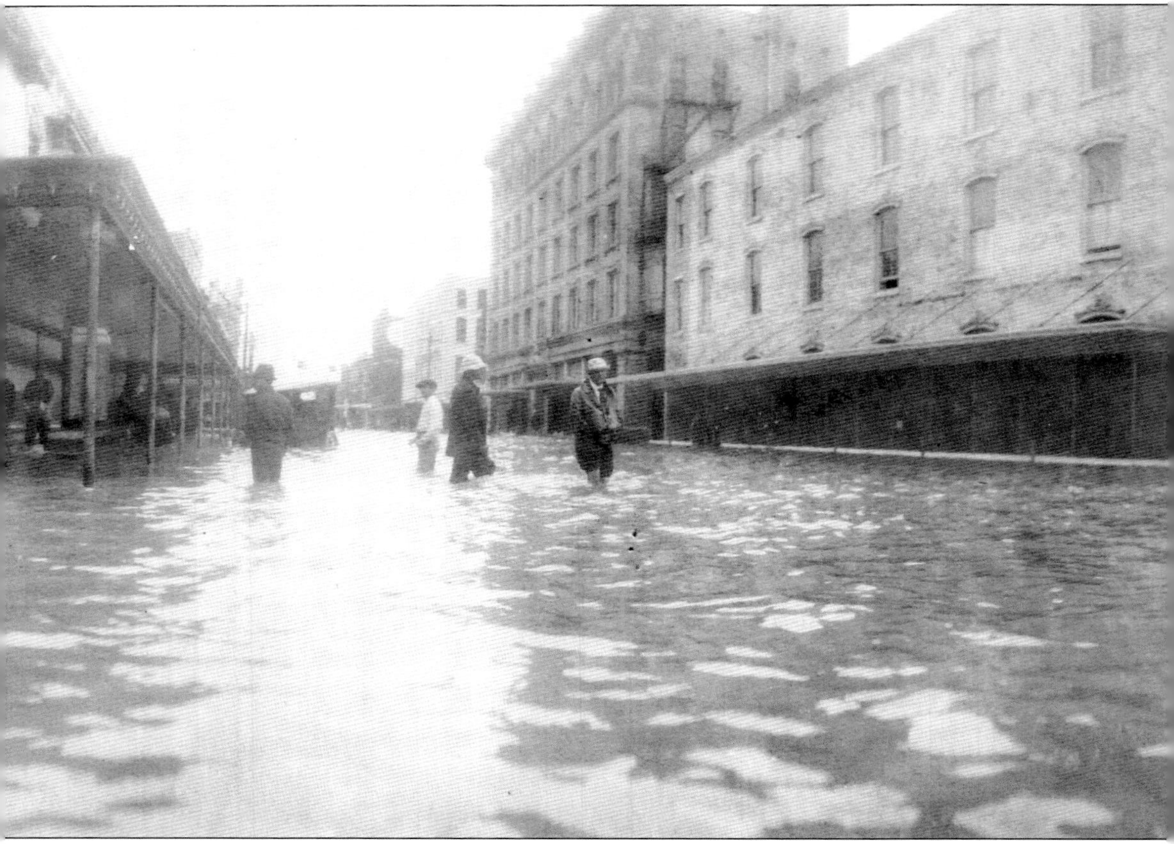

Unlike the hurricane of 1900, the hurricane of 1915 came with plenty of warning to the citizens of Galveston. Most took refuge behind the seawall, which extended to Fifty-third Street. Many, however, decided to leave the island. The hurricane hit on August 16, 1915, centered fifty miles west of Galveston. The barometric pressure dropped to 28.63 inches. Its wind strength was similar

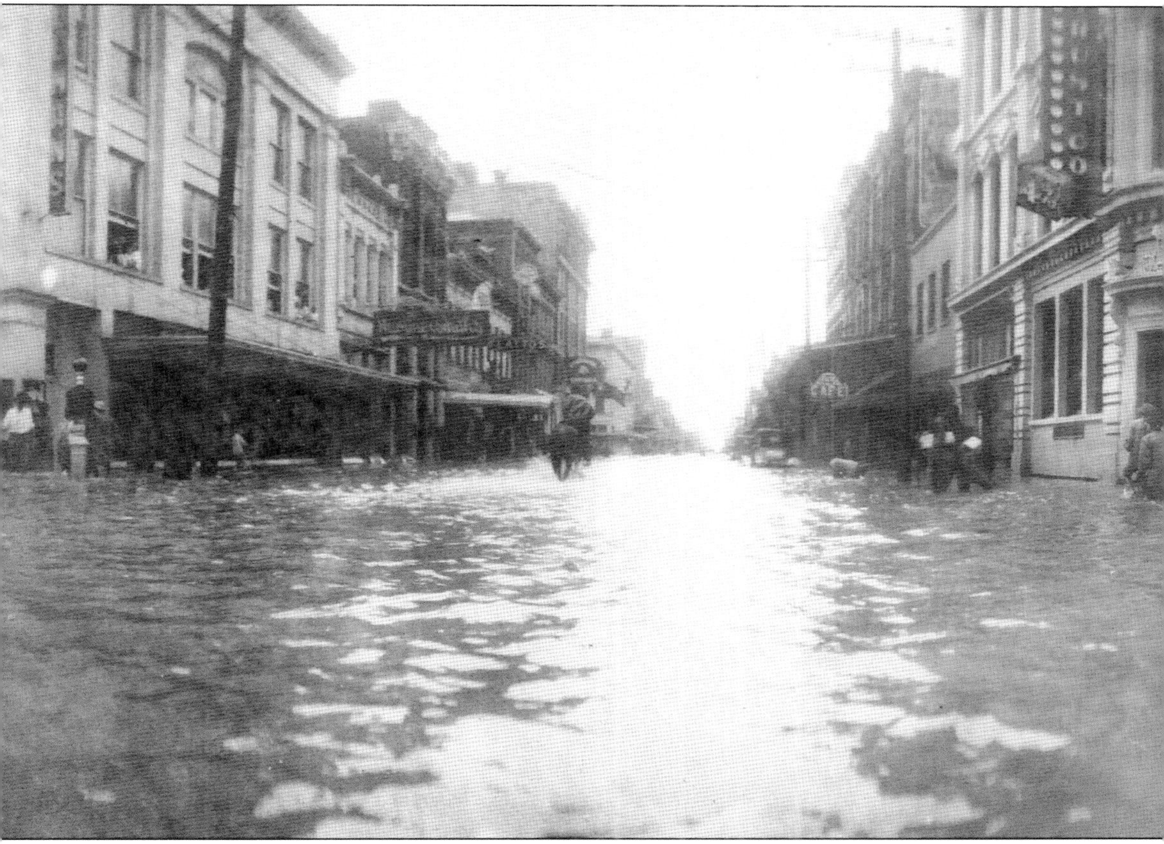

to that of the 1900 Storm, but it had a completely different effect on Galveston. This photograph, taken at the corner of Twenty-first and Market, shows water damage in downtown. (Photograph courtesy Galveston County Historical Museum, Galveston, Texas.)

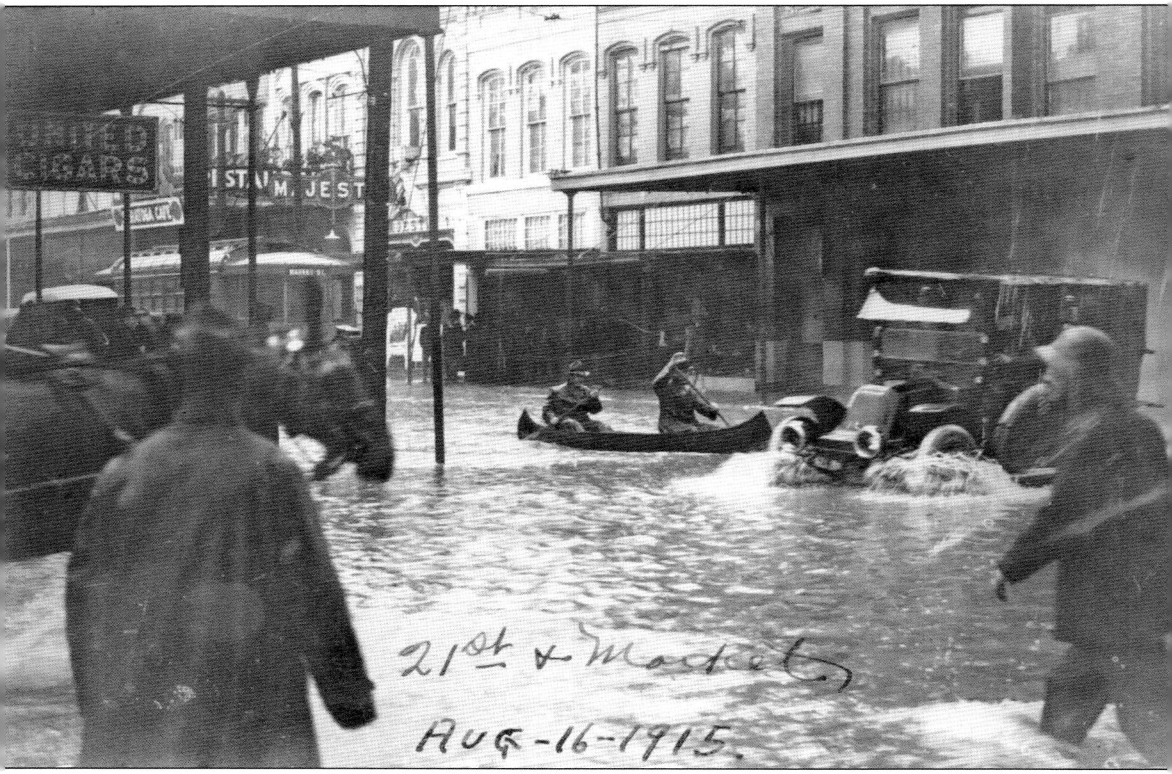

The hurricane of 1915 left 5 to 6 feet of water in downtown Galveston. Wind from the storm took out all telephone and telegraph lines. A water main was broken, and more importantly, access to the island via the causeway was damaged. The jetties built as part of the grade raising stayed intact. Remarkably, only eight people died. In true Galveston fashion, it did not take long for services to be up and running. Reports say that it was within 10 days that the streetcars and electricity were both running again, and a temporary system for water was put in on the damaged causeway. The construction of the seawall and grade raising surely helped Galveston escape heavy damage. With the 1900 Storm only happening 15 year earlier and sill fresh on the minds of many citizens, the newly built seawall was defiantly a heroic build. As noted in many books and editorials, the seawall and grade raising helped to sustain Galveston as a functioning city. (Photograph courtesy Galveston County Historical Museum, Galveston, Texas.)

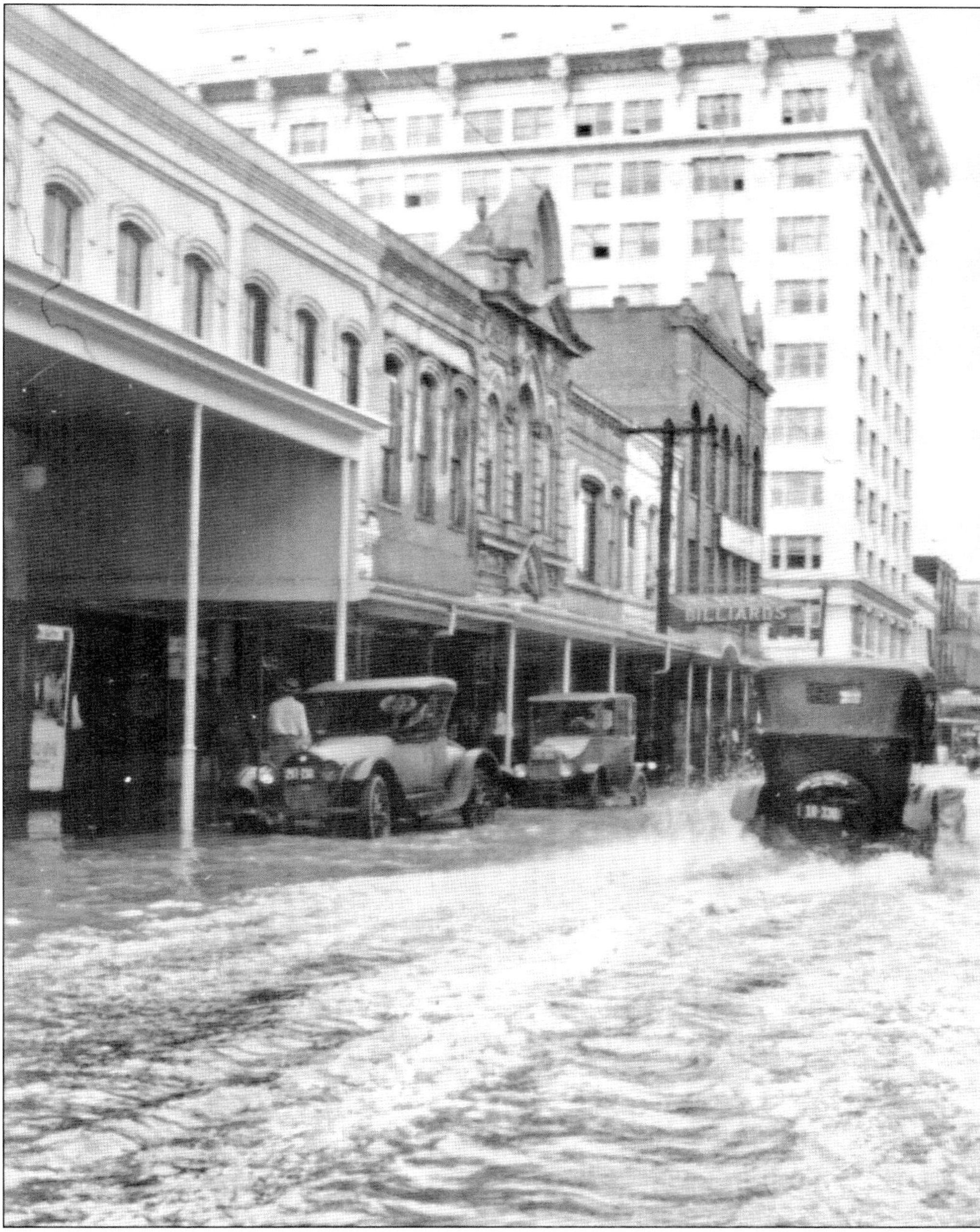

After the hurricane of 1915 struck Galveston, many more occurred in the following years: 1943, 1949, 1957, 1961, 1983, and 2008. Each hurricane brought a different set of challenges for Galveston. Carla in 1961 hit with 80-mile-per-hour winds and a massive tornado that destroyed 120 buildings and killed six people. Alicia in 1983 killed not a single person in Galveston, but left an estimated $300 million dollars in damages. Alicia had 12-foot tides and 102-mile-per-hour winds. This hurricane, like Ike, eroded away yards of beachfront and left many buildings out of the reach of the seawall in perilous conditions. (Courtesy of the Galveston County Historical Museum, Galveston, Texas.)

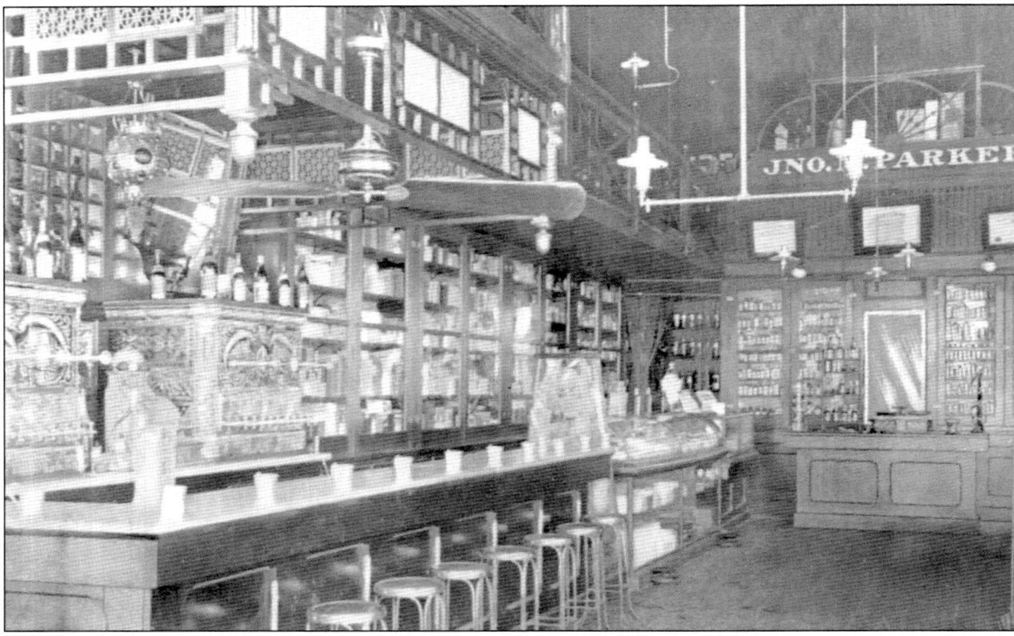

Parker Drug Store was located at Twenty-first and Market. Market Street was a retail street in the 19th century. Drugstores at this time acted like modern day pharmacies and sold compounds, medicines, and goods to help ailments. Most drugstores took on the same appearance as Parker Drugs, lined with shelving, glass cases, and glass bottles of medicinal remedies.

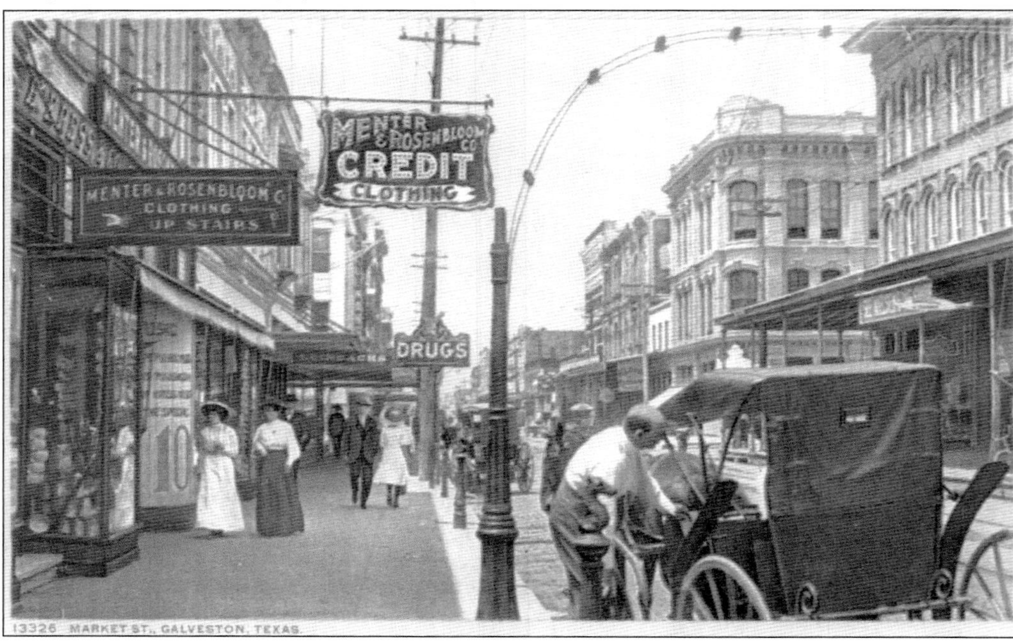

This postcard shows ladies walking and enjoying shopping along Market Street. As the signs shows, there was a mixture of clothing, music, and drugstores along the street. Market Street was also very dense with properties lining both sides of the street. Unlike the Strand, Market Street suffered multiple demolitions, and this streetscape is no longer intact.

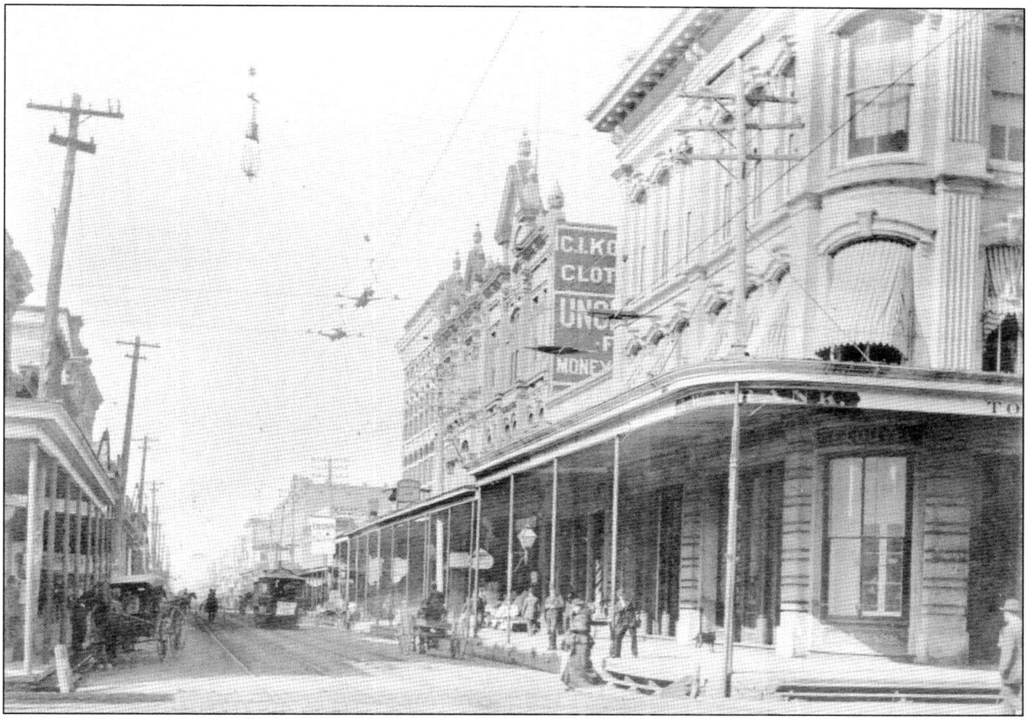

With the population of Galveston swelling in the late 1800s, the construction of new buildings marched south to Market and Postoffice. As noted in Clayton's Galveston, "they (buildings) displayed a lack of concern for proportion, coupled with an exuberant but hardly discriminating use of applied ornament, frequently in contract to the rawness of the building fabric itself." The buildings along Market in this photograph show a penchant for ornamentation. Brick streets of Strand are considered historic today. Brick streets became common as a way to ease traffic long downtown streets.

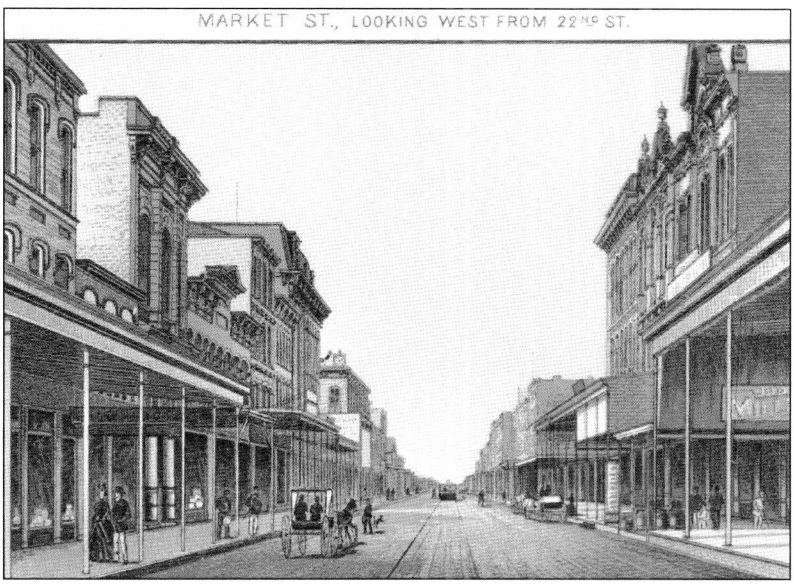

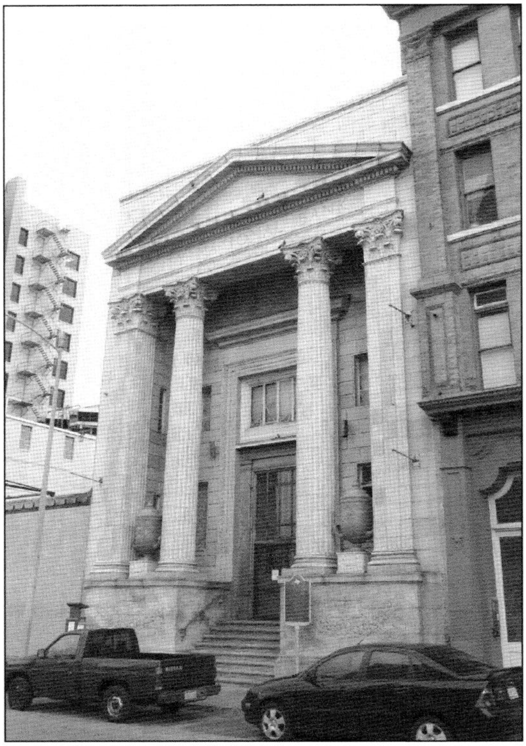

At 2219 Market Street stands the W. L. Moody Jr. City National Bank Building, built in 1920 by Weary and Alford Architects of Chicago. By opening this bank on Market Street, the banking focus was shifted off the Strand. The exterior material is decorative terra cotta. The building was built for banking operations, and the flooring on the interior still shows wear from patrons visiting the teller booths.

Originally, on the corner of Twenty-third and Market was the Tremont Opera House. Thomas H. Adams designed this building constructed in 1870 and 1871. This opera house was abandoned to build the opera house and hotel on Postoffice Street. The design of the opera house on Twenty-third Street was described as bleak, and the narrow windows made the building seem crowded. The building was demolished to make room for the E. S. Levy Building, which stands on this site today.

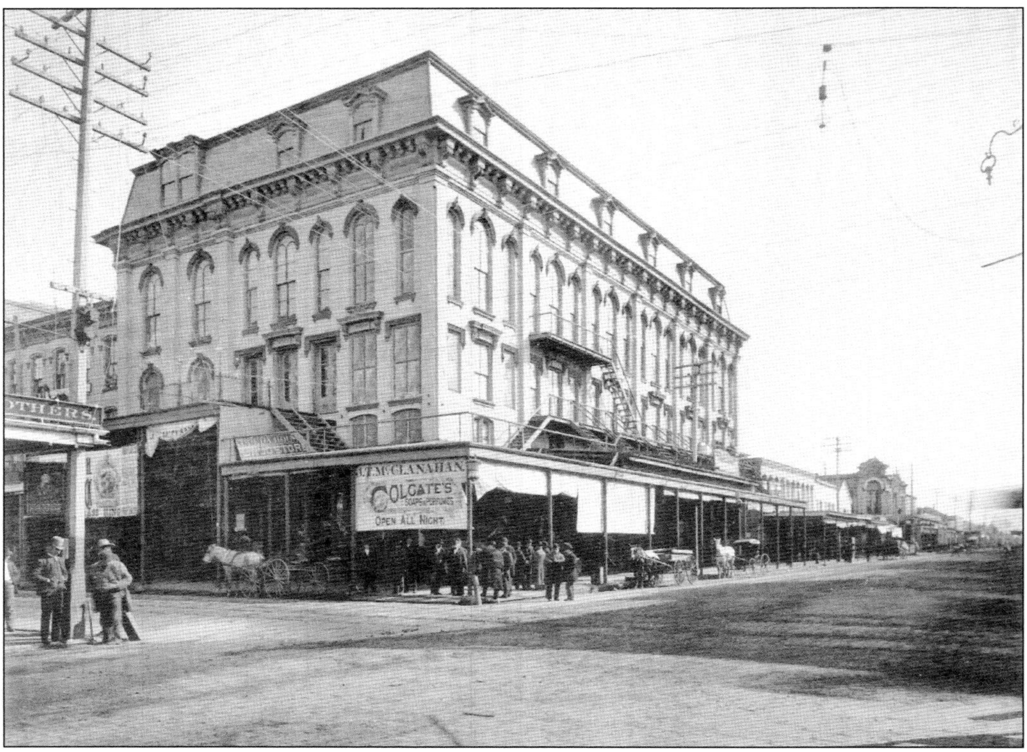

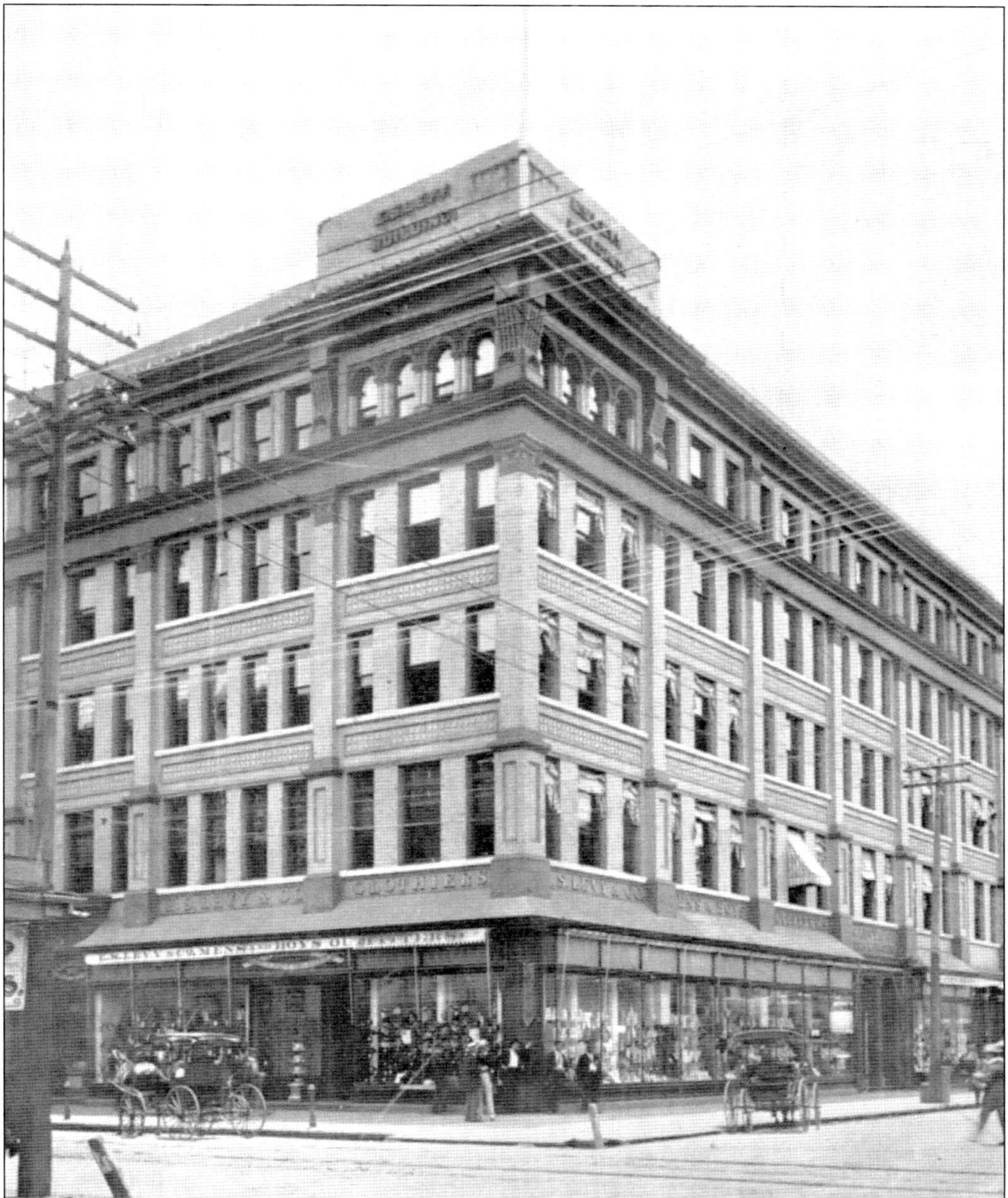

C. W. Bulger was the architect for the E. S. Levy building, constructed in 1896. When constructed, it did not have the high Victorian detail, as did many of Nicholas Clayton's buildings. Located at 2221 Market Street, many of its neighbors have been lost. The top floor was an addition in 1900. The Levy Building was able to remain extant, even though many of the buildings along Market Street were lost to urbanization and the need for more space. Artist lofts occupy the building, along with various retail and restaurants. The building has never regained its individual window awnings.

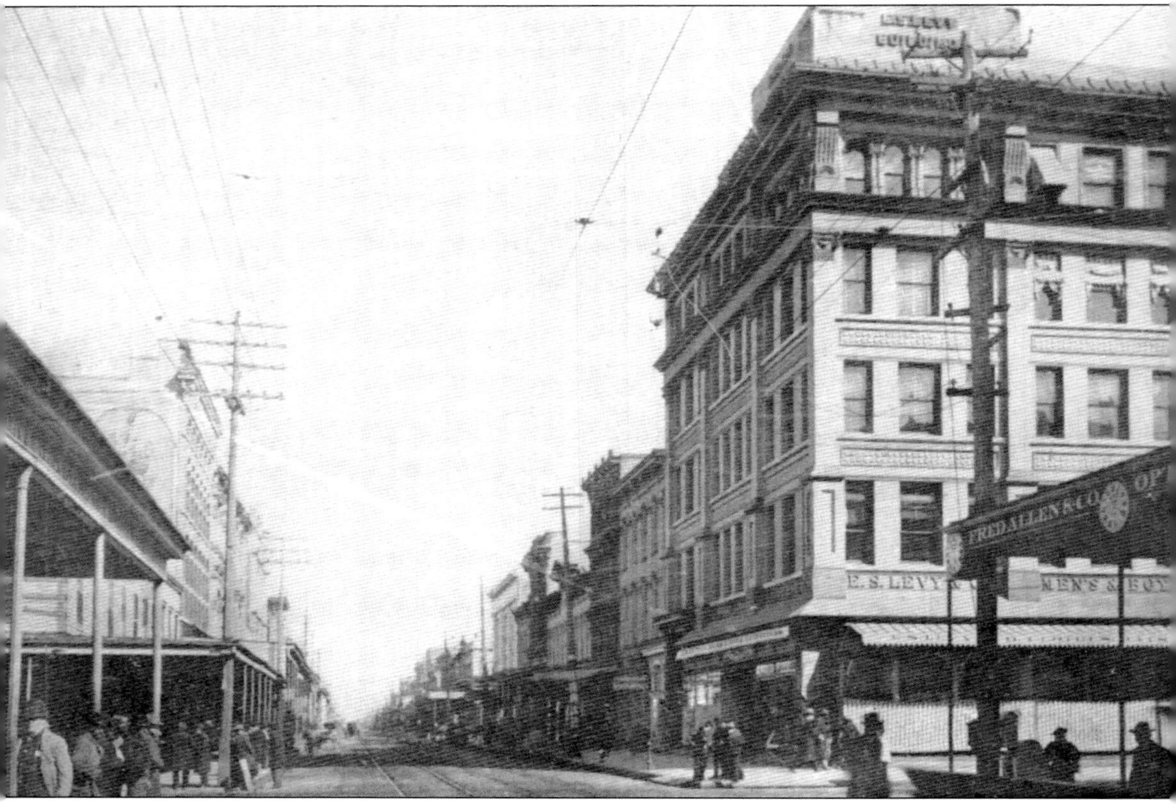

Most street scenes from Twenty-third and Market take the angle of looking directly at the opera house and Levy Building; however, this scene gives a glimpse of the entire block, showing small two-story structures to the east of the Levy Building. This was taken before the City National Bank was constructed in 1929 and offers up a look at the north side of the street. All of the buildings on the north side are no longer extant.

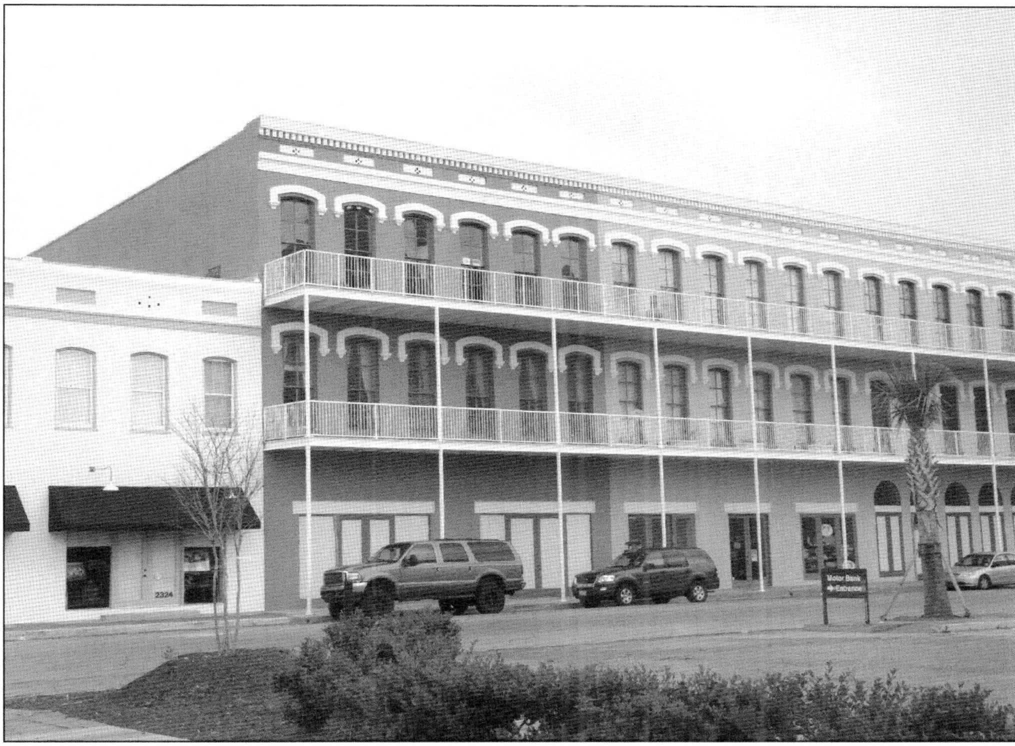

The Dubie, Schulte, A. Flake, and Company and Engleke Buildings were constructed in 1874, located along 2326–2314 Market Street. It was only in the early 1990s that these buildings started to receive attention. Now the buildings are brightly painted condominiums and have their first floor sidewalk balconies back in place.

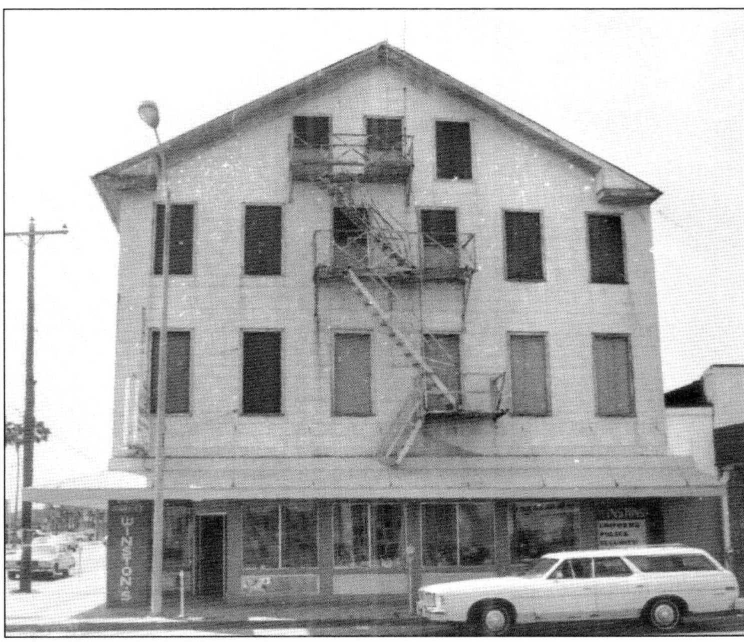

This building is an unusual survivor of wood-frame construction at 2401 Market. The fire of 1869 destroyed the original building, and the owner re-built the building by claiming repairs to the original. This building typifies buildings of the early 1840s and 1850s. It does have cast-iron supports along the first floor storefront.

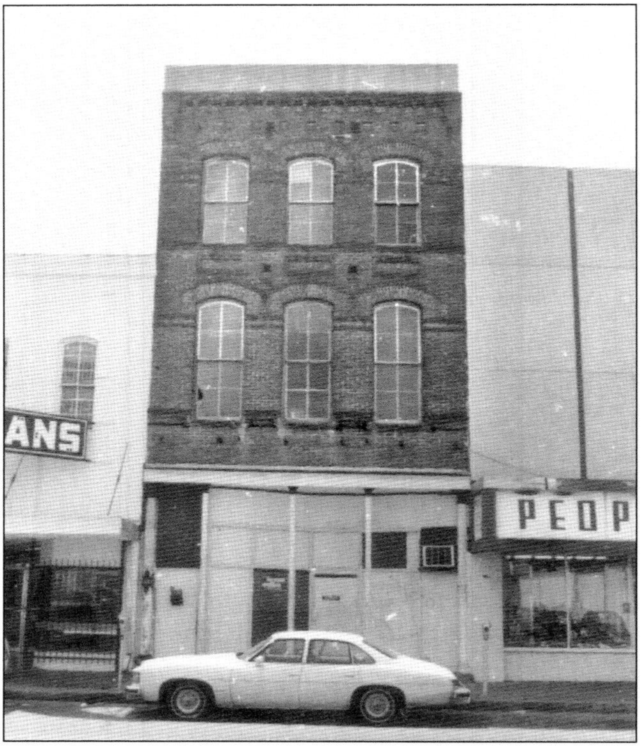

Located at 2415 Market Street, the Trube Building was constructed in 1894. The structure has cast-iron storefront and is three stories tall, which is taller than many of the buildings surrounding it. This photograph, taken during the decline of Market Street, shows a mostly boarded up first floor.

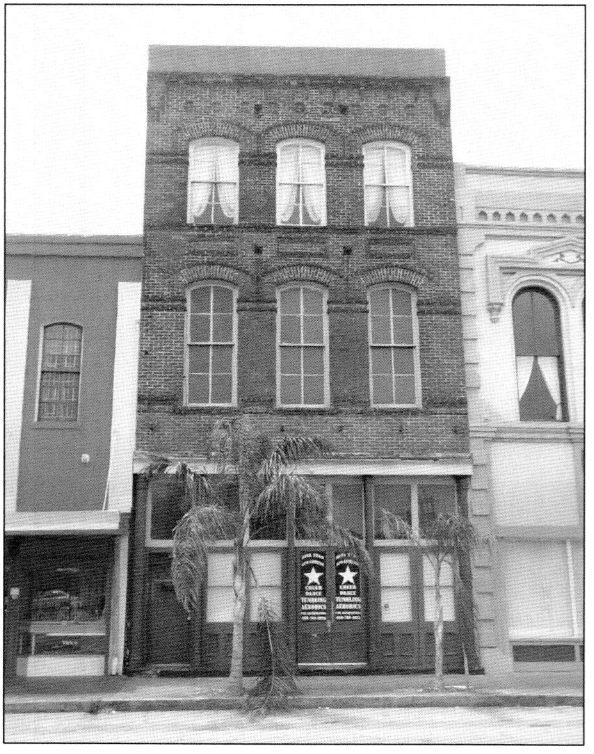

A current-day photograph shows the Trube Building after undergoing renovation, with special attention given to the cast iron. This block is reminiscent of the time of 19th-century Market Street; however, facing the building on the north side of the street is a modern-day stucco building that does not have the same charm as the 19th-century buildings across the street.

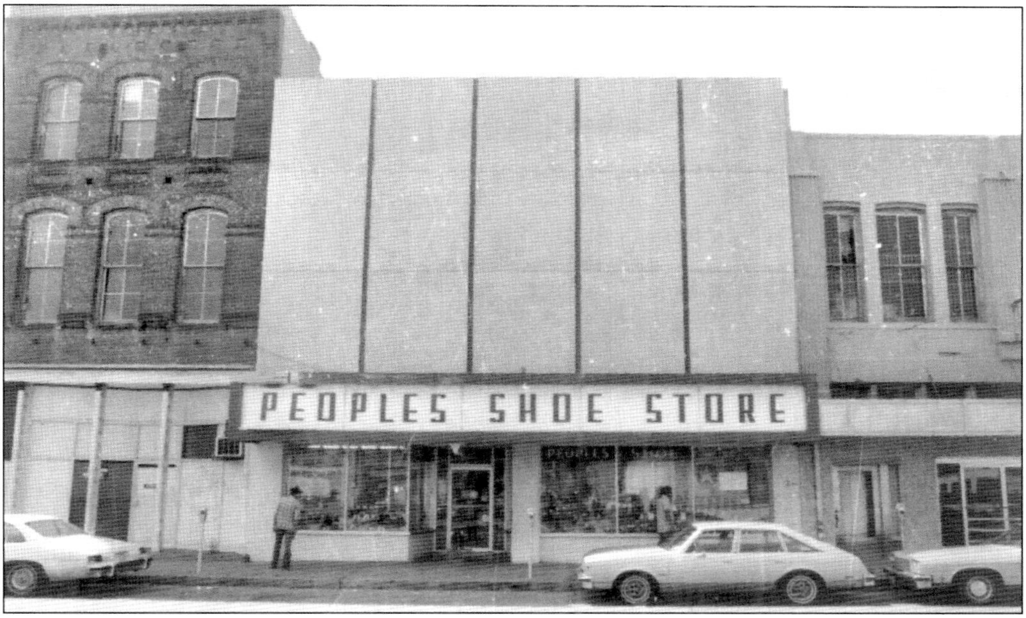

Located at 2417 Market Street, the Lalor Building was constructed in 1894. There is no evidence identifying the architect of this handsome building with Victorian details. As with many buildings in downtown Galveston, a facade cover was a way to dress up a building to make it seem more current and fashionable.

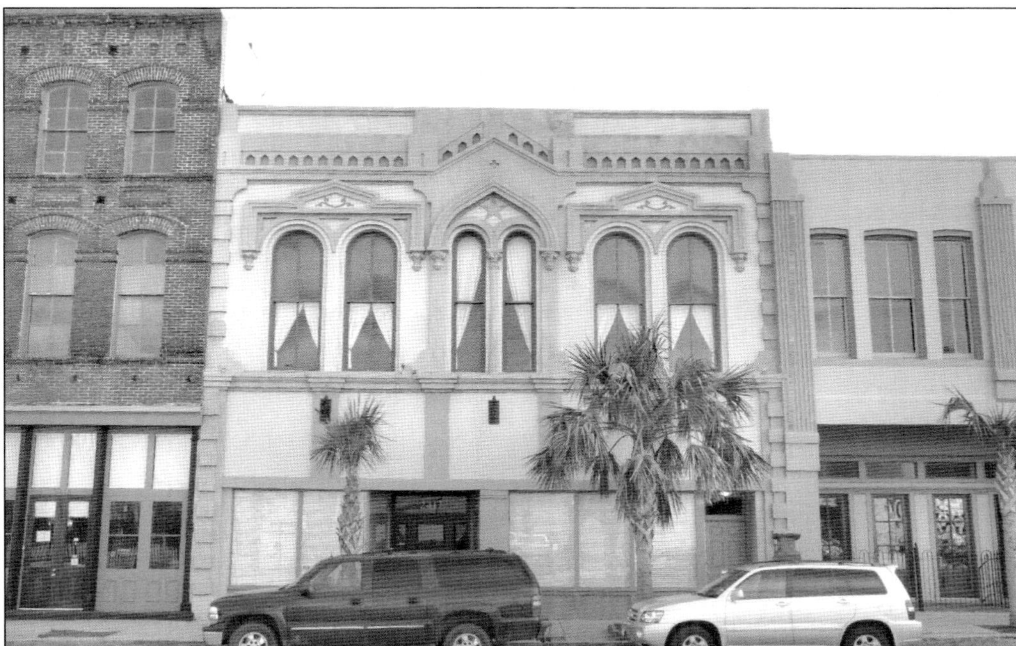

The facade cover of the Lalor Building was removed prior to 1995, and subtle Victorian details were uncovered. The building shows similarities to the Wegner Brothers Building at 1921 Market, but there is no known connection between the two.

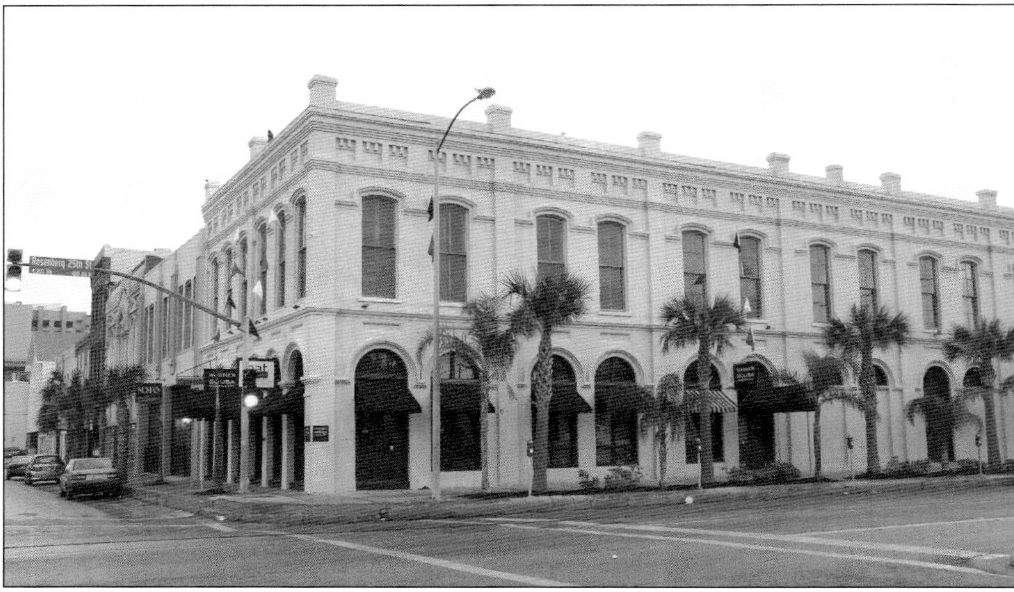

Galveston's red-light districted started on the west side of Twenty-fifth Street, along Market and Postoffice, but the R. F. Martin and Company Building was constructed in 1878 and housed a bordello on the second floor. Many of these establishments were in business until the 1950s. It was not until 1957 when the Attorney General of Texas shut down gambling, prostitution, and other vices that the area west of Twenty-fifth saw decline.

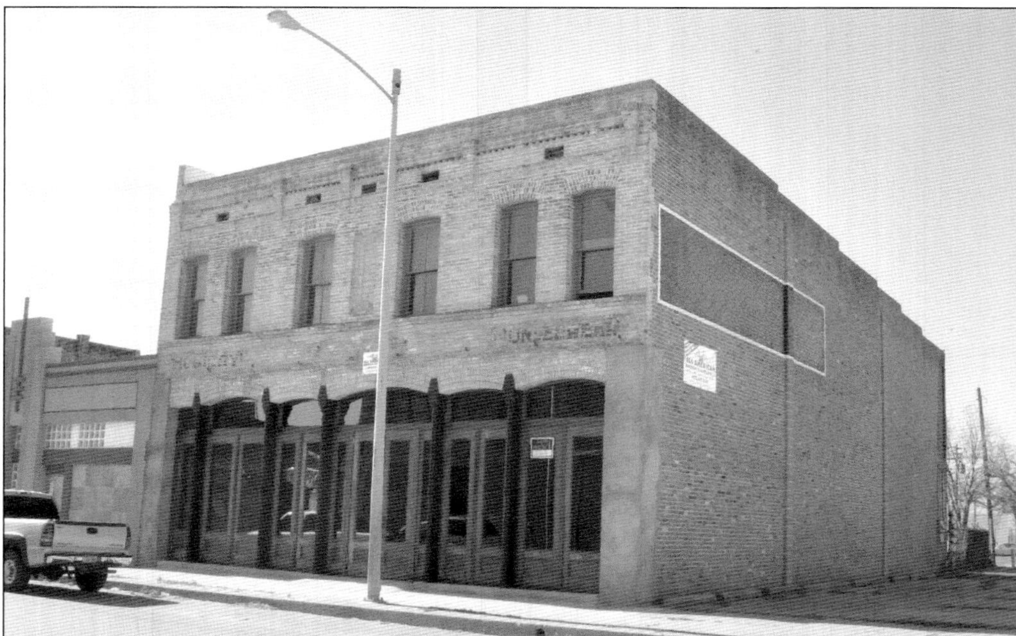

African Americans, immigrants, and visitors to the Port of Galveston would flock to Market and Postoffice Streets, west of Twenty-fifth Street. Businesses on this side of town did not conform to the same standards as those located on the Strand. This building at 2510 Market is an example of the hearty and utilitarian style of buildings in this section of downtown.

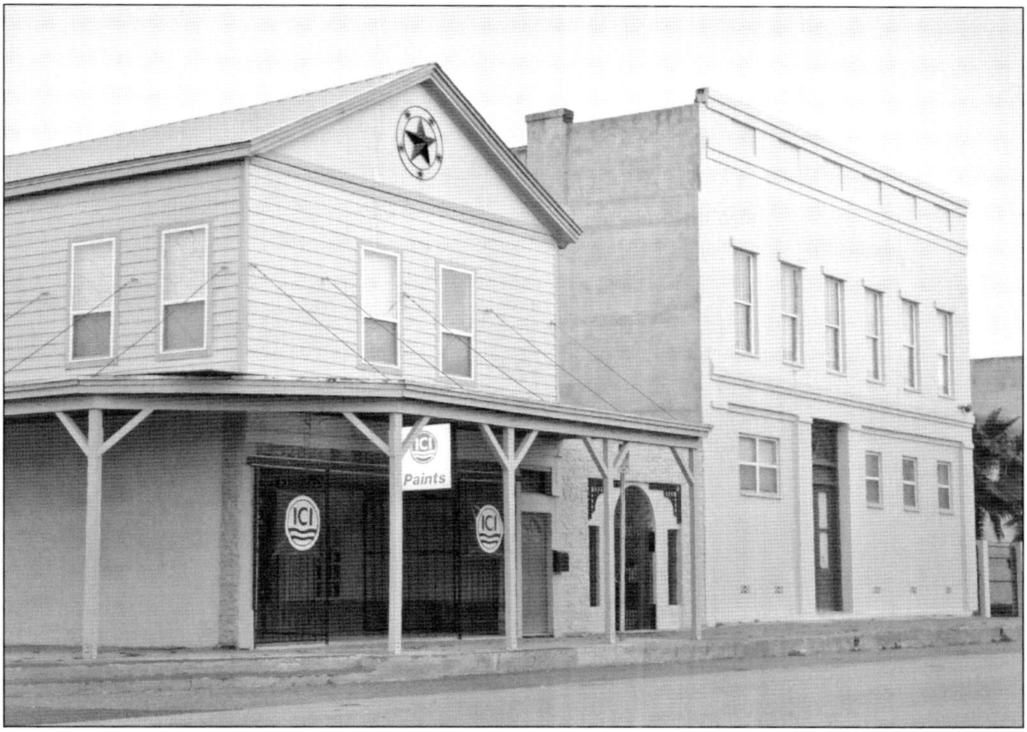

The buildings on 2528 and 2526 Market were constructed about 1870 and 1876, and the building located at 2522–2524 was built in 1891. All are called the Scott Building and were built by investor Mitchell L. Scott. The building to the left is one of the last standing wood-framed buildings on Market and is similar to the Central Hotel, only a few blocks to the east.

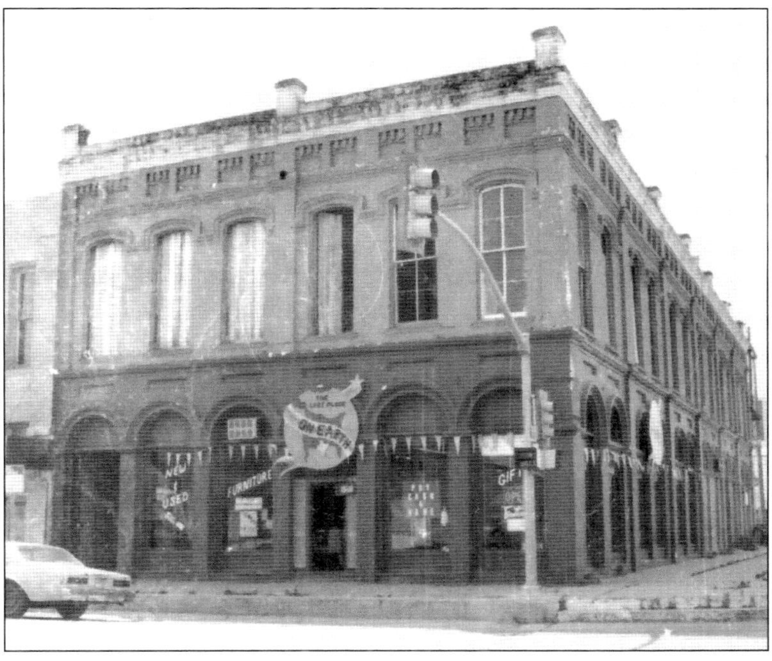

Located at 2501 Market, the Hall Scott Buildings were constructed in 1906, designed by George Stowe. This area has seen substantial investment in recent years.

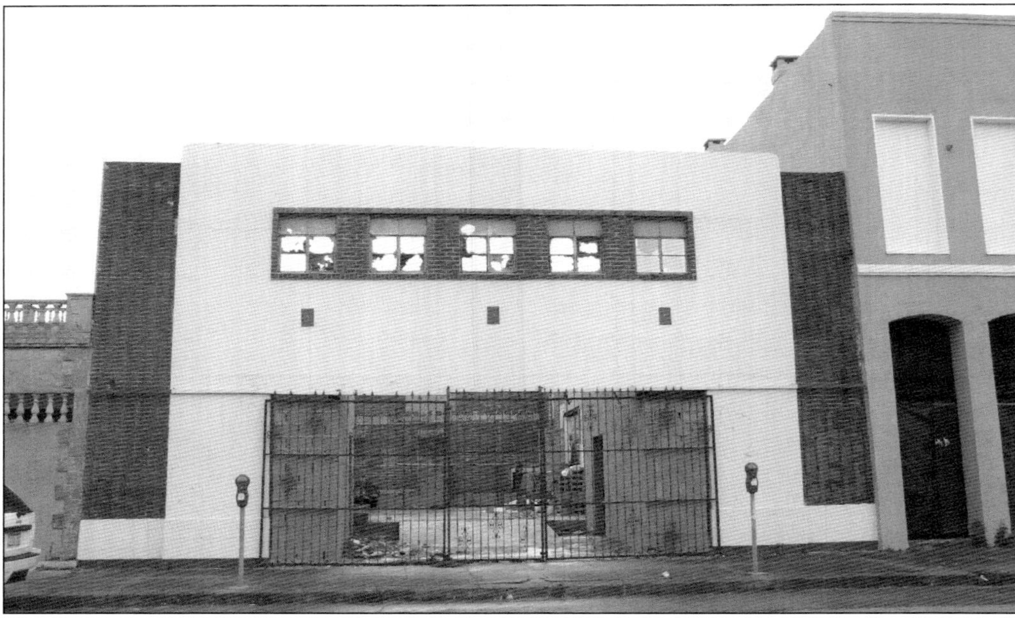

The Carver Theater was primarily a theater for African American patrons. Giouse Martini built it in 1948. The Martini family ran theaters in Galveston from the 1920s until the 1970s. Also, located near here was the headquarters of the Lone Star Cotton Jammers of Texas, a union of African American cotton workers.

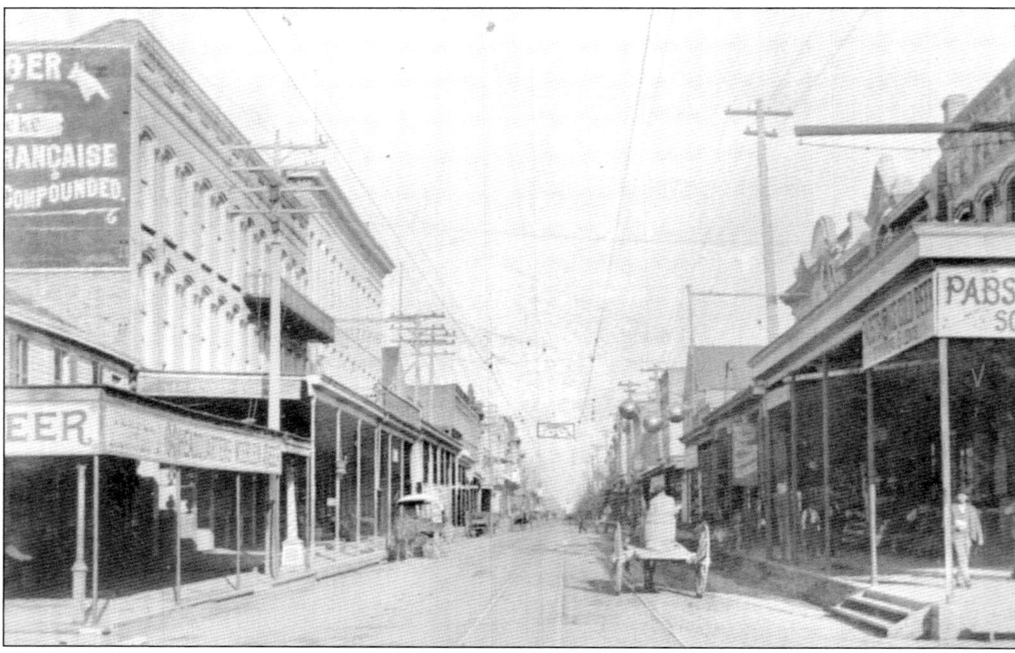

Taken in 1894 of Market Street, looking east from Twenty-fifth Street, this photograph shows the R. F. Martin and Company (1878) and Lalor (1894) Buildings, which are located along the right of the photograph. Without awnings, the flavor of the street is completely different. The two larger buildings on the left-side of the photograph have been demolished.

Five

AVENUE E, POSTOFFICE

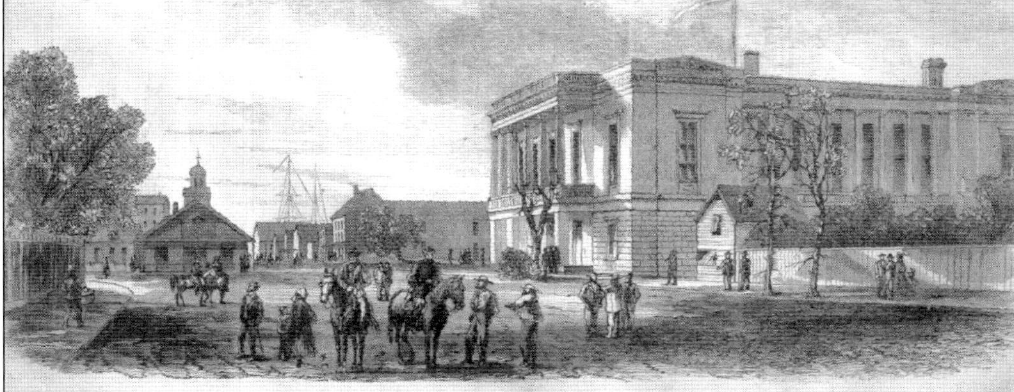

Postoffice Street has long been known as Galveston's shopping street. In the 1880s, Postoffice Street was developed after spaces along Market Street were occupied. In the 1970s, Galveston tried the urban mall concept along Postoffice and closed the street to vehicle traffic. Many of the stores closed, and it has only been since the beginning of the 21st century that Postoffice Street has seen redevelopment with art galleries, housing, and restaurants.

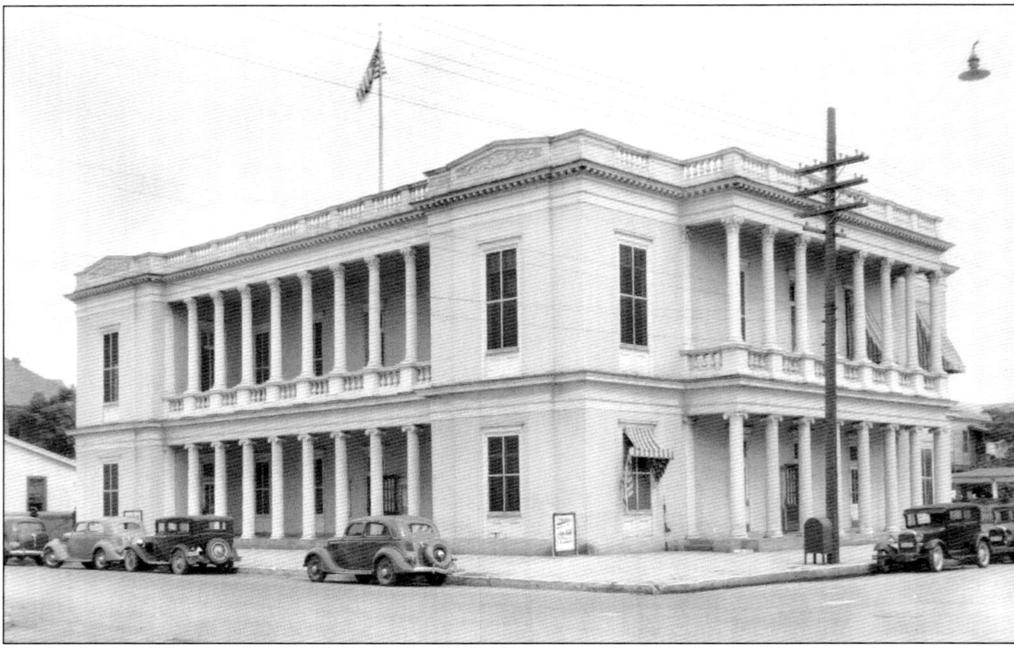

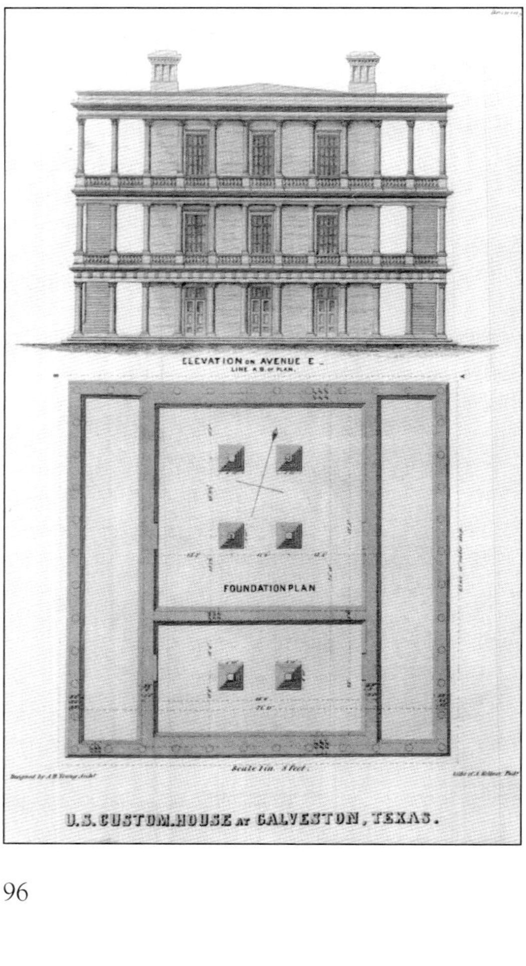

The U.S. Custom House was built on the eve of the Civil War outbreak in Galveston, completed in 1861. The federal government's first civil building in Texas, the Custom House was designed by A. B. Young, who was then the supervising architect of the Treasury. Escaping the East End fire of 1885 and undergoing multiple rehabilitations, shown whitewashed in this 1933 photograph, the Custom House is now the headquarters for the Galveston Historical Foundation. (Library of Congress, Prints and Photographs Division, Historic American Buildings Survey.)

Original plans for the U.S. Custom House called for a three-story building to be constructed. A mix of factors caused the building to be scaled back to its current two stories. One reason might have been its expense. Construction costs escalated to $97,000 in 1858, and the Civil War was bearing down on Galveston. The Custom House is located at Twentieth and Postoffice. (Courtesy of the Library of Congress, Prints and Photographs Division, Historic American Buildings Survey.)

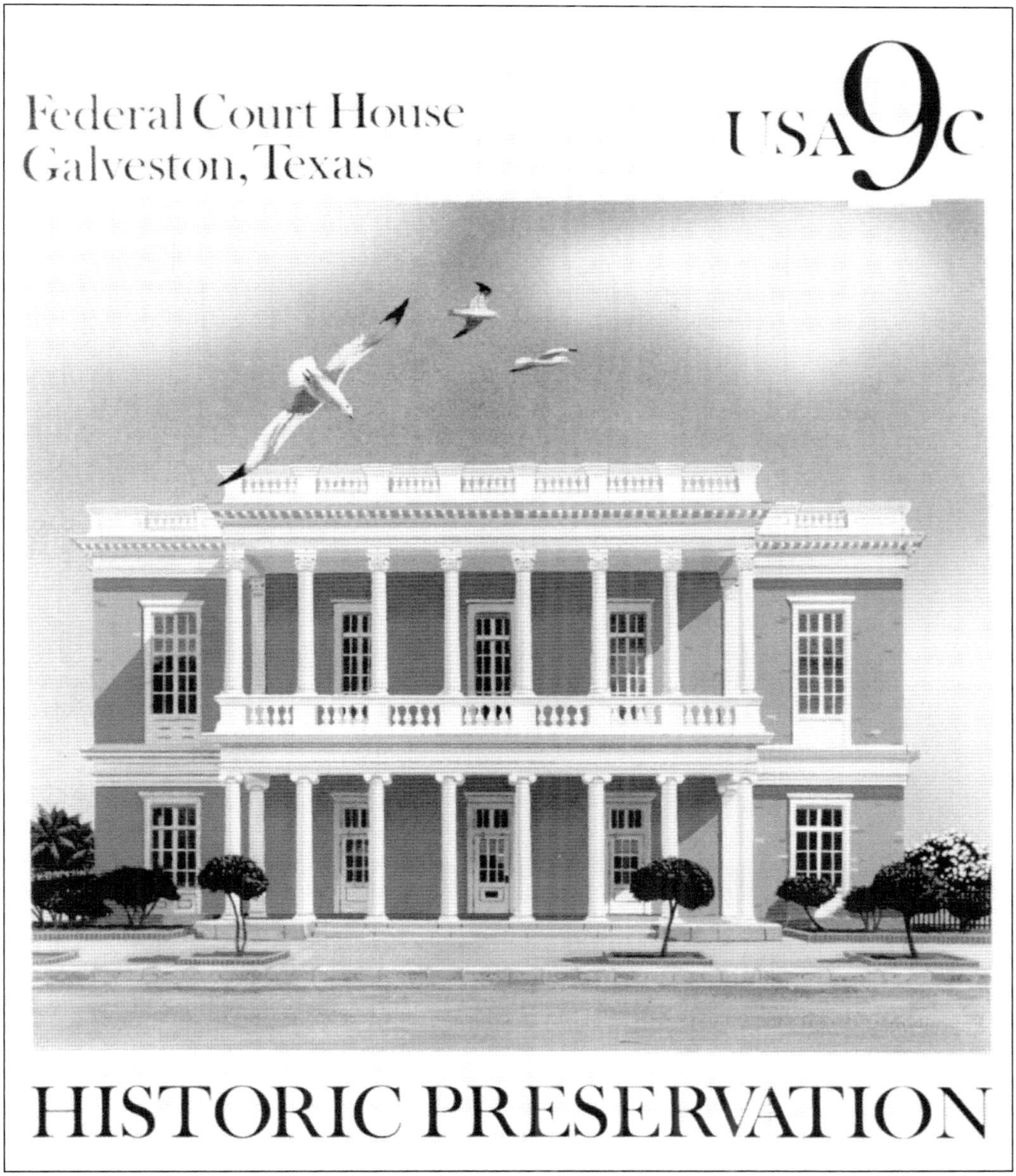

The U.S. Custom House was constructed between 1860 and 1861 in a total of four and a half months, being completed before Texas seceded from the Union in March 1861. Cast iron was used for the columns on three sides of the building, window frames, and cornice. The building also has grey-granite offsetting the white of the cast-iron columns with a salmon colored brick. This building was designed for the ever-changing climate of the Gulf Coast, with porches shading most of the office space and large window openings to catch the breeze. The interior spaces are held strong with wrought-iron beams and brick walls that are 12 inches thick. The Custom House was illustrated with a U.S. Post Office postcard in 1977. The Custom House escaped the East End fire of 1885 but sustained damage from a boiler accident in 1978.

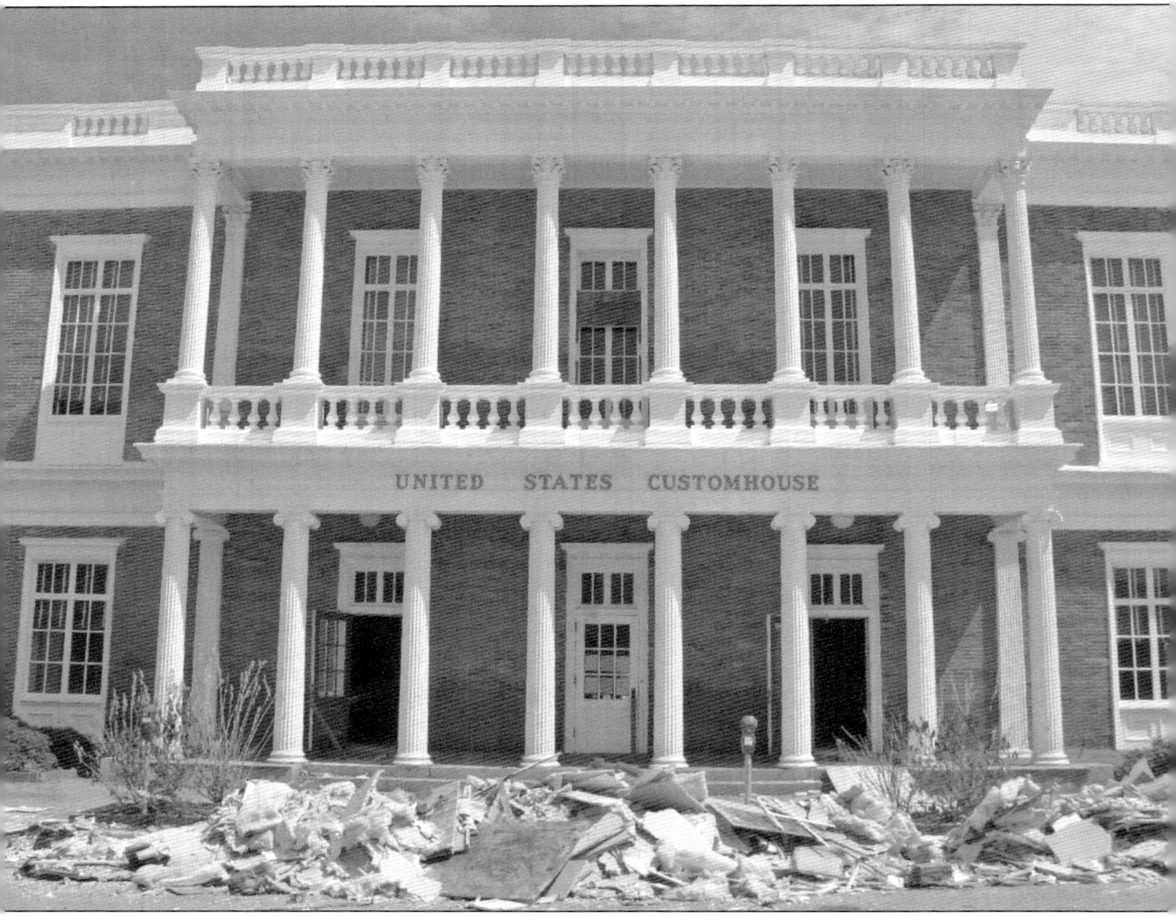

Galveston Historical Foundation staff returned five days after Hurricane Ike to find its office building filed with inches of sludge. With over 5 feet of water in the building, all first-floor offices, including the Preservation Resource Center Library were destroyed; 50 years of research on properties in Galveston turned to mush in the salty water. Debris filled the street, and ironically, an exhibit on the 1900 Storm was part of debris field. All of the interior spaces in the Custom House underwent extensive renovation. The eastern half of the building was reconstructed with new wiring, all new HVAC systems, flooring, and electrical were installed. Still in the year 2010, the plaster walls in the western portion of the building, where the walls are 12 inches thick, continue to hold water from the storm in 2008. The Custom House is now owned by the Galveston Historical Foundation.

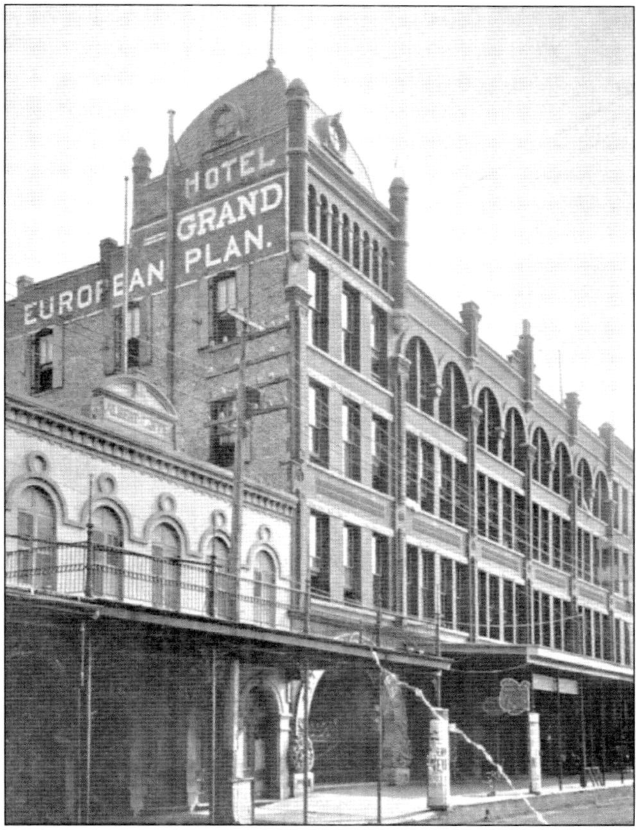

Frank Cox designed the Galveston Opera House and Grand Hotel, and the building was constructed between 1894 and 1895. The opera house was designed with 1,500, seats and the hotel was constructed with 56 rooms. With its grand arches and red brick, the building has similarities to the Richardsonian Romanesque work of famed architect H. H. Richardson. This photograph was taken in 1894.

The aftermath of the 1900 Storm was felt widely in downtown Galveston. Many of the buildings suffered damages from the high winds. Located at Twentieth and Postoffice, the 1894 Grand Hotel and Galveston Opera House sustained minor damages to its top floor. The building was designed by New Orleans architect Frank Cox, with the help of Nathaniel Tobey Jr.

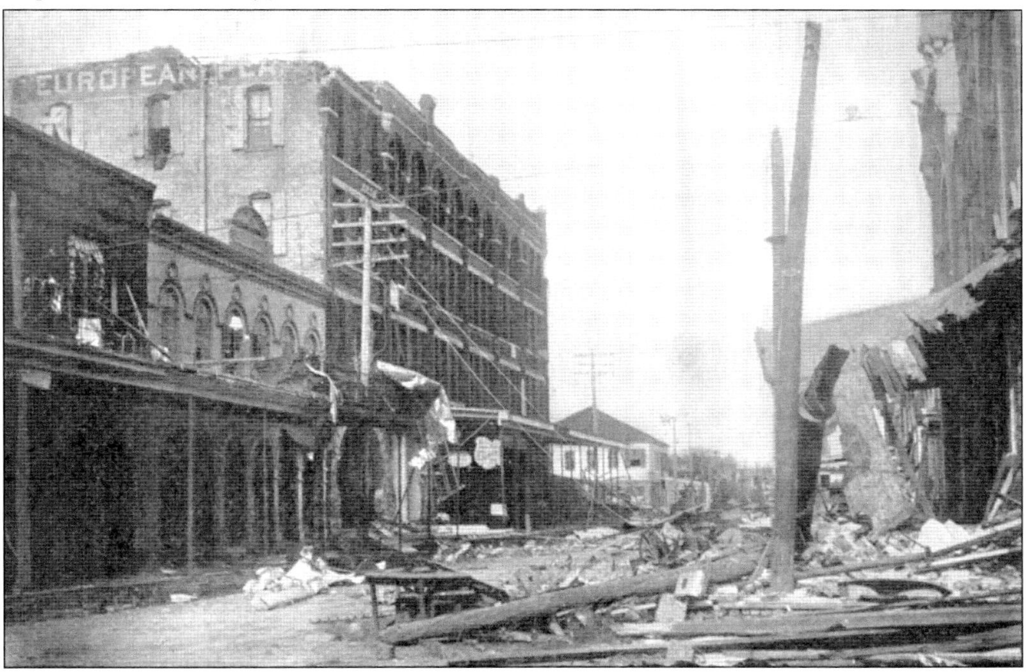

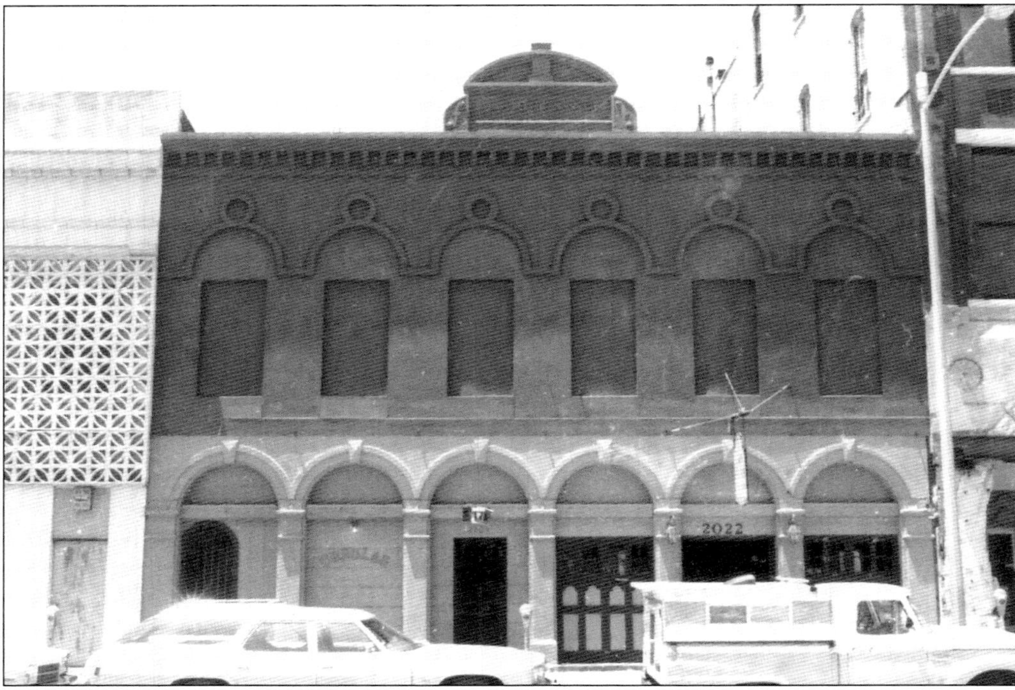

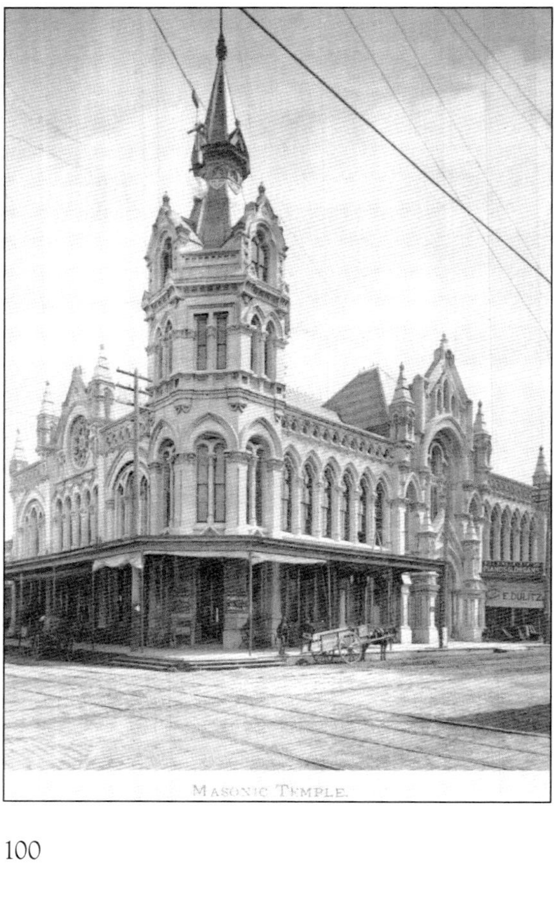

MASONIC TEMPLE.

The small building next door to the opera house is visible in both the 1894 photograph and the 1900 Storm photograph. The building still stands today. It is more representative of buildings along Postoffice Street, being smaller in nature with detailed stucco arch work on both the first story arcade and second-story window details.

Nicholas Clayton designed the Masonic Temple in the early 1880s, and it was constructed by 1884. Although no longer standing, this building shows how grand of a street Postoffice was poised to become. Located at the southwest corner of Twenty-first and Postoffice, the Masonic Temple suffered damages in the 1900 Storm and eventually succumbed to fires in 1942 and 1966. The Masons of Galveston were one of the first Masonic organizations in Texas.

Nicholas Clayton and Company designed the Harmony Club Building at 2109 Postoffice in 1895. The Harmony Club was an elite Jewish social club. The group once occupied the now Scottish Rite Temple on 2128 Church Street but moved into the upper floors of this building as a cost saving measure. The bottom floor was used as rental space.

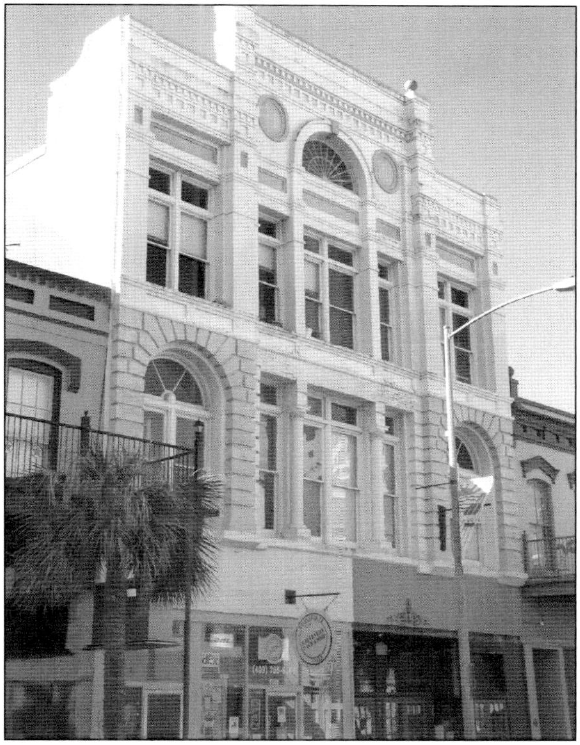

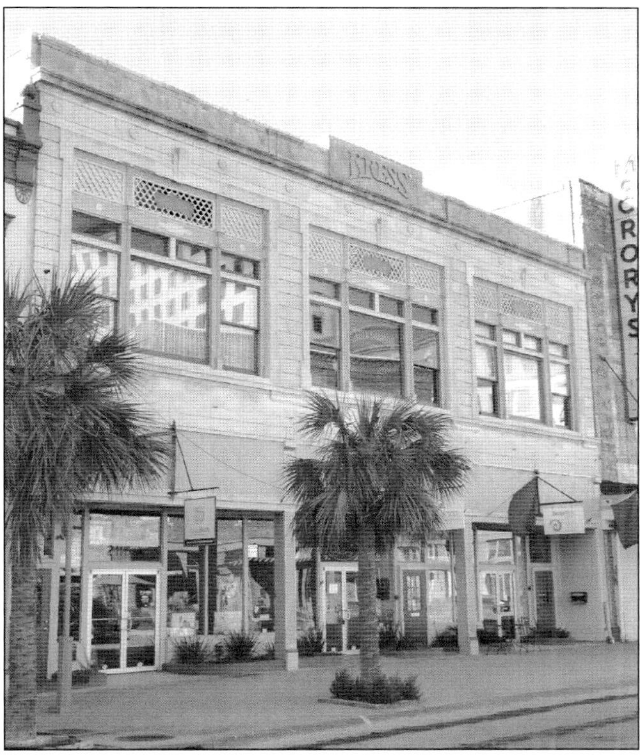

S. H. Kress and Company was a department store chain that operated from 1896–1981. Samuel Kress was known to employ architects to design his buildings and felt architecture was like a work of art. Galveston's Kress Building was constructed in the early 20th century. Many Kress Buildings around the country are still in use.

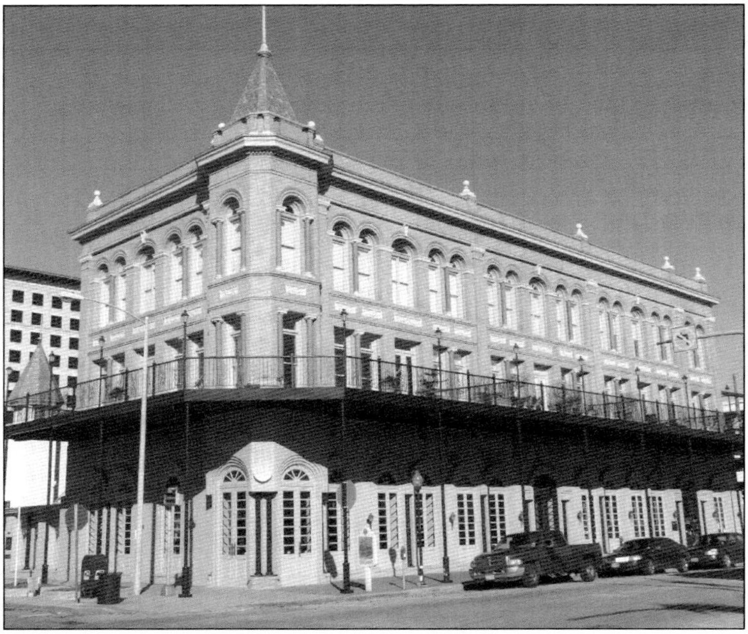

Originally, called the Ikelheimer and Company Building, the 1898 George B. Stowe building at 2102–2104 Postoffice helped Postoffice Street gain more style in the 20th century. The building was constructed for Marx Marx as an income property. For Galveston born architect George Stowe, this was his first major commission in downtown, and he took inspiration from Victorian design.

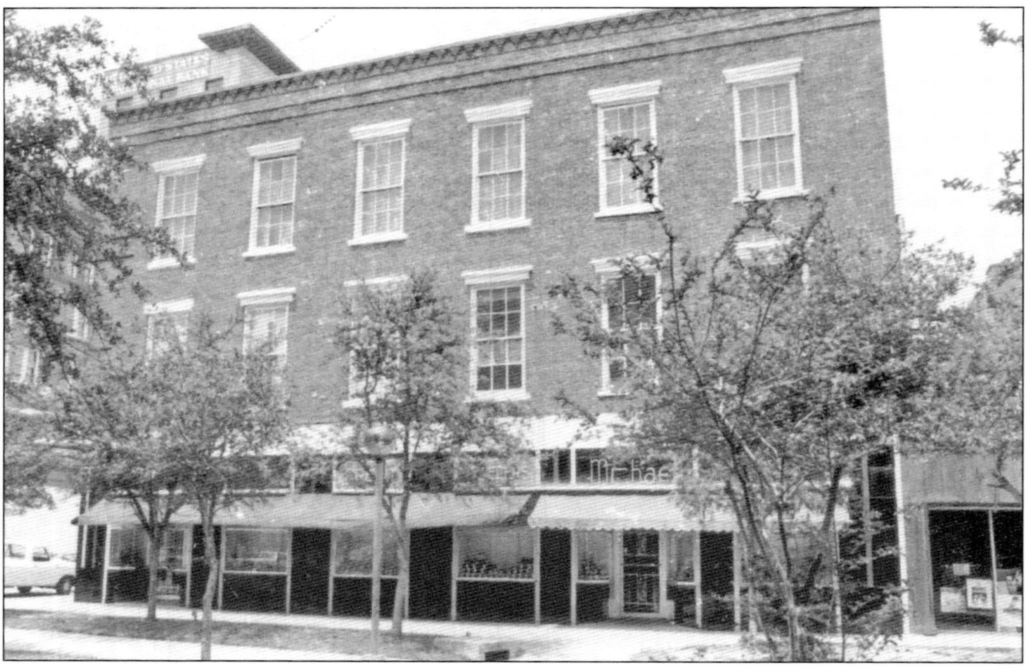

The Pix Building, constructed in 1858, is one of the few pre–Civil War buildings in downtown Galveston. Charles Pix, a merchant and ship's broker built it. The building features cast-iron lintels on the windows and structural cast-iron columns as an interior feature. The Pix Building is similar in appearance to the Hendley, Berlocher, and Davie Buildings, which were all constructed within the same two-year time span.

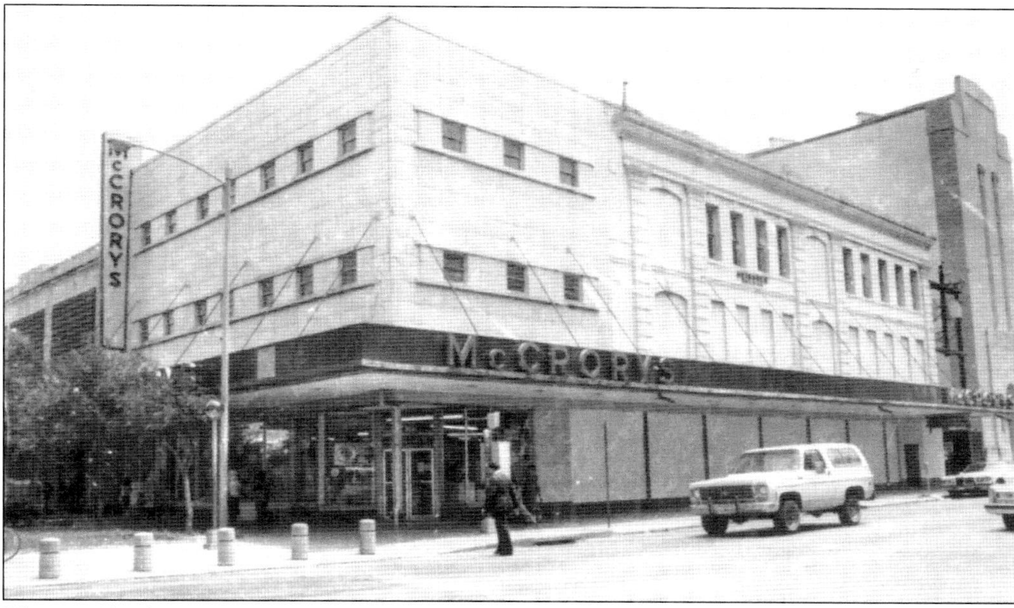

The 1885 bird's-eye view of Galveston shows this space with several small-framed buildings. The McCrory's Building on the corner of Twenty-second and Postoffice still stands vacant in 2010 and is one of the last remaining buildings along Postoffice that has not seen reinvestment. The back of the Scottish Rite Temple, designed by Nicholas Clayton for the Jewish Harmony Club, can be seen on the left side of the photograph.

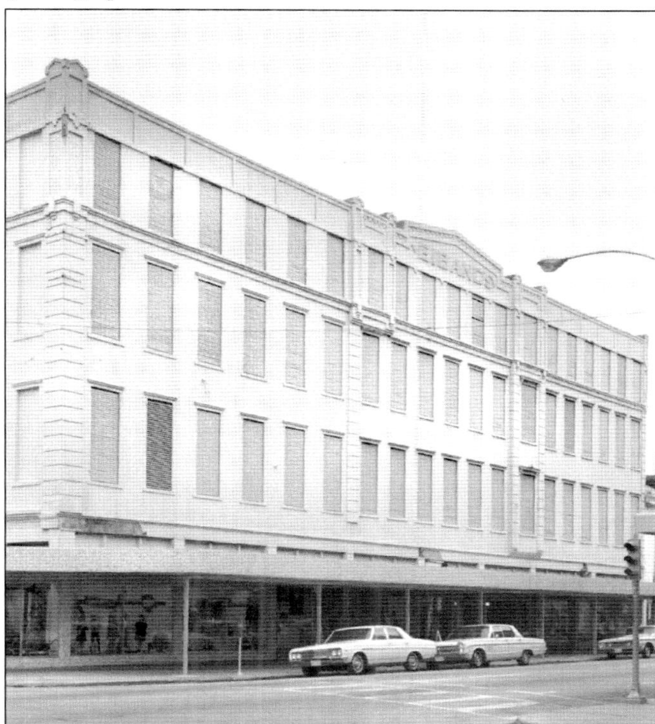

Postoffice Street suffered a dramatic decline in business, as seen in this 1966 photograph. The Garbade, Eiband, and Company Building was constructed in 1914, and L. S. Green designed it. This shows how many Galveston businesses combined their buildings into one unit. The center section along Postoffice was built as a three story building in 1870s; however, Eibands clothing store expanded it by building a fourth floor and connecting all of the buildings. (Library of Congress, Prints and Photographs Division, Historic American Buildings Survey.)

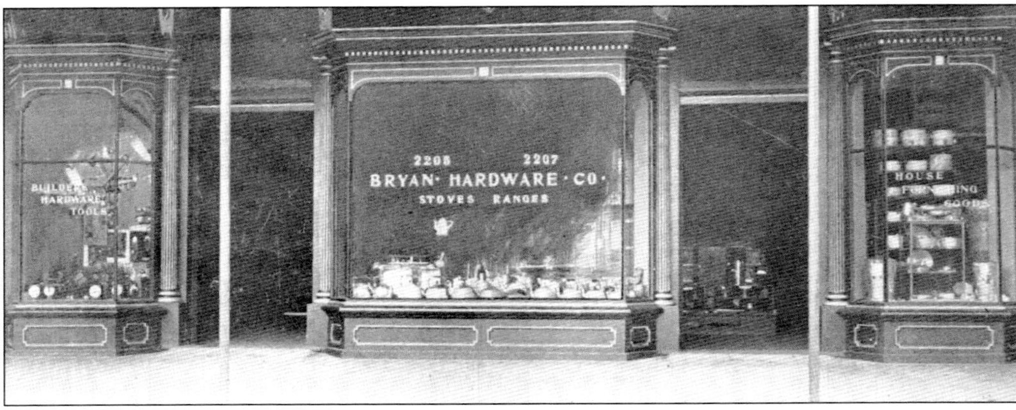

This detailed photograph of Bryan Hardware at 2205 Postoffice shows the type of goods sold along Postoffice. Glass display windows were very popular at the time. In the 1900 Storm, Bryan Hardware suffered losses of up to $12,000 and the store had already placed an order for new goods on September 10, 1900, which was only 2 days after the storm hit.

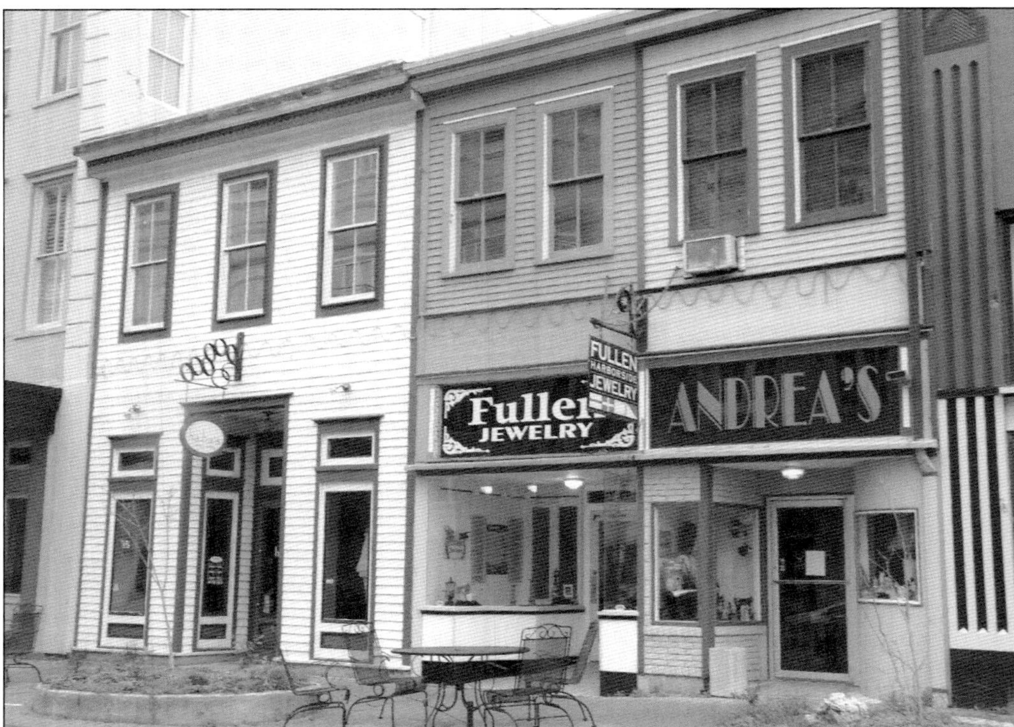

In November 1885, Galveston suffered a traumatic fire. The fire started near the business district and burned 43 city blocks from roughly Harborside to O1/2 and from Twenty-first to Sixtieth Streets. Intermittently, there were buildings that survived, and the Salzmann-Houlahan Building at 2213–2215 was one of those. These buildings are made with wood-frame construction, which only adds to their remarkable survival.

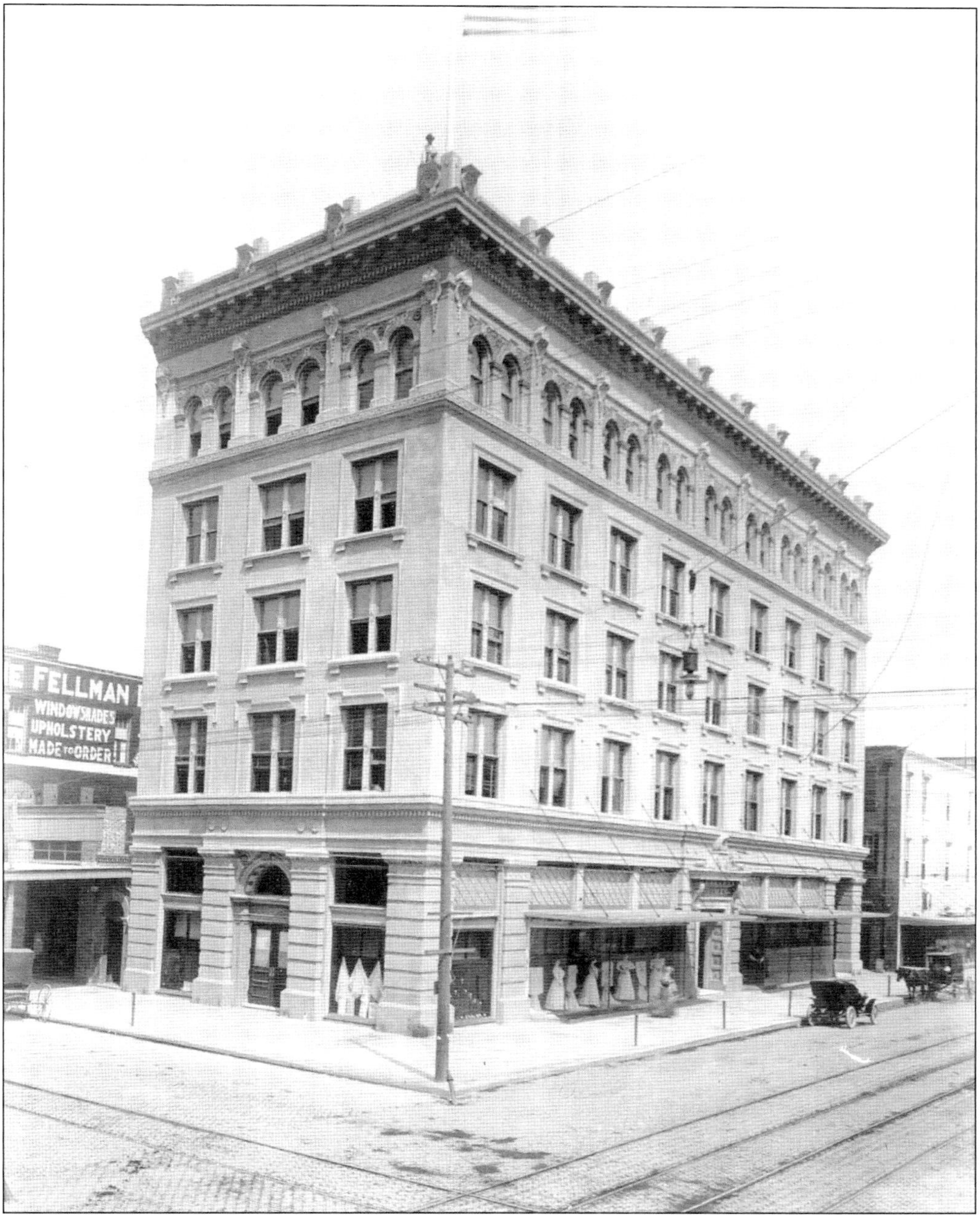

Located at 2202–2204 Postoffice Street is the Fellman Dry Goods Company Building, built in 1906 with Charles W. Bulger as architect. Fellman's Dry Goods store inhabited all five floors of this building. Bulger practiced in Galveston from 1891 to 1904, designing a number of commercial and residential buildings. Along with his family, Bulger survived the devastating 1900 hurricane, as they took shelter in the Levy Building, which he designed in 1896. In 1904, the family moved to Dallas, which is where Charles W. Bulger and his son are credited with designing numerous buildings. One of them, the 15-story Praetorian Building was the first true steel-framed skyscraper in Texas, built in 1907.

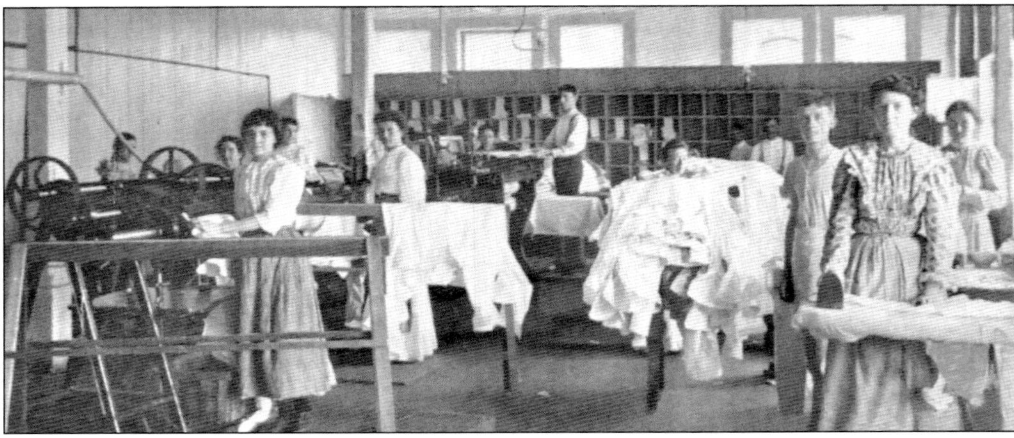

The proprietors of the Trimble Brothers Laundry were three brothers, Edward, Charles, and Horace. They operated in different locations throughout the years, the first being on Eighteenth and Ships Mechanic Row, followed by this location at 2214 Postoffice, then moving to 2326–2328 Postoffice Street around 1902–1903. The name changed to Model Laundry, and the brothers began selling hats and clothing. The family lived on the 2317 P 1/2 and 2419 Q 1/2. William Johnson, who was well known in the laundry business, took over the Trimble Brothers business and moved it to the corner of Twenty-fifth and Market.

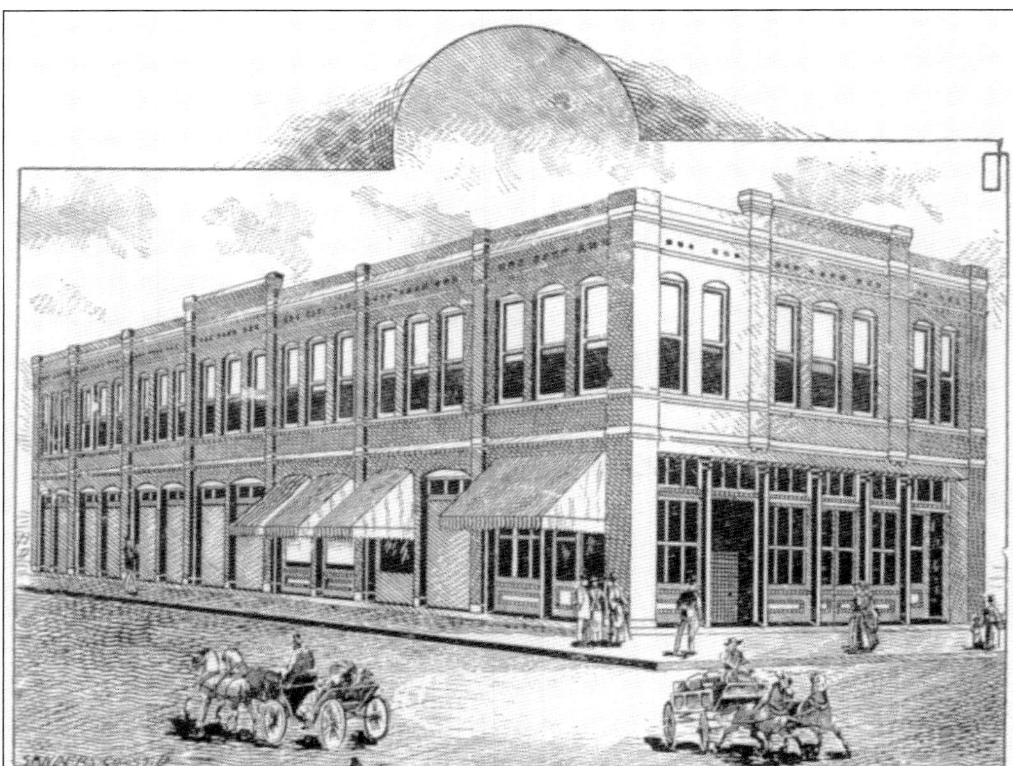

Six

North and South Cross Streets

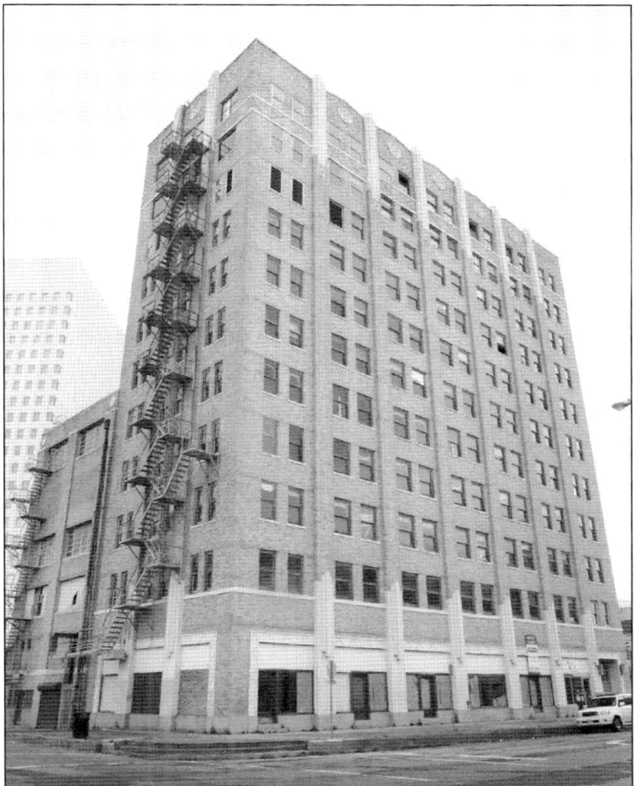

Andrew Fraser designed the Medical Arts Building at 308 Twenty-first Street. The building was constructed in 1929. The building was constructed as an annex to the now demolished American National Insurance Company (1913). Fraser worked on several buildings in downtown Galveston and the seawall and did residential design of smaller apartment buildings and individual homes.

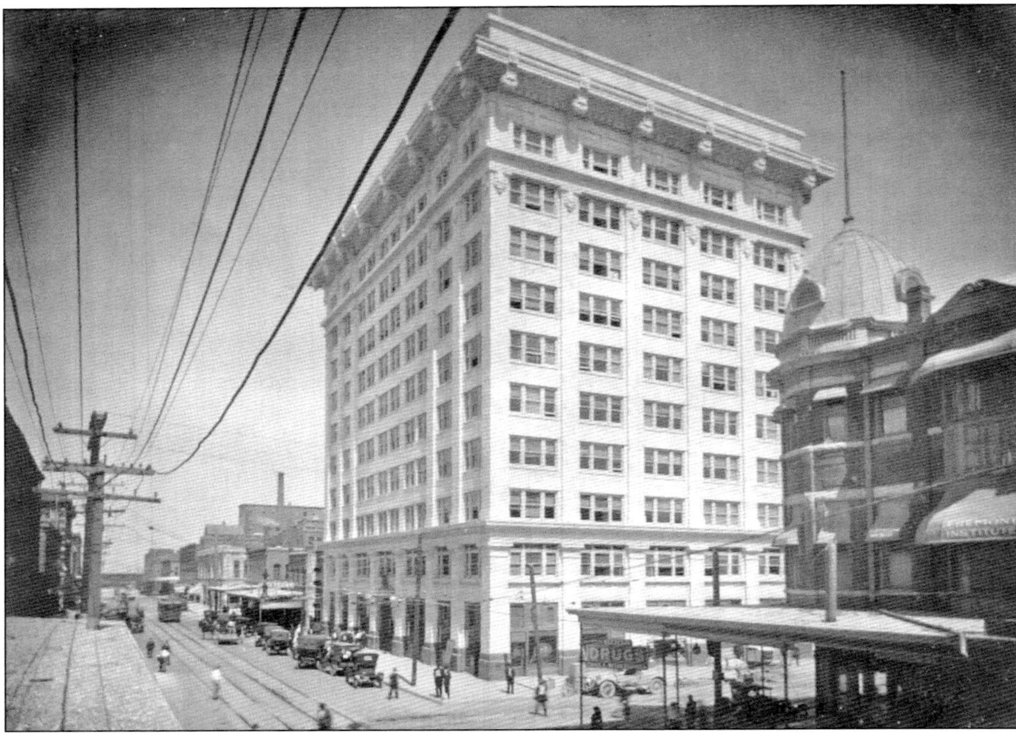

The American National Insurance Building, built by the Moody's, stood 11-stories tall at Twenty-first and Market Streets. Built in 1914 and demolished in 1972 for the current-day high rise, the 1914 building was very reminiscent of the Chicago Style of Architecture, which used large windows to let in light. (Courtesy of the Galveston County Historical Museum, Galveston, Texas.)

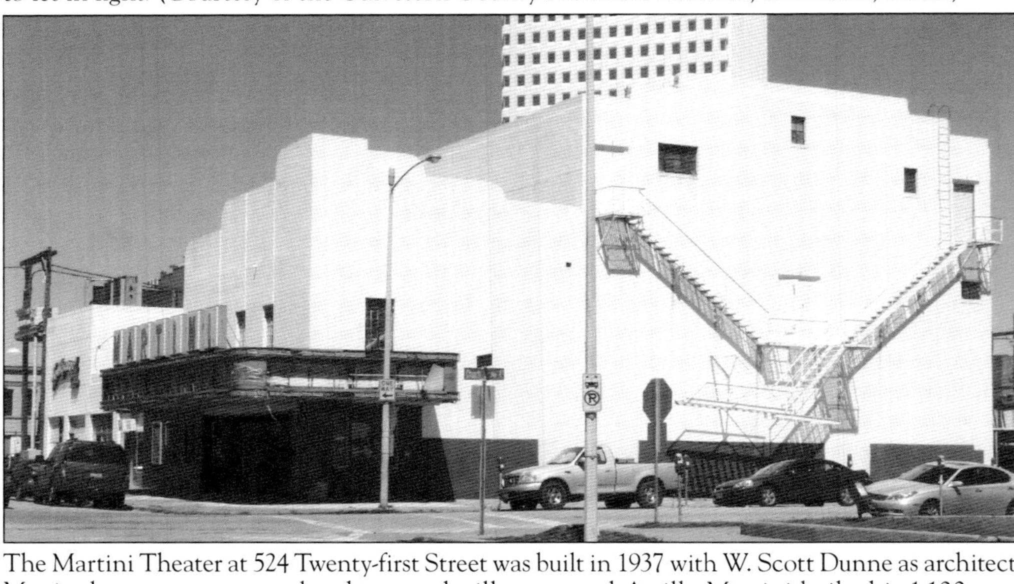

The Martini Theater at 524 Twenty-first Street was built in 1937 with W. Scott Dunne as architect. Movies became more popular than vaudeville acts, and Attillo Martini built this 1,100-seat, single-screen theater to meet the growing demand. At one time, this theater had a large, colorful, art deco sign. W. Scott Dunne designed theaters across Texas.

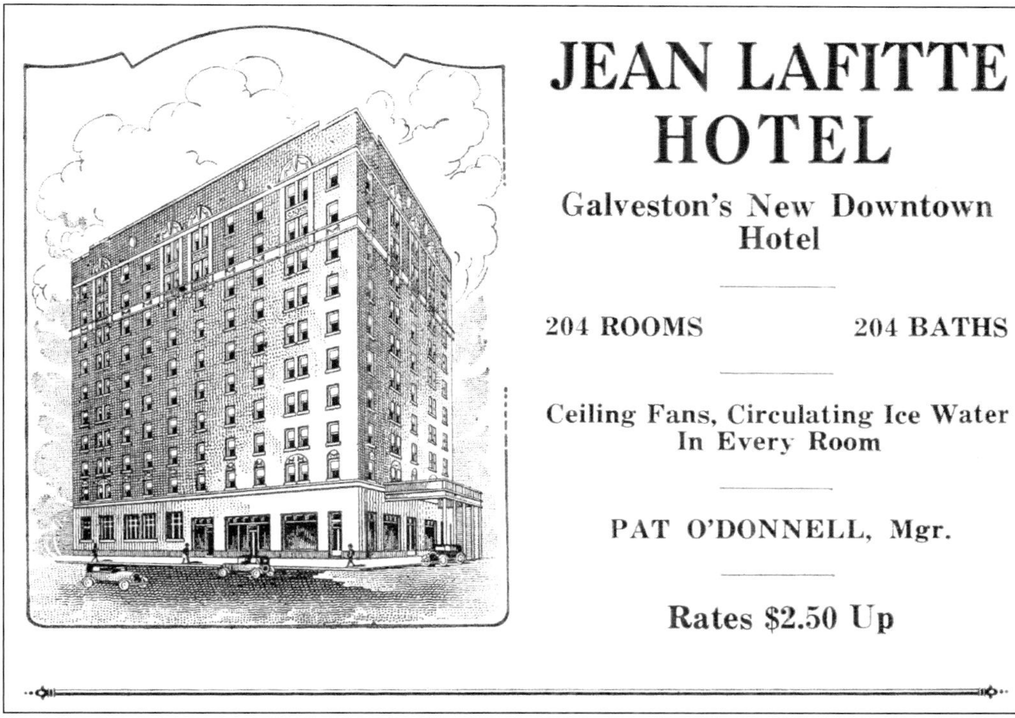

Andrew Fraser designed the Jean Lafitte Hotel. The Jean Lafitte Hotel was built in 1927, and its opening would have been one cause of the Tremont Hotel, only a few blocks away, to lose customers. Marshall, Tyler, Mineral Wells, Big Spring, Abilene, and countless others have hotels in their downtowns similar to the Jean Lafitte. The Jean Lafitte was named for one of Galveston's most notorious pirates.

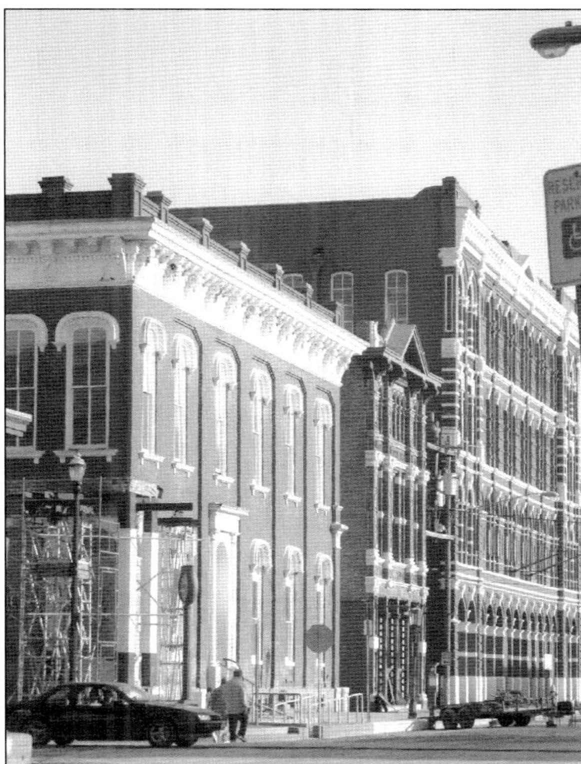

The First National Bank Building (1878), the Truheart-Adriance Building (1882), and the Kauffman and Runge Building (1882) are three architectural treasures that can be viewed as a cohesive block, situated along Twenty-second Street, between Strand and Ships Mechanic Row. Although all buildings were constructed for different investors and were used for different purposes, the slender styling of the Truheart-Adriance Building ties the three together.

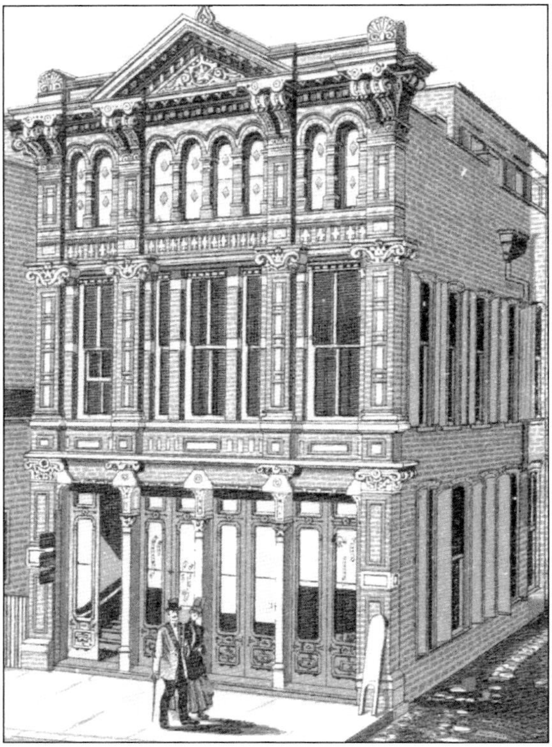

Promotional books about Galveston showing photographs and etchings of downtown, residential, and beach scenes were very popular in the 19th century. This drawing is from a Galveston souvenir book, which was then published after the 1900 Storm in one of the many books about the storms awesome effects, this book in particular called *Galveston in 1900*.

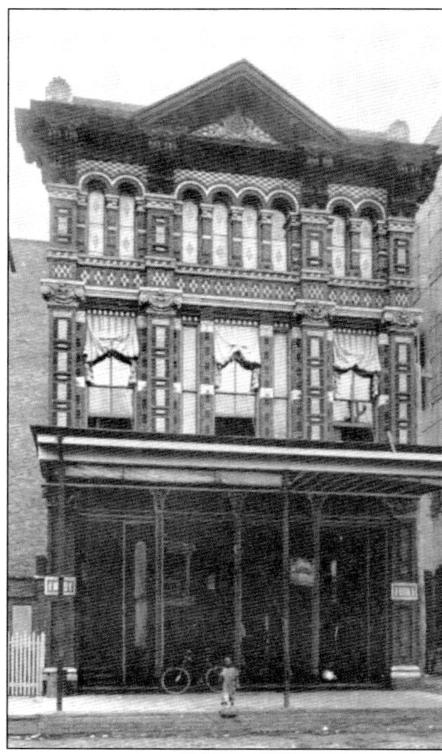

The offices of the H. M. Trueheart and Company Buildings are small, but hold a mighty punch its attention to detail. Architect Nicholas Clayton built this structure in 1882. Now known as the Trueheart-Adriance Building and home to the Galveston County Junior League, it is one of Historic Galveston's treasures. Clayton used considerable brick detail and contrasting trim.

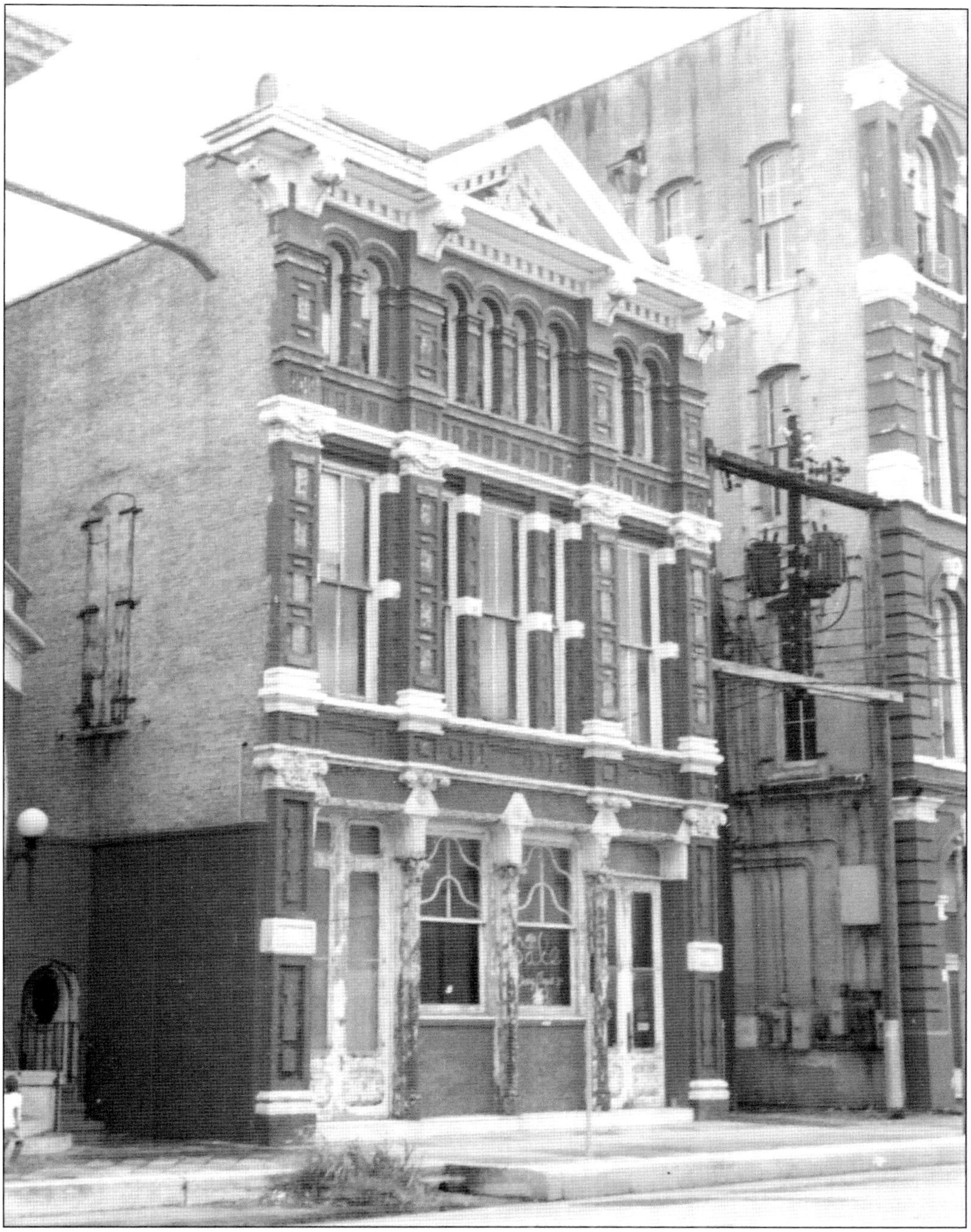

The Truheart-Adriance Building was one of the first historic structures to undergo restoration work in 1971. As shown in this mid-1960s photograph, the building had lost most of its detail work, the cast iron was deteriorating, and the essence of the multilayer bricks playing off the light was diminished. Henry Martyn Truheart was an early Galveston settler and was a soldier in the Battle of Galveston. When the Confederate forces took the city, he was appointed Assistant Provost Marshall. John Adriance became a member of the firm after the death of Trueheart. When Adriance joined, the Trueheart Company Realtors was renamed John Adriance and Sons.

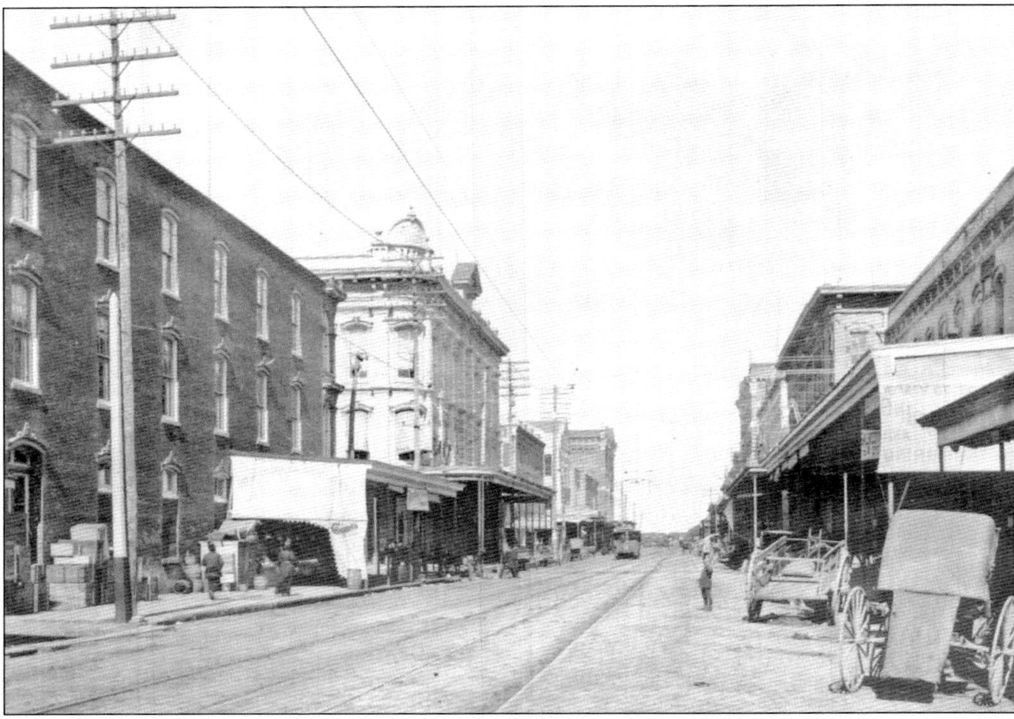

This street scene on Twenty-second Street, looking north from Postoffice, shows the trolley tracks and again the canopies that shaded the sidewalks from dust and debris. The buildings on the left were demolished for the United States National Bank Building, now at Twenty-second and Market. The buildings to the right are now parking lots.

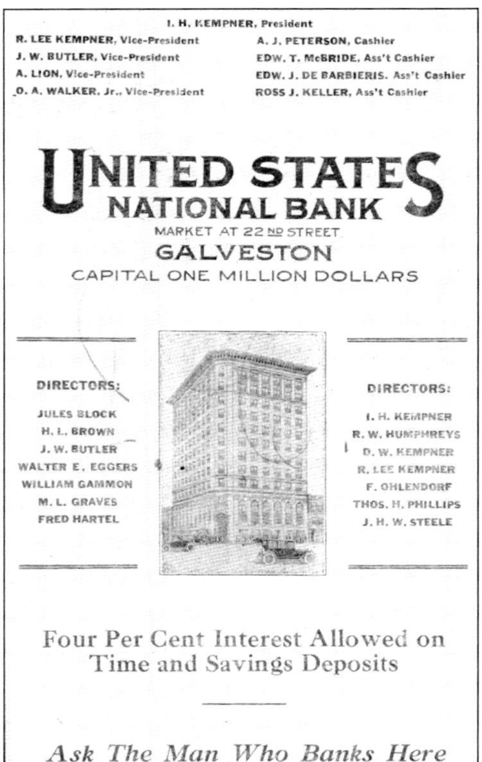

Alfred C. Bossom, along with Sanguinet, Staats, and Hedrick, designed the United States National Bank Building in 1925 at the corner of Twenty-second and Market Streets. This building, like many others at the time, addressed the corner with its main entrance straddling the corner. The building is 11 stories tall and has a limestone facing.

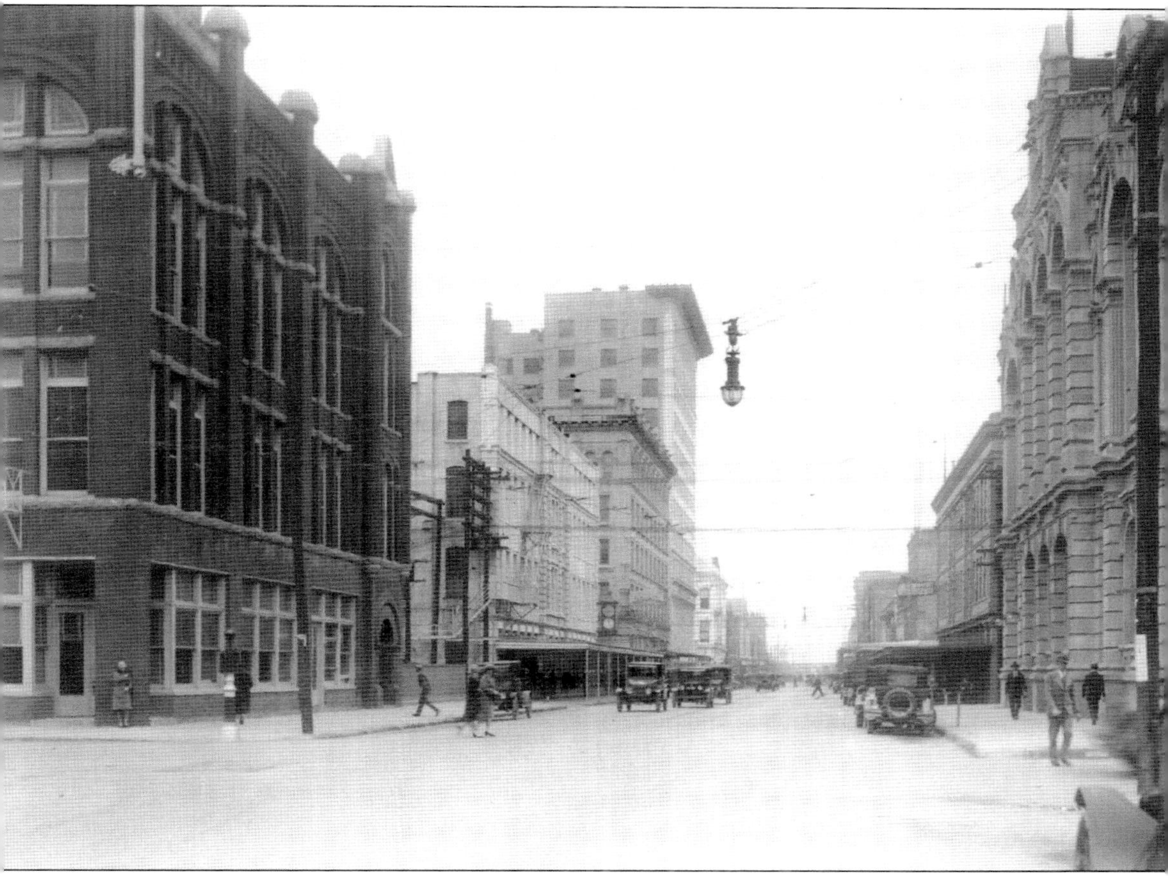

At 2202–2206 Church Street (Twenty-second and Church Streets) is the Telephone Building, constructed in 1896, with Alfred Muller as architect. Alfred Muller was born in Prussia in 1855. Unlike Clayton, Muller received formal architectural training at the Royal Academy of Fine Arts in Berlin. Muller immigrated to the United States and worked for the Washington, D.C., architectural firm of E. H. Didden and Company. He established his own practice in 1887 after working with Nathaniel W. Tobey Jr. Muller died of typhoid fever in 1896, the same year the Telephone Building was built. He is buried at Lakeview Cemetery in Galveston. The Telephone Building is his only extant major commercial work in downtown Galveston. (Courtesy of the Dolph Briscoe Center for American History, The University of Texas at Austin.)

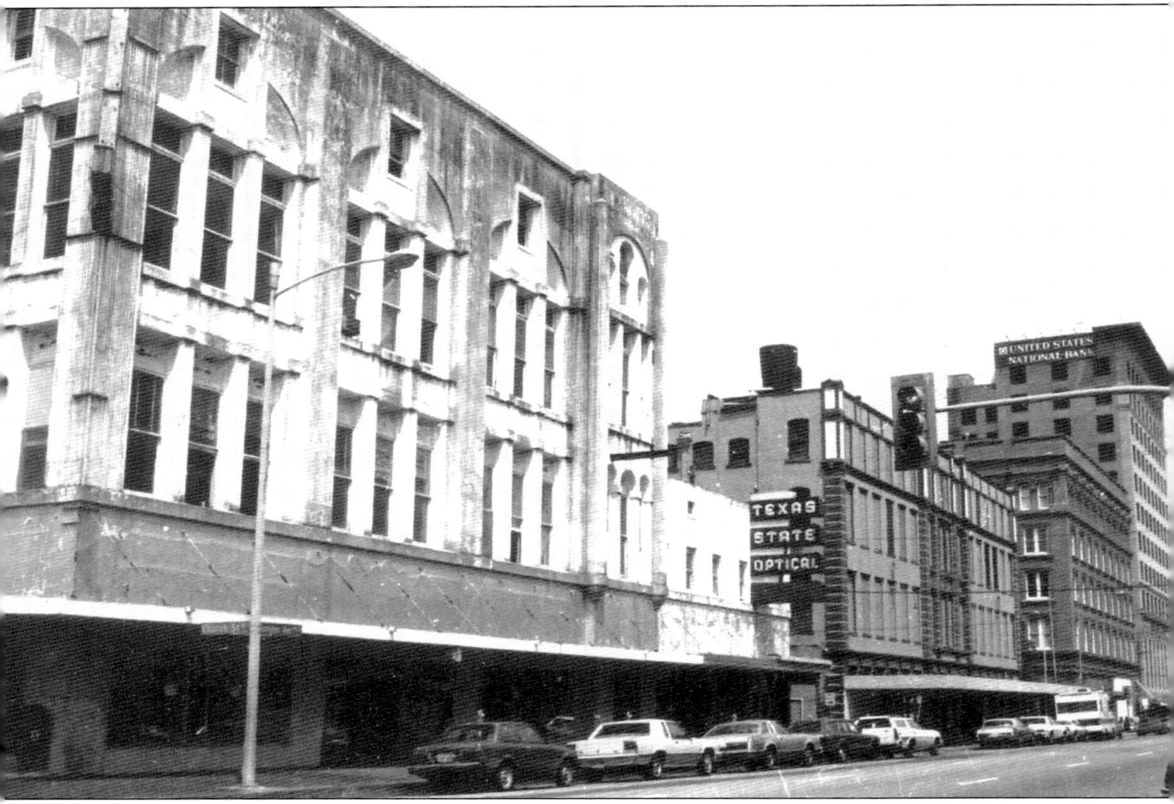

This street scene shows the decline of Twenty-second Street in the late 1970s and early 1980s. The Telephone Building is shown with peeling white paint, along with the art deco Texas State Optical Center, Eibands, Fellman Dry Goods, and the United States National Bank Buildings. All of the buildings on this block have now been restored and are occupied.

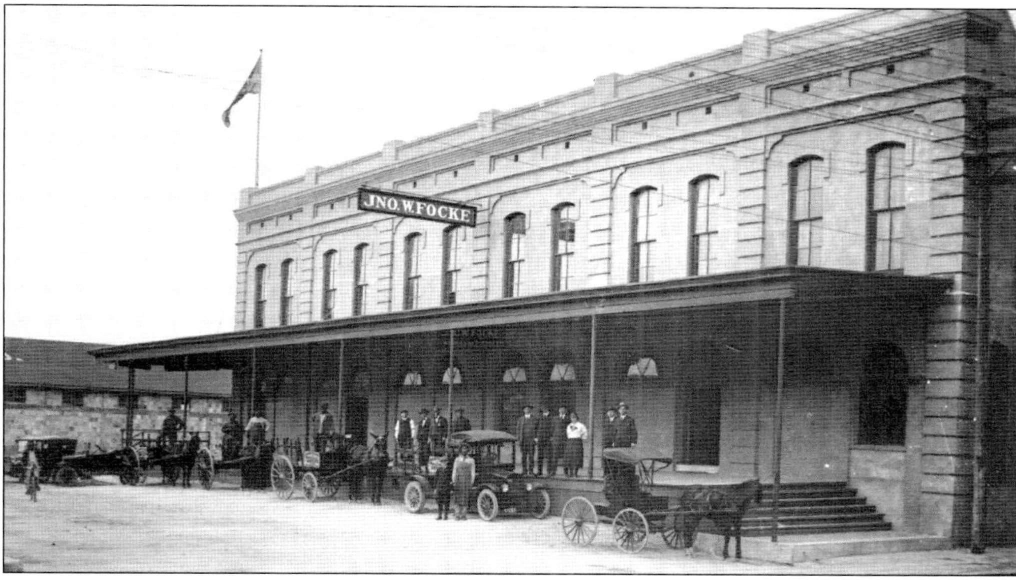

Cotton merchants Wolston, Wells, and Vidor hired Nathaniel W. Tobey to design their warehouse building at Twenty-third and Water Street, now Harborside Drive, in 1877. The location of this firm was once in the T. J. League Building, across the street. Charles Vidor was born in Hungary and immigrated to New York before settling in Galveston. The first tenant of the building was R. F. George, a wholesale druggist. (Courtesy of the Dolph Briscoe Center for American History, The University of Texas at Austin.)

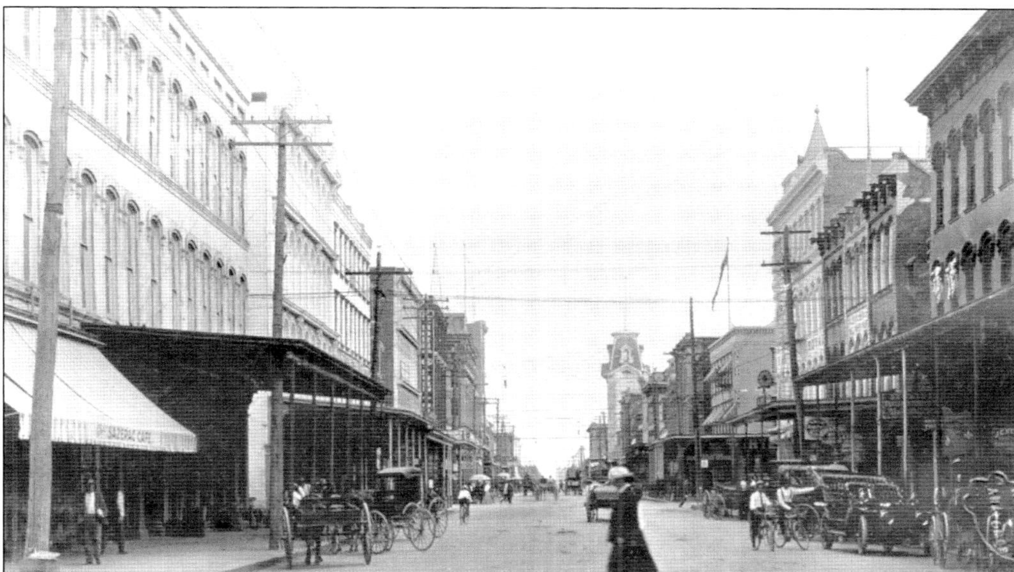

This vibrant photograph shows a very busy Twenty-third Street, looking south. The T. J. League Building is on the right, followed by the Rice and Baulard Buildings, next the McDonnell, then the Ufford Building, with the Tremont House Hotel in the distance. The left side of the photograph shows the handsomely clad cast-iron building at 302 Tremont, with the backside of the Washington Hotel showing.

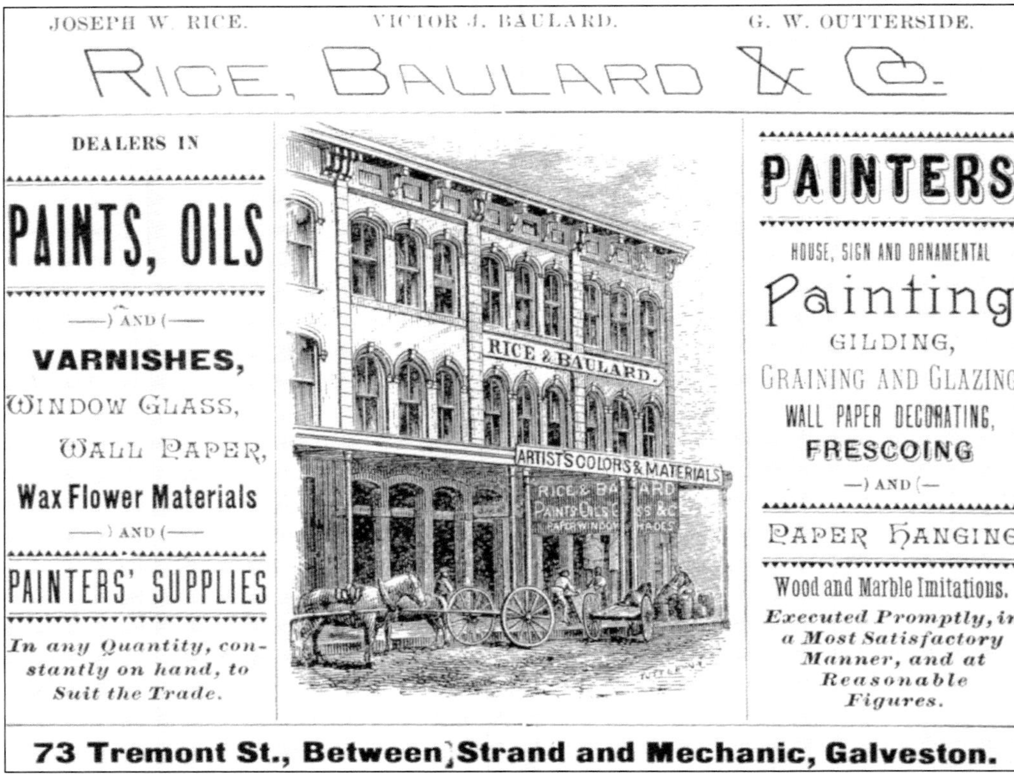

Jos. W. Rice and Victor J. Baulard were both early residents of Galveston, both being in Galveston by 1845. Rice, Baulard, and Company sold paints, oils, and glass. They engaged in grinding of paints, had the patent right for Bemin's oil, and carried a full line of wallpaper, window shades, varnishes, and paints.

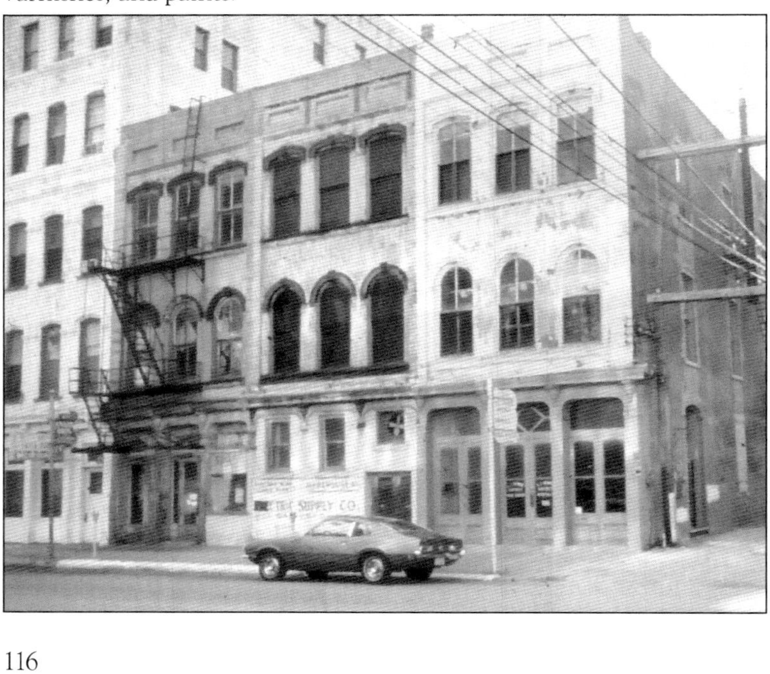

These buildings were constructed at the same time in 1870, which was after the Moro Castle fire in 1869, but are three separate buildings. With decorative cast-iron storefronts, these buildings have undergone multiple renovations. Now cast iron is seen on only one of the three storefronts. These buildings were also the first historic buildings downtown to undergo loft conversion in 1975.

Clarke and Courts originally occupied this structure before it moved to a larger location on Twenty-fourth and Ships Mechanic Row. Clark and Courts was Galveston's largest stationers, printers, and lithographers. They were established in 1879. Like many businesses of the time, traveling salesmen crisscrossed the region selling their products. They employed 75 to 100 employees in 1887.

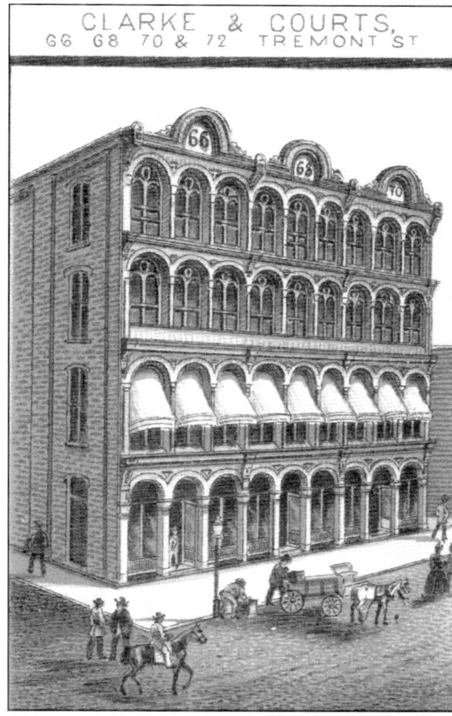

Another business also inhabited the 302 Tremont space, Outterside, Eimar, and LaFrance paints and paint supplies. George Outterside was once in partnership with Rice and Baulard, a business that once inhabited the buildings directly across the street from this location. Unfortunately, this cast-iron storefront building is no longer in existence.

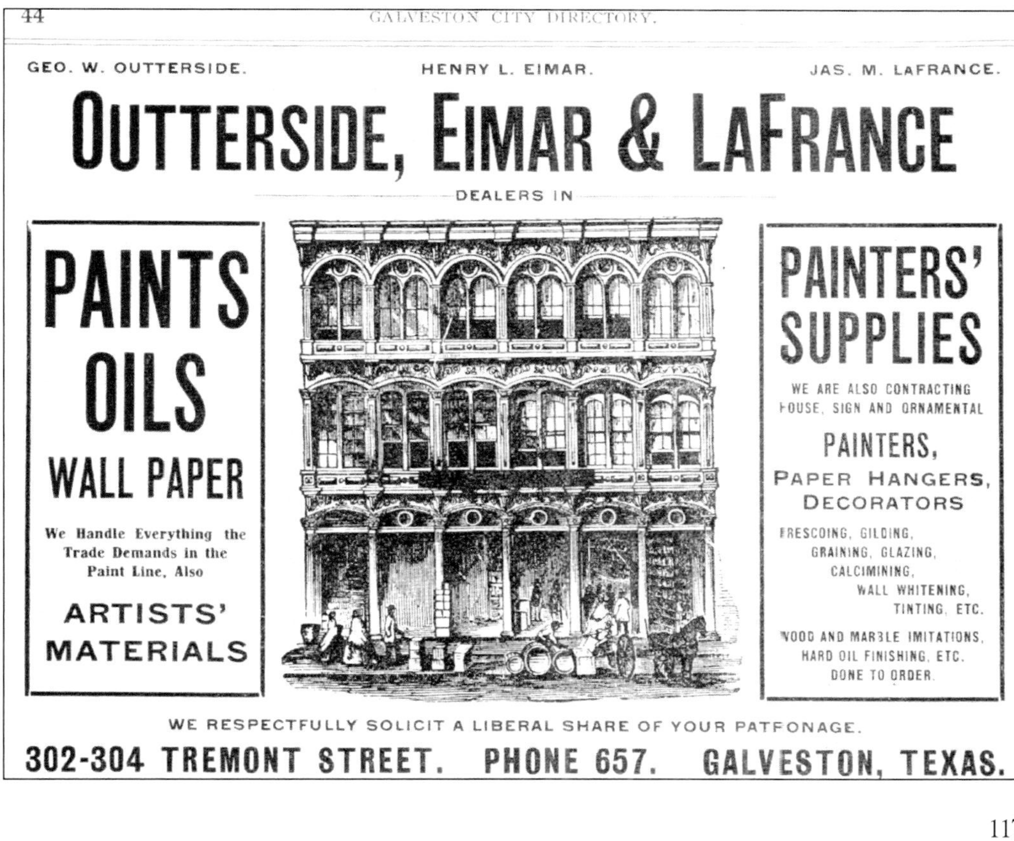

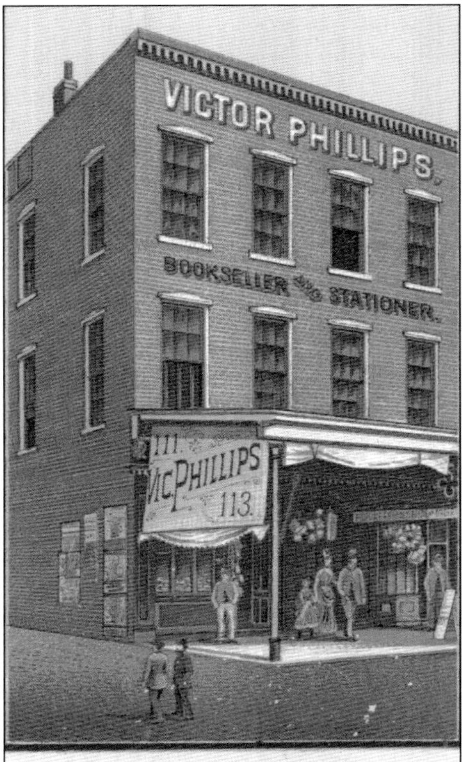

VICTOR PHILLIPS STORE.

The Victor Phillips Stationary store was located on the middle of the block, between Ships Mechanic Row and Market on Twenty-third Street. Many of the Galveston souvenir books were published for Victor Phillips. He included his own building in the publication. Attractive, small, souvenir albums full of lithographed illustrations of cities and scenery appeared throughout the United States and Canada in the late 19th century.

In the first building to the left, T. E. Thompson was in the business of being a watchmaker, jeweler, and dealer of watches, clocks, jewelry, diamonds, and silverware. Further down the street, George F. Jr. and Charles A. Schneider sold groceries and were seed dealers. On the right, notice a wooden-frame building, a rarity on Twenty-third Street in the late 1800s. This is of Twenty-third Street, looking north from Market.

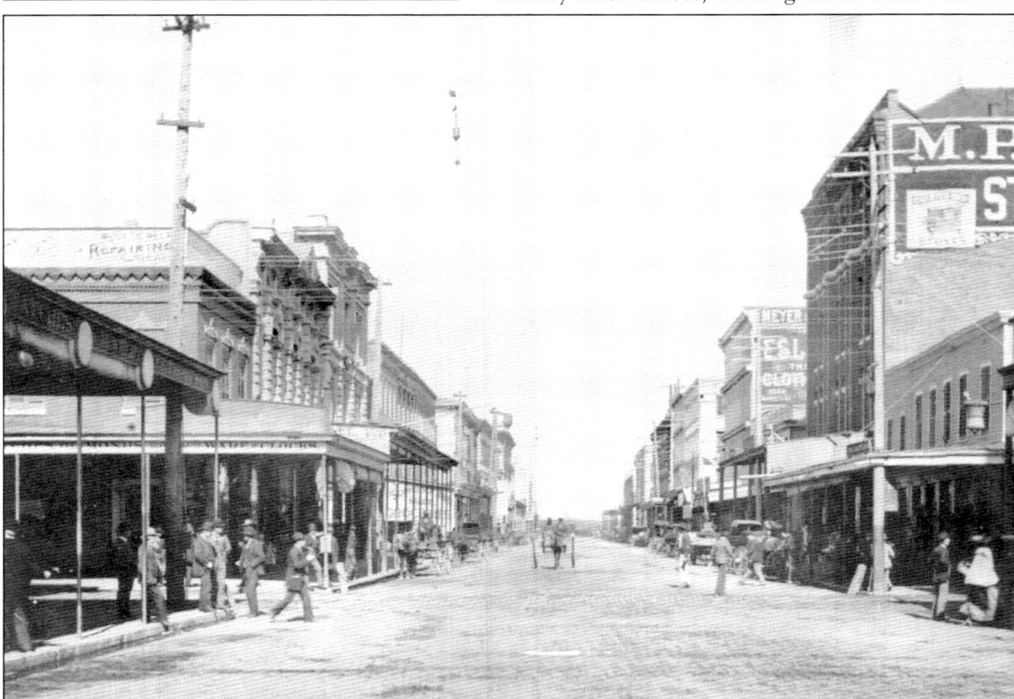

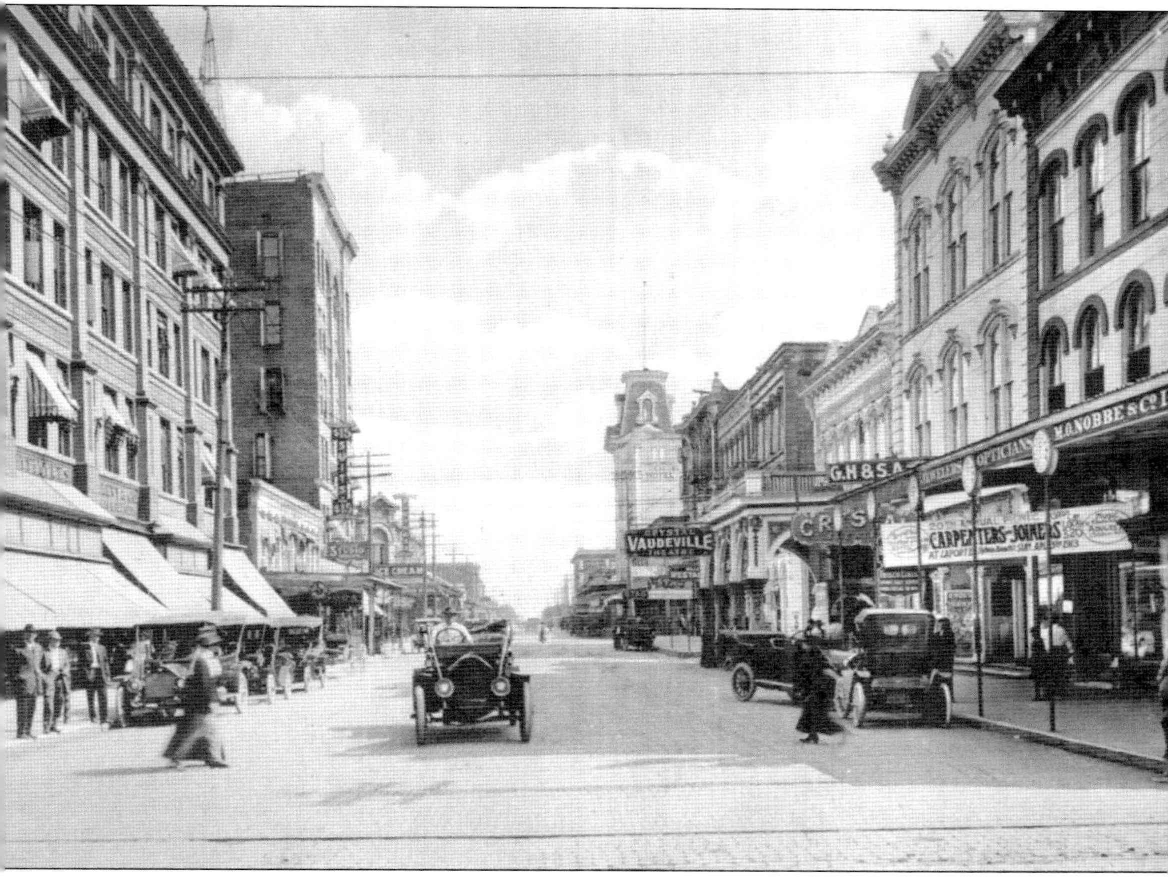

This photograph is another charming street scene, showing Twenty-third Street, looking south from Market Street. Taken in the early part of the 20th century, it shows the influence that theater and live shows were having on building tenants. Vaudeville acts were very popular until the mid-1920s. The Levy Building is the large structure on the left. The Clympia Frebye Building (1886) is noticeable on the left side of the photograph by the sign for "ice cream." The Tremont Hotel is visible to the right.

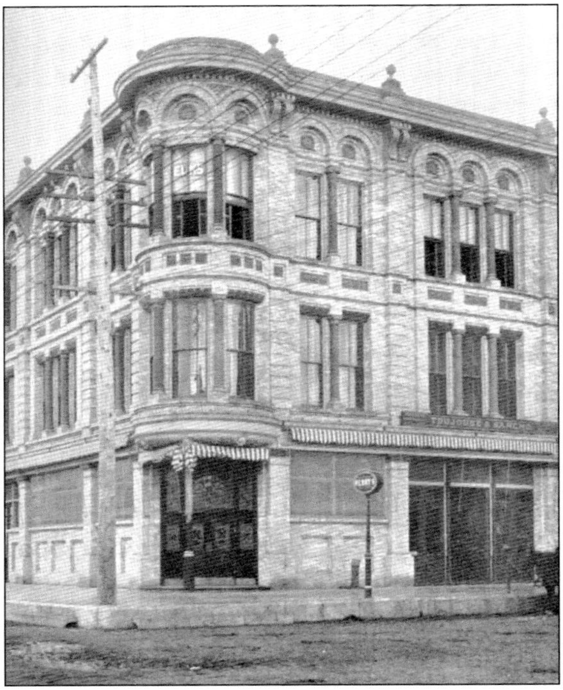

Henry Toujouse operated the Stag Hotel on the upper floors of this structure, located at the northwest corner of Twenty-third and Postoffice Streets. The firm of Toujouse and Sancho was made up of importers and wholesale and retail dealers in wines, liquors, cigars, and table luxuries. Nicholas Clayton completed the interior spaces in 1898 for Marks Marx. It was built for $14,000. The building was demolished in 1960.

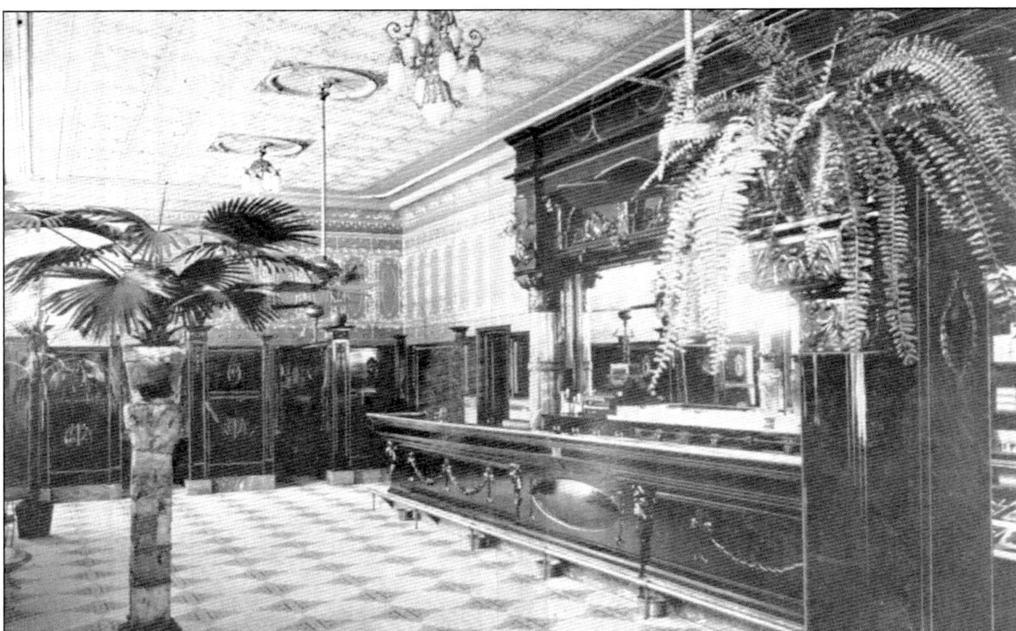

The photograph caption from *Picturesque Galveston* reads, "interior of the Henry Toujouse Bar Palatial Saloon, Showing One-Half of Bar (One of the Handsomest in America)." After the building was torn down, the bar bounced around locations in downtown. The Galveston Historical Foundation received the bar as a donation. It is now on permanent loan inside the Tremont House Hotel on 2300 Ships Mechanic Row.

George B. Stowe designed the Improvement Loan and Trust Company Building at the northeast corner of Twenty-third and Postoffice Streets. It claimed to be one of the first skyscrapers in the southwest with six floors. Construction was completed in 1900. The "Trust Building" was demolished in June 1956, when the owners felt it would be costly to modernize.

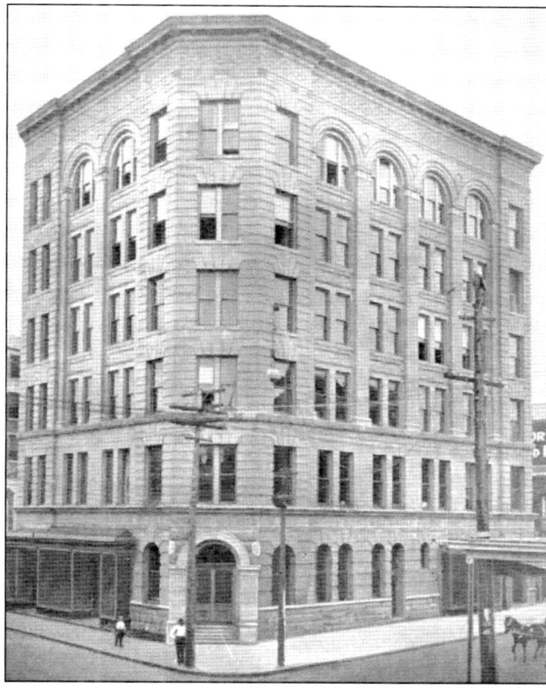

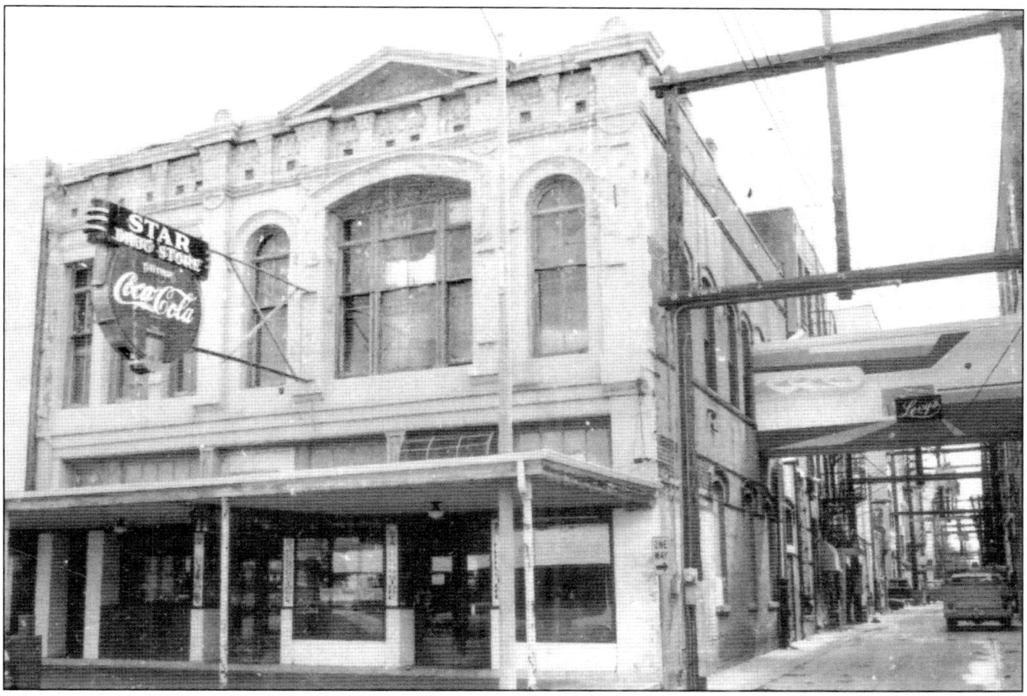

The Star Drug Company Building at 512 Twenty-third Street was designed by Nicholas Clayton and built in 1909 to seamlessly match the Olympia Freybe Building, which was constructed on the corner of Postoffice and Twenty-third Streets. The Star Drug Company has remained a tenant and still has its 1917 interiors intact.

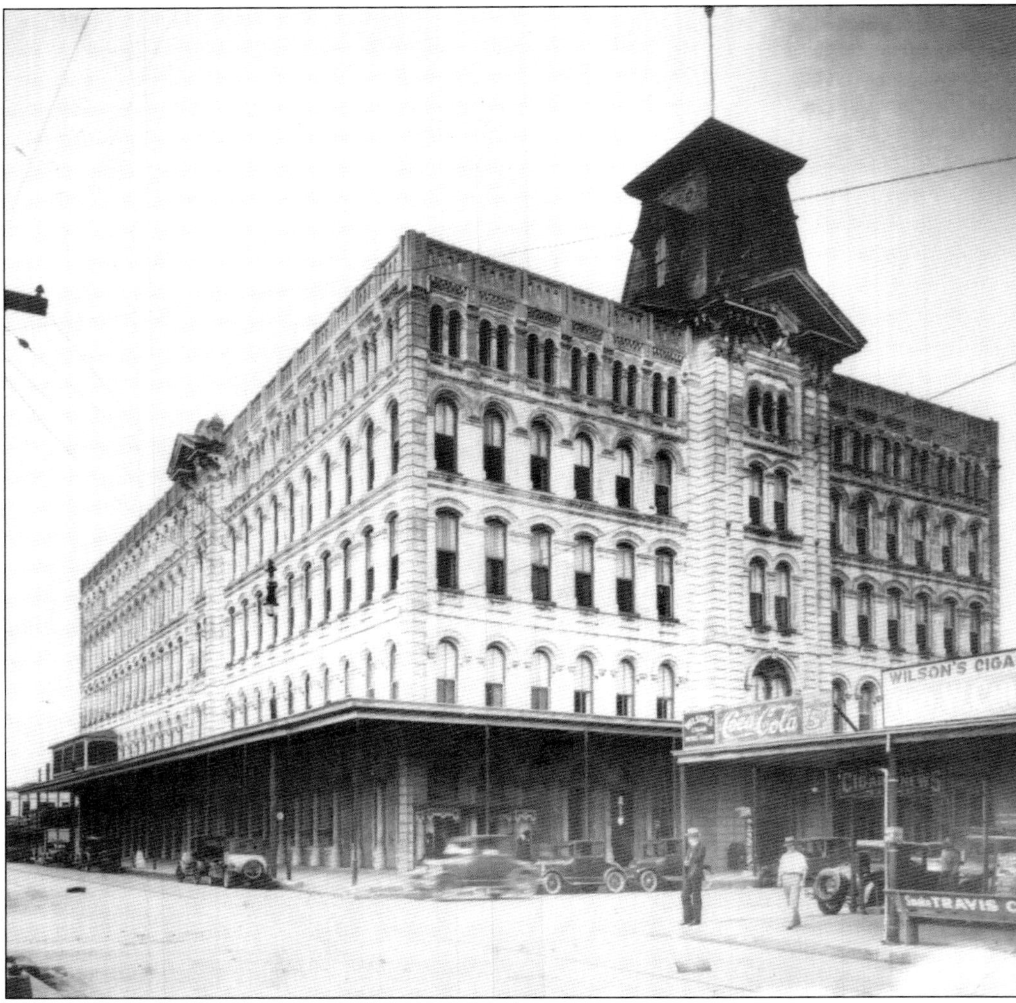

The second Tremont Hotel had beginnings by architect Fred S. Steward in 1872. Steward practiced architecture in Galveston in the early 1870s. He was also the architect for the Masonic Temple Building at 816 Twenty-second Street. When Steward started building the Tremont, only two floors were completed, and the building was not finished for four years. Nicholas Clayton and his partner Michael Lynch revised the plans, and the stockholders of the Tremont wanted those plans followed. The hotel finally opened in 1877. The Tremont Hotel seems to be one of the most famous hotels Galveston has ever seen. Unfortunately, not famous enough, the building was demolished in 1928. Work for demolition began on December 11, 1928, and several odes were written to the Tremont Hotel in the *Galveston Daily News*. (Courtesy of the Dolph Briscoe Center for American History, The University of Texas at Austin.)

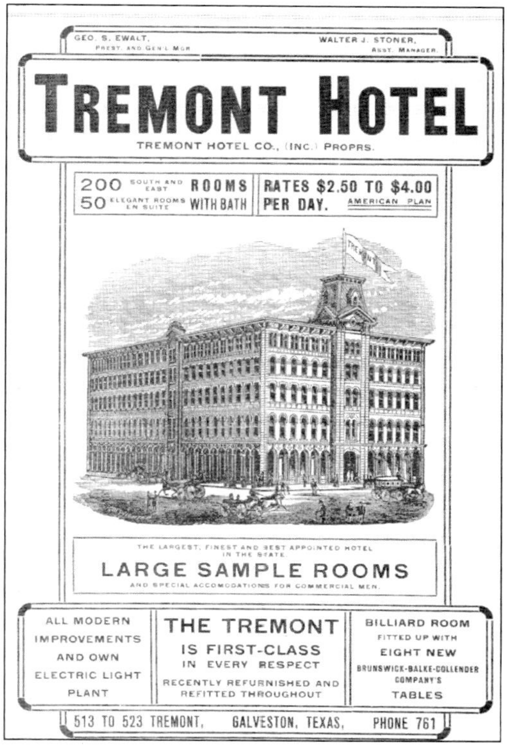

Clayton and Lynch continued to work on the Tremont, completing rehabilitation contracts in 1884 and 1896. The Tremont Hotel was the scene of most elite social functions, as well as operating as a hotel for business travelers. As noted in the advertisement, the Tremont operated with electricity and had the most modern amenities, including baths in some rooms, an elegant bar, and gaming room. Being the most elegant hotel in Galveston, European nobility and famous politicians stayed at the Tremont. It was said that new laws were proposed and plans for many of the great railroads in the state had originated here. The Tremont Hotel was also a place where many wedding receptions took place. The interior of the Tremont Hotel was elaborately decorated. It was reported that the interior was decorated with marble from Italy.

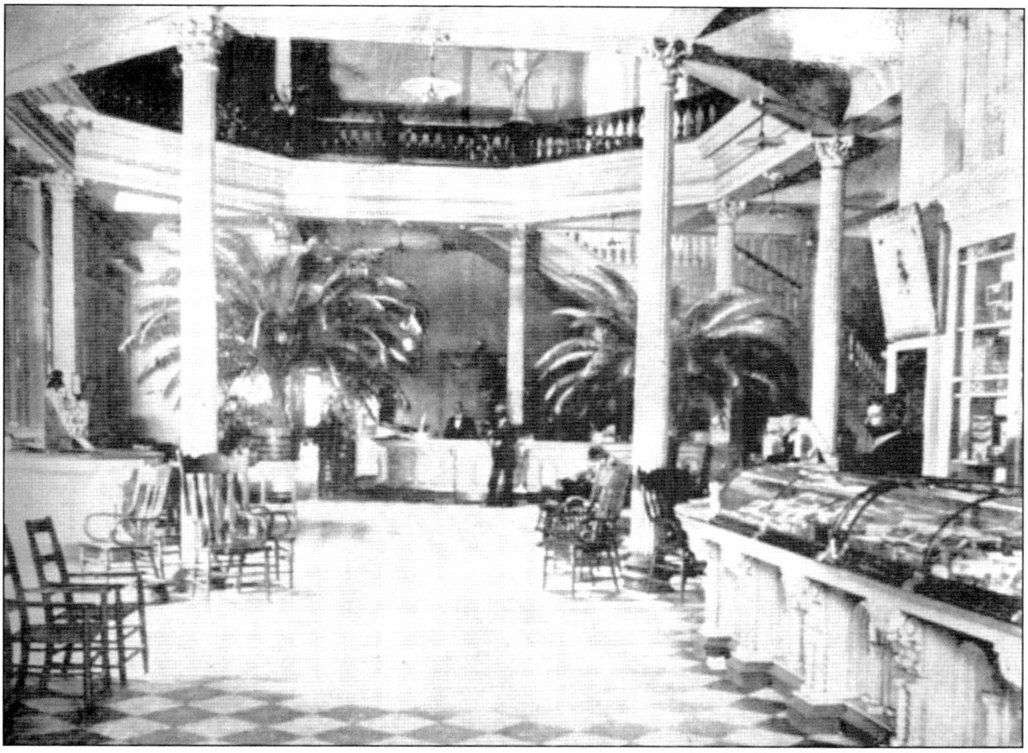

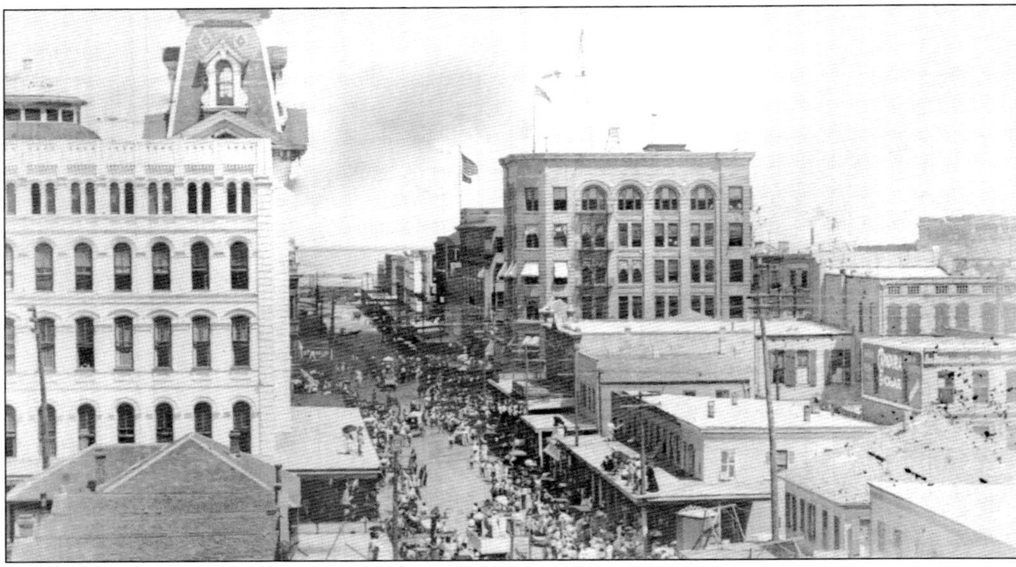

Streets in Galveston often carry double, and sometimes triple, names. Twenty-fifth Street began as Bath and now carries the name Rosenberg Avenue, Twenty-fourth Street became Mitchell Avenue, Twenty-third Street is known as Tremont, and Twenty-second Street is known as Kempner. This photograph was taken during a parade near Twenty-third and Church, looking north.

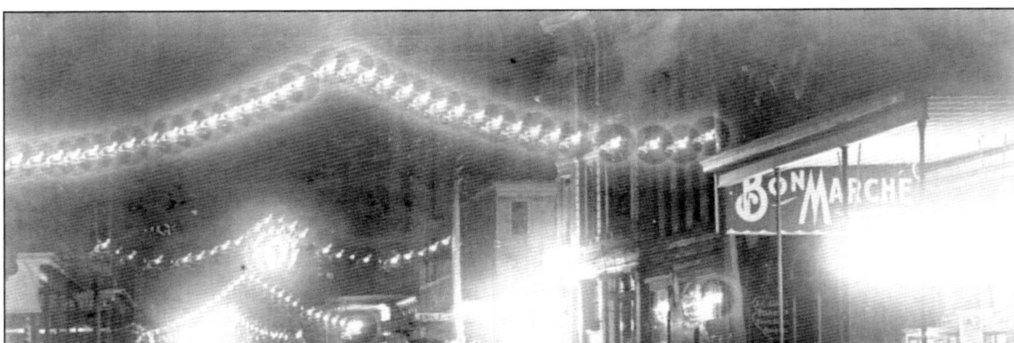

Taken from the Ashton Villa postcard collection, this is a remarkable scene of nighttime in Galveston. This fascinating postcard shows Twenty-third Street at night, including the Bon Marche Store sign that is visible left of center in the previous photograph. Isidor Davidson was the manager, and he and his wife Helen lived at 1602 Sixteenth Street.

In the 1920s, this firm of wholesale grocers liquidated their stock and went out of business. Members of the Focke family went on to be wholesale grocers, the members of Wilkens family were cotton factors and steamship agents, and Alvin T. Lange became a member of the real estate firm of Arnold and Lange. This was a large warehouse that took up a city block on Twenty-fourth Street and Avenue A. The building is no longer extant.

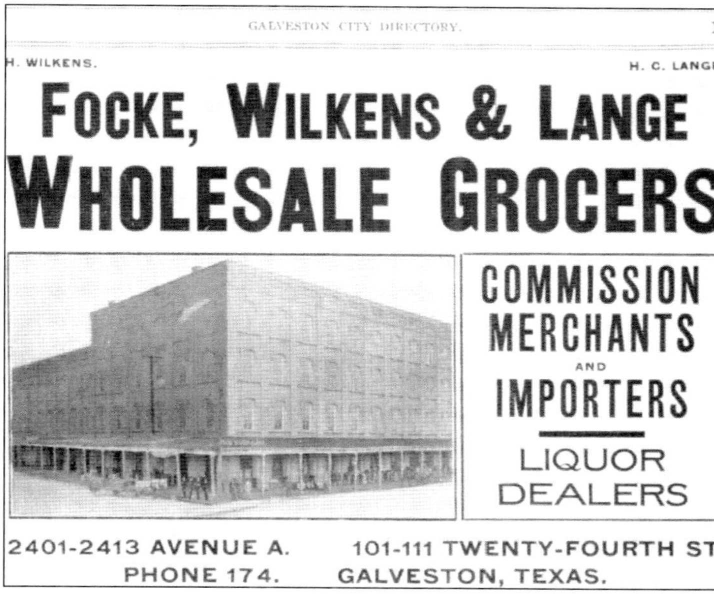

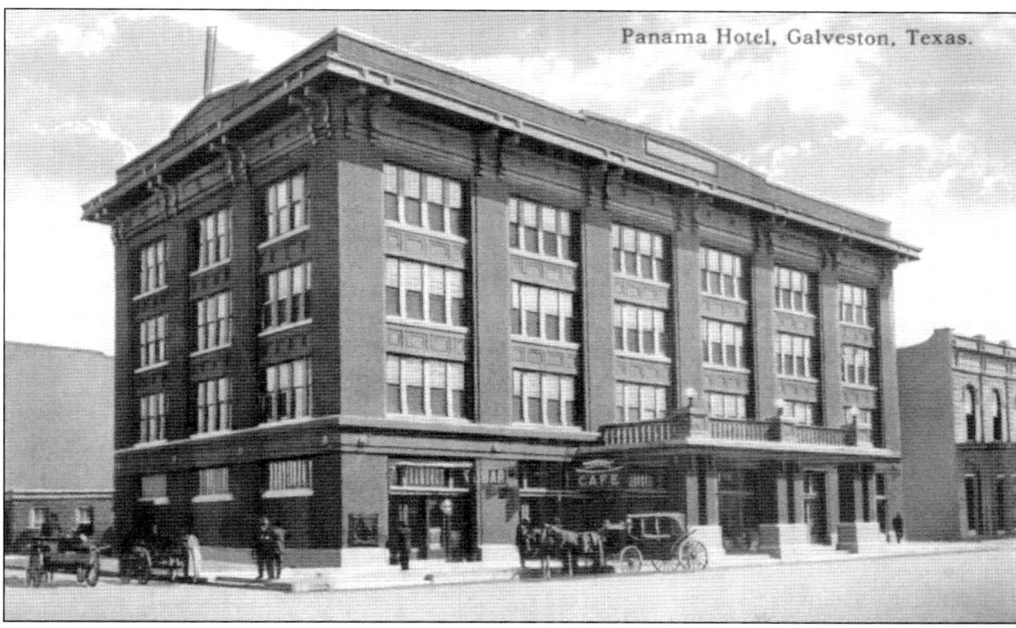

Built in 1913, across the street from the railroad station, the Panama Hotel was constructed as a business traveler hotel by Green and Finger Architects of Houston. The Panama Hotel was named for the newly constructed Panama Canal. Galveston at that time was the closest U.S. port. The building has been converted to condominiums. (Courtesy of the Galveston County Historical Museum, Galveston, Texas.)

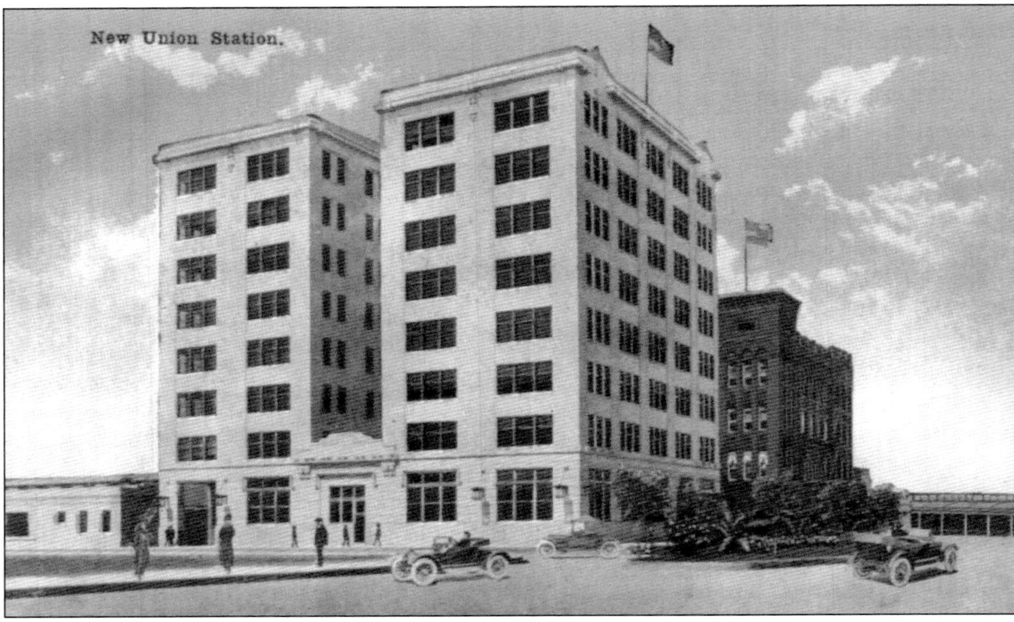

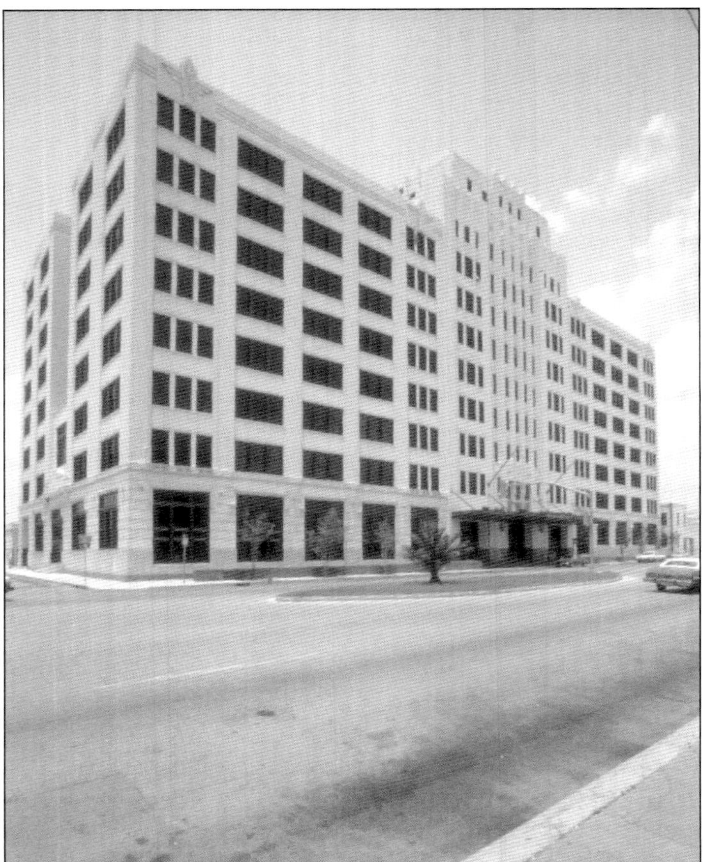

At the intersection of Twenty-fifth and Strand sits the Santa Fe Building. This building is a textbook case for companies merging and then making the decision to expand their building to fit their growing business. The first portion of this building was the eight-story rear wing, built in 1913, with Dalbert Simpson as architect. The original 1897 terminal was demolished to make way for the 1932 E. A. Harrison Building, which is an 11-story terra cotta clad building that can still be seen today. It is in unusual to see the art deco style in Galveston. The 1932 building was constructed for the Santa Fe Railway, and the railroad used the building until 1967. The building was left vacant until 1976, when the Moody Foundation purchased the building.

About the Organization

Incorporated in 1954, the Galveston Historical Foundation (GHF) is one the nation's largest local preservation organization. During the past 50 years, the foundation has expanded its mission to encompass community redevelopment, public education, historic preservation advocacy, maritime preservation, and stewardship of historic properties. Today the Galveston Historical Foundation has more than 2,000 memberships representing individuals, families, and businesses across Texas, the United States, and abroad, and exerts a profound impact on the culture and economy of Galveston.

The work of GHF has earned the foundation recognition by prominent state and national organizations. Among the recognized efforts are the redevelopment of the Strand; the rescue and restoration of the 1877 iron barque the *ELISSA*; the revitalization of historic residential neighborhoods and creation of historic districts; and the conception of signature events including Dickens on The Strand and the Galveston Historic Homes Tour. Galveston Historical Foundation serves as the steward and operator of many of Galveston's most significant historic properties. The 1838 Michel Menard House, 1839 Samuel May Williams House, 1859 Ashton Villa, 1859 St. Joseph Catholic Church, 1861 U.S. Custom House, 1880 Garten Verein, 1887 Tall Ship *ELISSA*, 1892 Bishop's Palace, 1937 *Santa Maria* Shrimp Boat, and Rosewood Cemetery.

The Galveston Historical Foundation continues to be a driving force in the development and enrichment of the city of Galveston. The foundation is major voice of preservation advocacy both locally and throughout the state. The Galveston Historical Foundation's many departments, programs, events, and volunteers are all dedicated to its mission: preserving and revitalizing the architectural, cultural, and maritime heritage of Galveston Island for the education and enrichment of all.